IMAGES of America

NEW BERN

IMAGES
of America

NEW BERN

Vina Hutchinson

ARCADIA
PUBLISHING

ISBN 978-0-7385-0651-7

Published by Arcadia Publishing,
Charleston, South Carolina

Printed in the United States of America

Library of Congress Catalog Card Number: 00107121

For all general information contact Arcadia Publishing at:
Telephone 843-853-2070
Fax 843-853-0044
E-Mail sales@arcadiapublishing.com
For customer service and orders:
Toll-Free 1-888-313-2665

Visit us on the Internet at www.arcadiapublishing.com

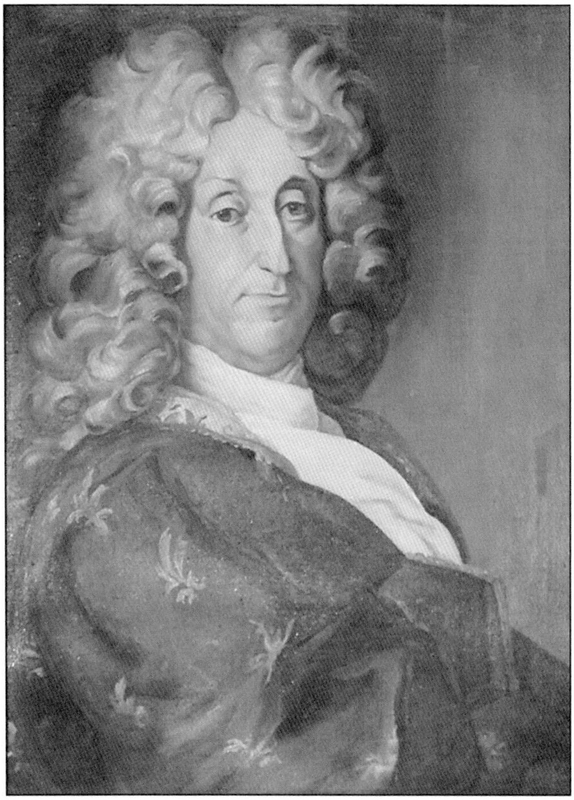

In 1710, Baron Christoph de Graffenried of Bern, Switzerland, led a group of Swiss and Palatine settlers to an area on the banks of the Neuse River. Graffenried, with the assistant of surveyor-general John Lawson, laid out a town and called it New Bern in honor of his hometown. This painting of the baron, by artist Grace Gilmore, hangs in the New Bern Firemen's Museum. (Courtesy of New Bern Firemen's Museum.)

Contents

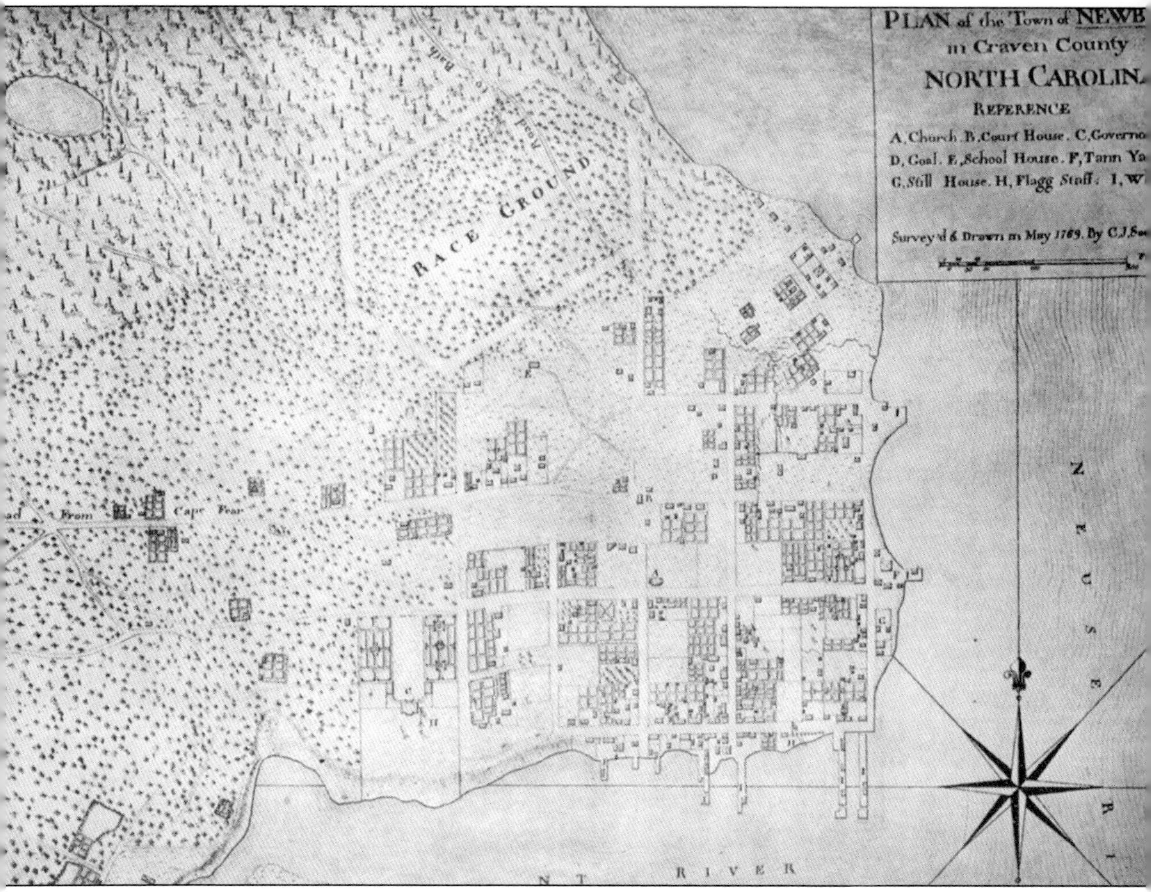

The governor's palace was still standing at the time this 1789 map was drawn. (Courtesy of New Bern Area Chamber of Commerce.)

INTRODUCTION

New Bern, the second oldest town in North Carolina, was settled in 1710 by German and Swiss colonists led by Baron Christopher DeGraffenried. He purchased the land from the Tuscarora Indians, who had a small settlement here known as Chattawka, which is believed to mean, "where the fish are taken out."

Named for the city of Bern, Switzerland, the town was located on the triangle of land where the Neuse and Trent Rivers meet. This is called the confluence of the Neuse and Trent Rivers. The original settlers suffered with the climate, a lack of provisions and supplies, diseases, and Indian problems. DeGraffenried and the surveyor John Lawson were taken prisoner by the Indians. Lawson was burned at the stake, but DeGraffenried was spared. Once the war with the Tuscarora Indians was ended, New Bernians looked to the natural resources for their support. Tar, pitch and turpentine, along with other native products, loaded down ships bound for England, New England and the West Indies. The ships would return with rum, molasses, sugar, and manufactured goods.

When King Charles II had been restored to the English throne in 1660, he issued a "Carolina Charter" granting eight of his loyal supporters (called the Lords Proprietor) wide areas of land in the New World. The area spread from Virginia to the Spanish border of Florida and from the Atlantic Ocean to the "South Seas," or the Pacific Ocean. It was called Carolina, from the word "Carolus," the Latin word for "Charles," as a way to honor the king. William, Earl of Craven, was one of the original Lords Proprietor, and it's from his family that Craven County got its name. New Bern became the seat of the Craven Precinct (now Craven County) in 1772.

By the mid-18th century, the river port had grown in size and importance. Because New Bern is centrally located between the Albemarle and Cape Fear, the Colonial Assembly often met here. The colony's first printing press was established in New Bern in 1749, and two years later, the printer, James Davis, published the colony's first newspaper, pamphlet, and book.

Royal Governor William Tryon saw the need for a permanent capital in the growing colony and selected New Bern as the site. Tryon Palace, first colonial and state capitol building of North Carolina, was designed by the English architect John Hawks. The palace, completed in 1770, made New Bern the political center of North Carolina, and that was important in the growth of the town. New Bern became the center of events leading to the Revolution. The first publicly organized assembly was called here in 1774, against the wishes of Royal Governor Josiah Martin, who fled the capital for safety in May of the following year. Throughout the Revolutionary War, the port sheltered many privateers.

Early in 1777, the first state government, under a new constitution, was begun under the leadership of Richard Caswell. In the 1790s, the growing population of the western counties led the General Assembly to move the state capital to a more central location. Jowl Lane's farm was purchased and there the present capital of Raleigh was established.

The Federal Era saw New Bern develop fully into a city. There was much more culture and wealth here after the American Revolution. The first school to be chartered in North Carolina, New Bern Academy, along with the Masonic Temple and Theater, the Episcopal church, and other churches built by Presbyterian, Baptist, Methodist and Roman Catholic congregations illustrate the educational, civic, and religious sophistication present in New Bern at that time.

All was relatively quiet until the outbreak of the Civil War. Union forces captured the important port city of New Bern on March 14, 1862, early in the war. Northern officers established headquarters in Neuse River mansions while other soldiers moved into other houses throughout the city. The Union forces occupied New Bern for the rest of the war, and for this reason, New Bern survived with less physical damages than many other small Southern towns.

After the difficult period of Reconstruction, New Bern entered its third era of development. Before and well after 1900, the fine quality pine, cypress, oak, and other hardwoods kept the lumber mills busy. By 1916, there were 16 lumber mills here. New Bern also became a source of seafood and what was not bought locally or shipped out was processed in fertilizer plants.

Construction started on the Marine Corps Air Station at Cherry Point on August 16, 1941, at a point located on the Neuse River halfway between New Bern and Morehead City. It now ranks as the largest United States Marine Corps Air Station in the world. The many personnel and Marines coming to the area helped to boost the local economy, a boost that continues to this day.

New Bern remains a progressive city, but much relating to its history can still be seen. Tryon Palace Historic Sites and Gardens can take a visitor back 200 years. The John Wright Stanley and Dixon-Stevenson exhibition houses further illustrate the early history of the city. The New Bern Academy Museum, New Bern Fireman's Museum, the Attmore-Oliver House, and the Birthplace of Pepsi all help illustrate the lifestyles of times past. The historic sites and old homes along the waterfront, large and small, make it easy to understand why we in New Bern say, "Our charm is historic!"

—Courtesy of Craven County Convention & Visitors Bureau

One

The Civil War

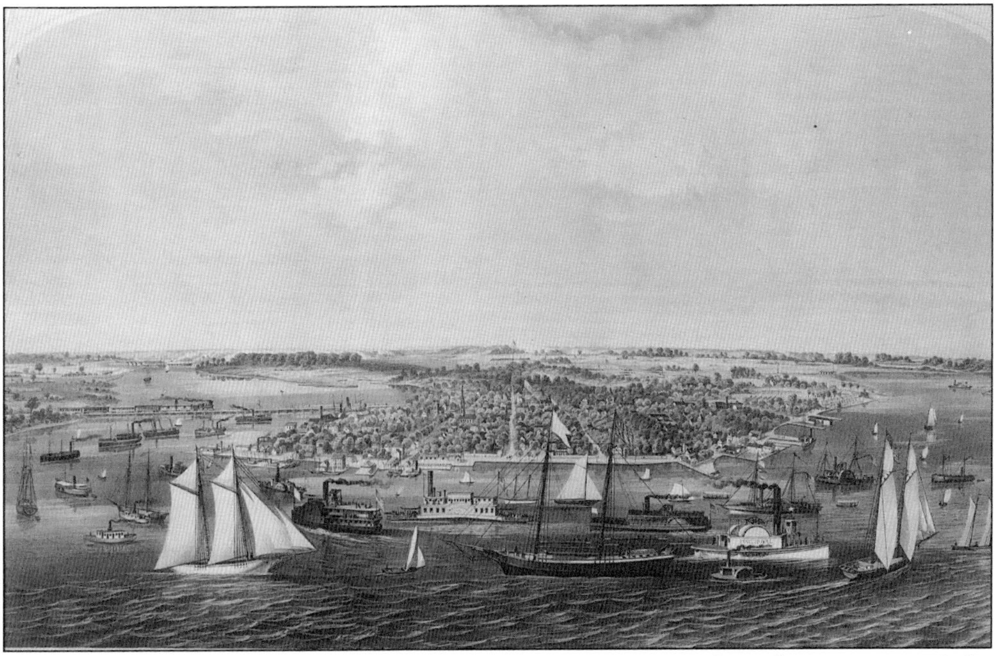

North Carolina seceded from the United States in May 1861 and, at that time, joined the Confederate States of America. In 1861, New Bern was the state's second largest city on the coast and thus an attractive target for the Union Army. By March 1862, New Bern had fallen into Union hands after the Battle of New Bern, led by Union general Ambrose Burnside. This lithograph, dated 1864, was by Major & Knapp of New York. (Courtesy of North Carolina Collection, University of North Carolina Library at Chapel Hill.)

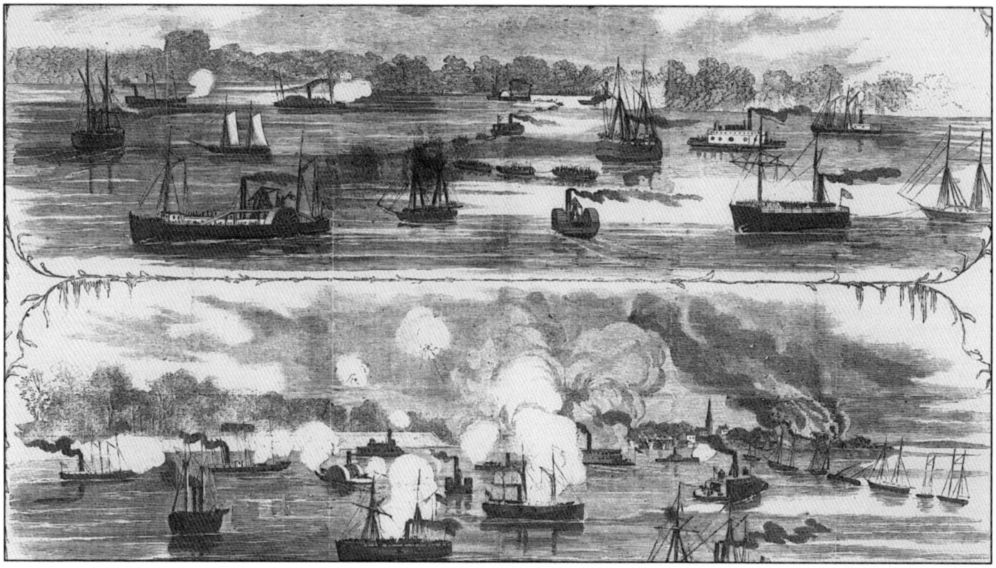

On March 12, 1862, Burnside and his force of 11,000 men had anchored their boats at the mouth of Slocum's Creek. John H. Johnson, a Confederate Army private who served in Company I, 7th Regiment, N.C. Troops, kept a diary of his daily experiences. He was an eyewitness to the Battle of New Bern. This illustration, titled *The Burnside Expedition—Bombardment of Newbern, North Carolina*, appeared in the April 12, 1862 issue of *Harper's Weekly*. (Courtesy of North Carolina Collection, University of North Carolina Library at Chapel Hill.)

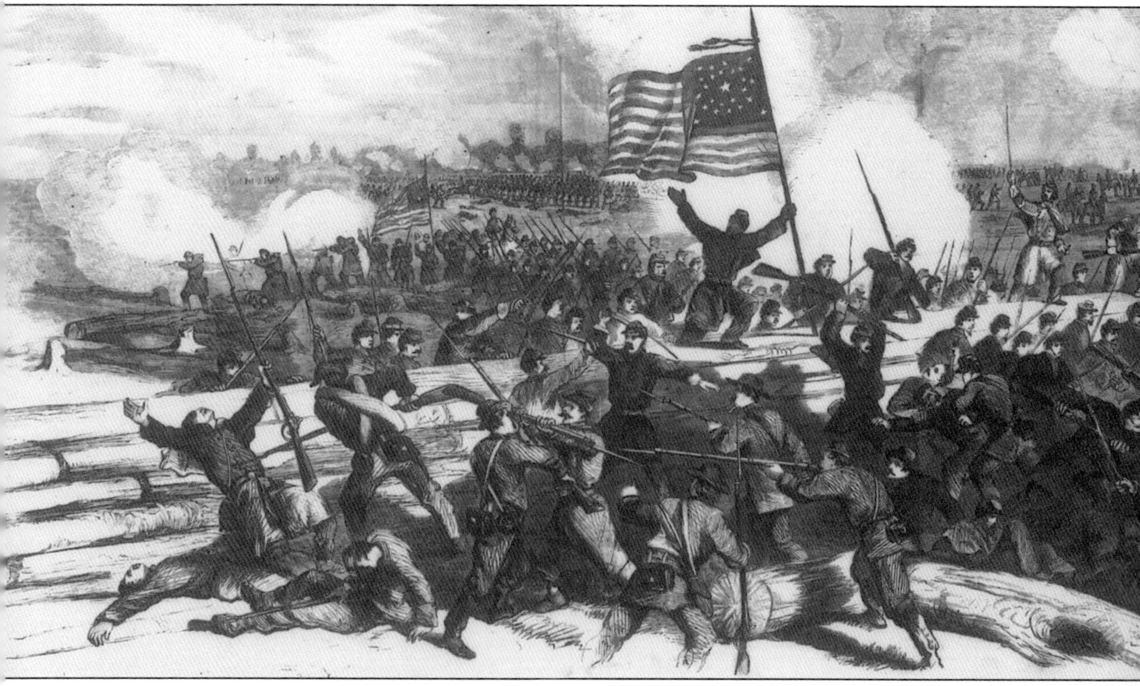

Johnson wrote on the morning of the battle that the soldiers of his regiment appeared "cool and calm although few of them had ever been in a battle and had little idea of how they would feel when facing the deadly weapons of such hostile foes." As the battle commenced, the

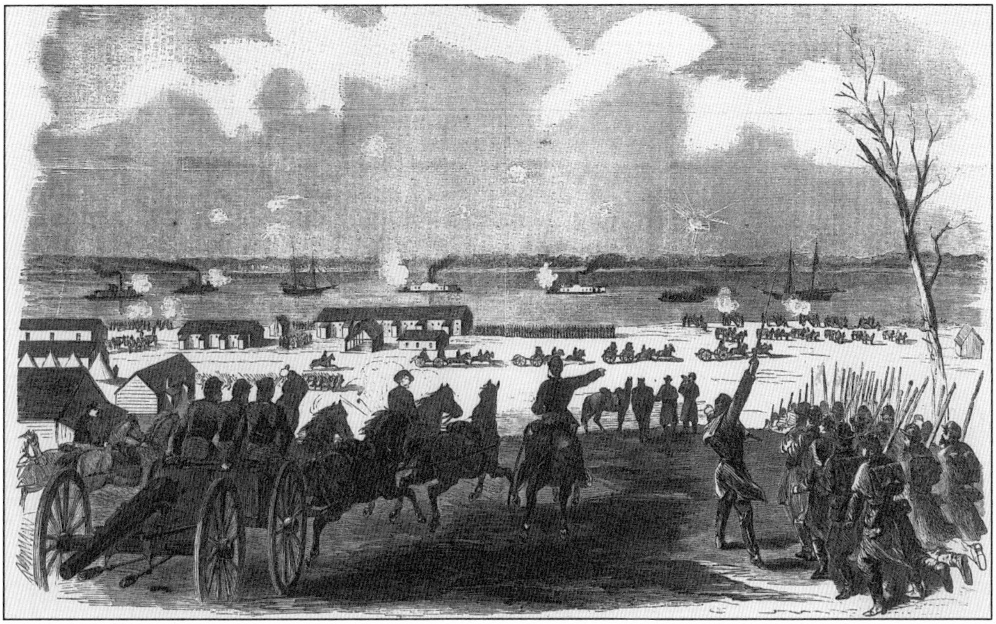

On the morning of March 14, Burnside and his forces converged on the waiting Confederates. Fighting lasted for about three hours as many New Bern residents watched from the rooftops. This illustration appeared in the April 11, 1863 issue of *Harper's Weekly*. (Courtesy of North Carolina Collection, University of North Carolina Library at Chapel Hill.)

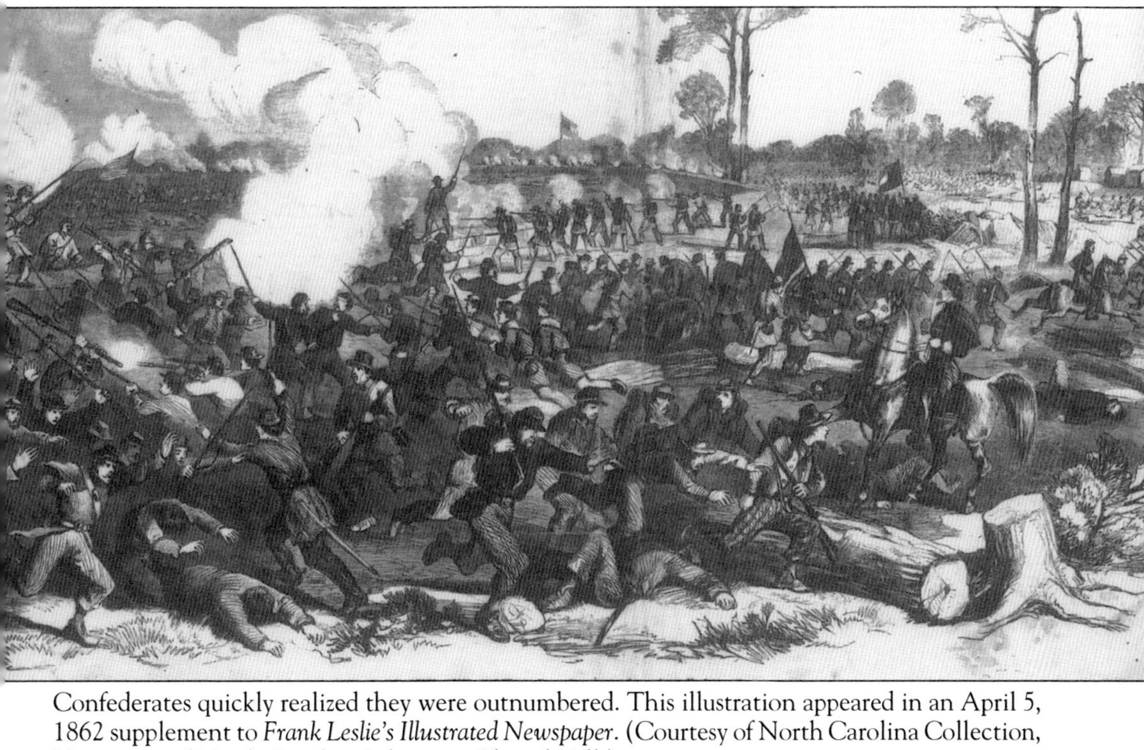

Confederates quickly realized they were outnumbered. This illustration appeared in an April 5, 1862 supplement to *Frank Leslie's Illustrated Newspaper*. (Courtesy of North Carolina Collection, University of North Carolina Library at Chapel Hill.)

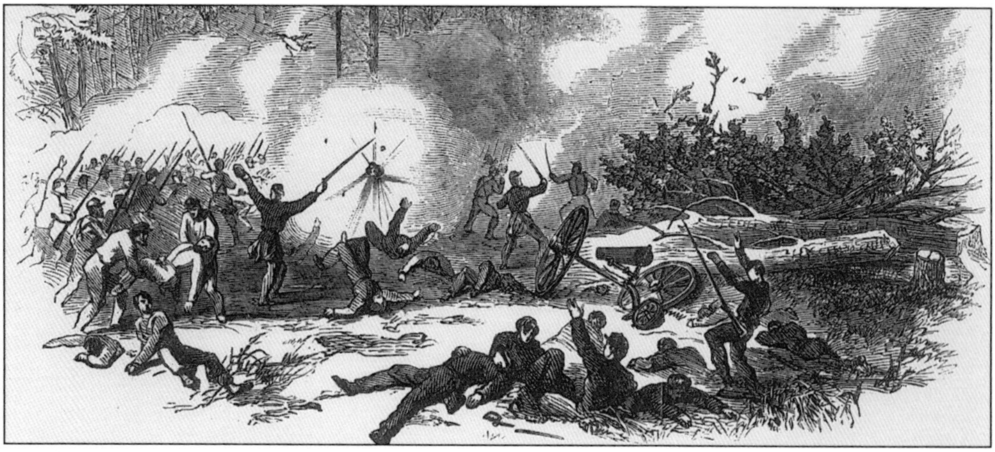

Outflanked, the Confederate Army began to retreat. Johnson wrote that many of the regiments "fought gallantly, though against a force many times their number." Many panic-stricken New Bern residents fled to a waiting train, which had been prepared the previous day in case an evacuation was needed. Many soldiers who had fled the front also boarded the train. Others retreated over land. Johnson described the retreat and the battle's end: "Our forces retreated to (Kinston), Our whole loss in killed, wounded (and) prisoners will not number more than four hundred . . . Thus New Bern has fallen into the hands of our enemy." The original printed source of this illustration of the Battle of New Bern is unknown. (Courtesy of North Carolina Collection, University of North Carolina Library at Chapel Hill.)

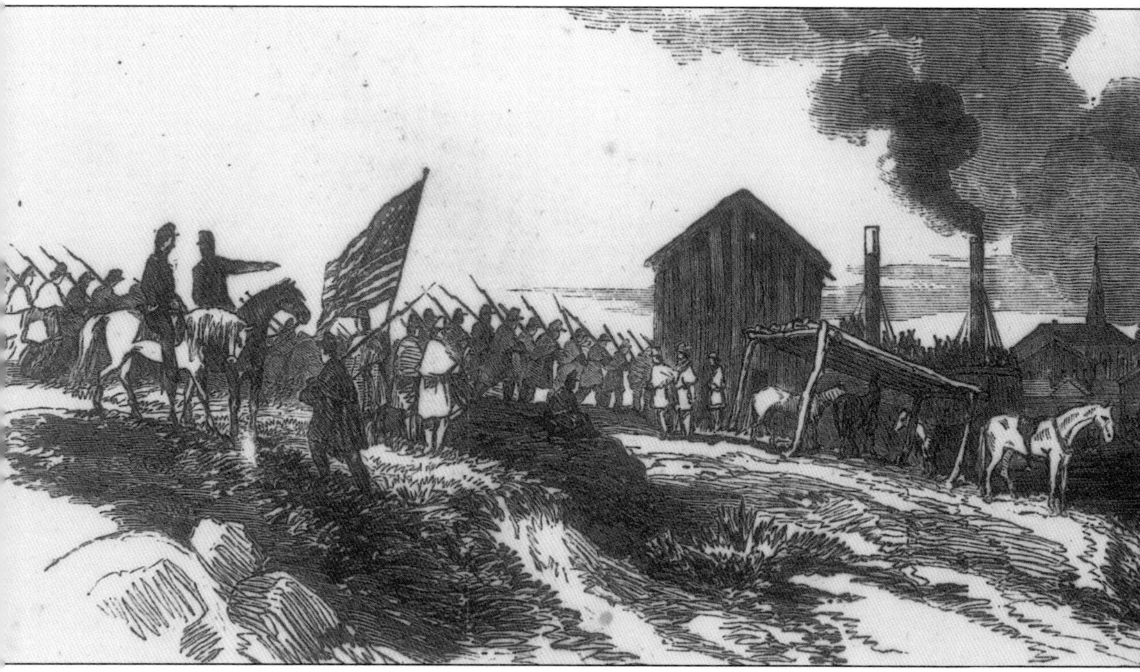

As New Bern fell into the hands of the enemy, some soldiers fleeing through town set fire to several buildings. Also, many panic-stricken residents tried to flee town, while African Americans celebrated the Union victory and pillagers began looting houses and stores. Chaos reigned for about a day until Union forces crossed the Trent (by boat, since retreating Confederates had

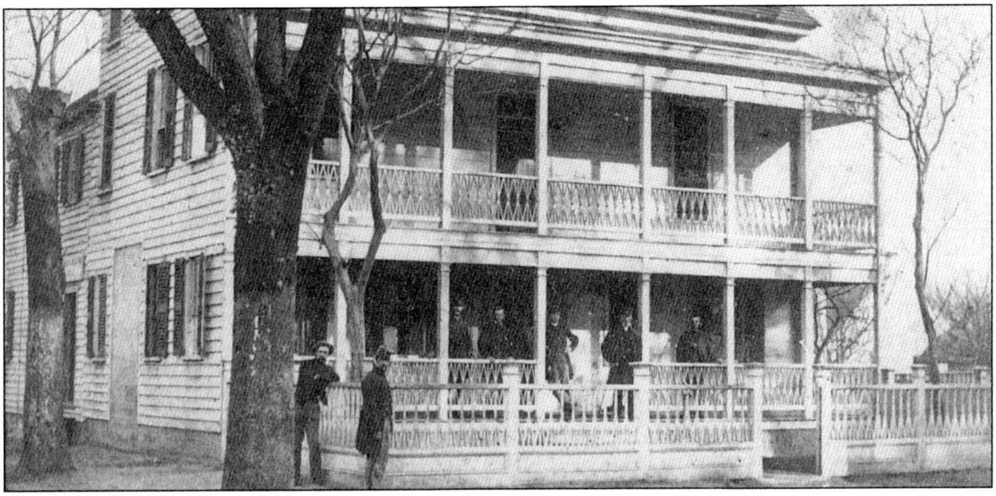

The Union Army maintained its control of New Bern until the war's end in 1865. Several homes were used by the occupying army as officers' quarters and hospitals. The house on the southeast corner of Middle and New Streets served as an office for Foster General Hospital, also called the Stanley General Hospital. The hospital complex itself was bounded by Broad, Craven, New, and Middle Streets. The Union Army only removed its military headquarters and offices outside of town once—in 1864, in response to an epidemic of what is believed to be yellow fever. This photograph is dated c. 1863 and is attributed to O.J. Smith, Union Photograph Rooms, New Bern. (Courtesy of North Carolina Collection, University of North Carolina Library at Chapel Hill.)

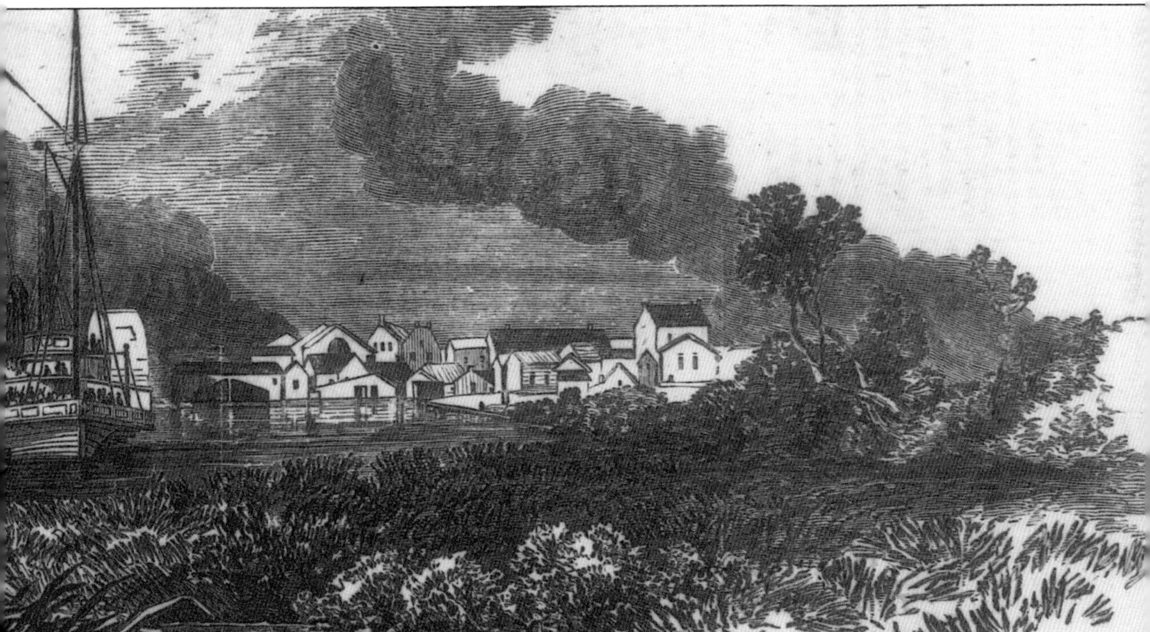

burned the railroad bridge) and took control of the town. This illustration of New Bern shows troops massing on the river bank, preparing for their passage into New Bern. The illustration appeared in the April 26, 1862 issue of *Frank Leslie's Illustrated Newspaper*. (Courtesy of North Carolina Collection, University of North Carolina Library at Chapel Hill.)

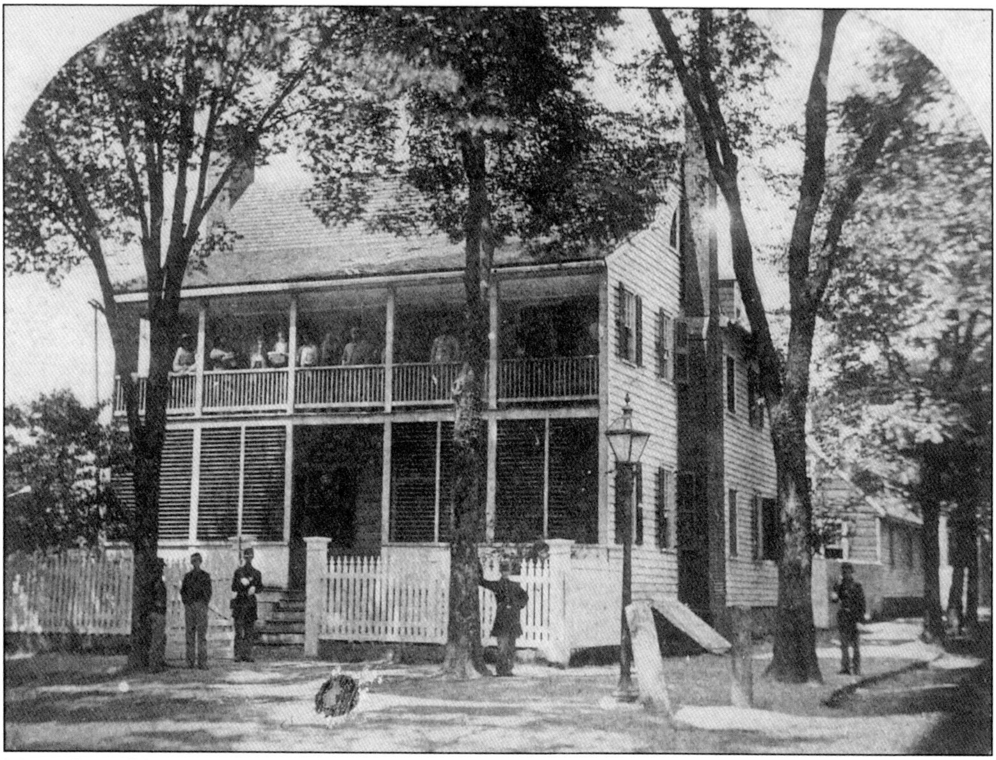

Many "secesh" prisoners were housed in the temporary "secesh" jail, located in the Jones house on the corner of Eden and Pollock Streets. This photograph, dated c. 1863, is attributed to O.J. Smith, Union Photograph Rooms, New Bern. (Courtesy of North Carolina Collection, University of North Carolina Library at Chapel Hill.)

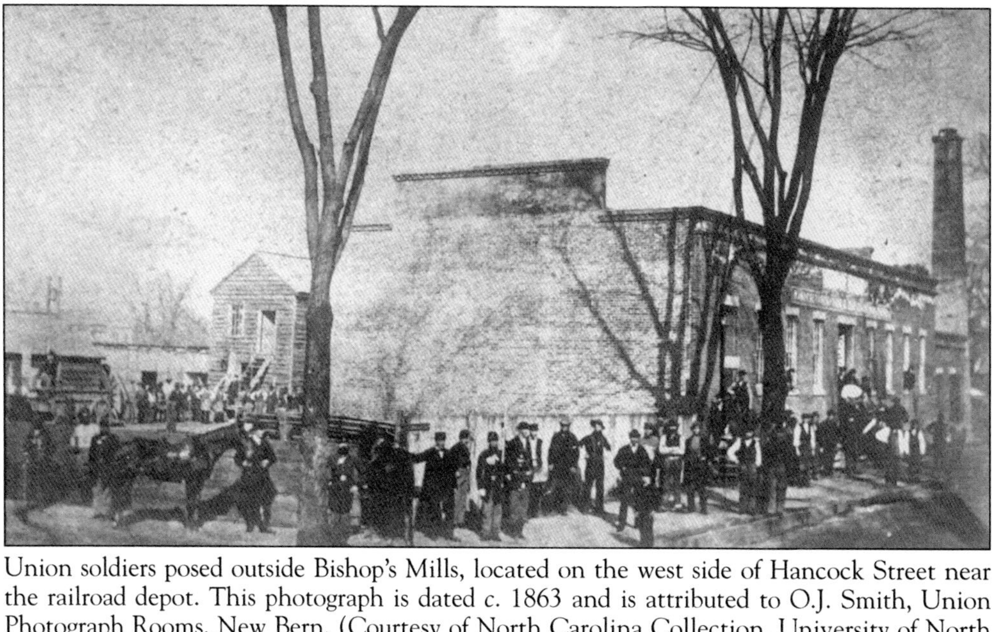

Union soldiers posed outside Bishop's Mills, located on the west side of Hancock Street near the railroad depot. This photograph is dated c. 1863 and is attributed to O.J. Smith, Union Photograph Rooms, New Bern. (Courtesy of North Carolina Collection, University of North Carolina Library at Chapel Hill.)

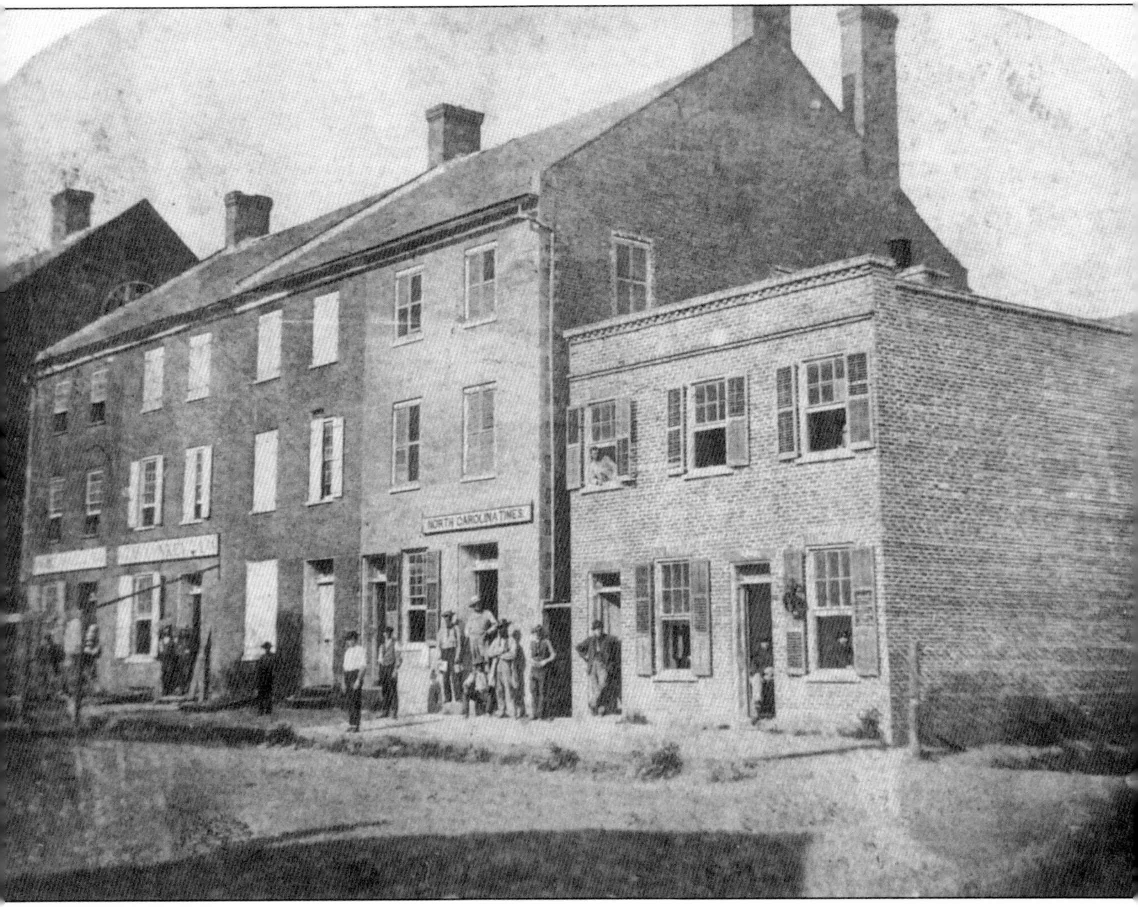

The *Newbern Weekly Progress* was a newspaper published by a staff of Union soldiers. The name of the newspaper was changed in 1864 to the *North Carolina Times*. It eventually became an afternoon daily, with about 1,200 copies printed daily. Delays in mail service sometimes led Corp. George Mills Joy, in charge of the publishing venture, to reprint old news as well as Bible passages. The *North Carolina Times* was located in the 200 block of Craven Street in Stephens' Brick Block, later renovated in 1888 to become New Bern City Hall. This c. 1864 picture is attributed to O.J. Smith, Union Photograph Rooms, New Bern. (Courtesy of North Carolina Collection, University of North Carolina Library at Chapel Hill.)

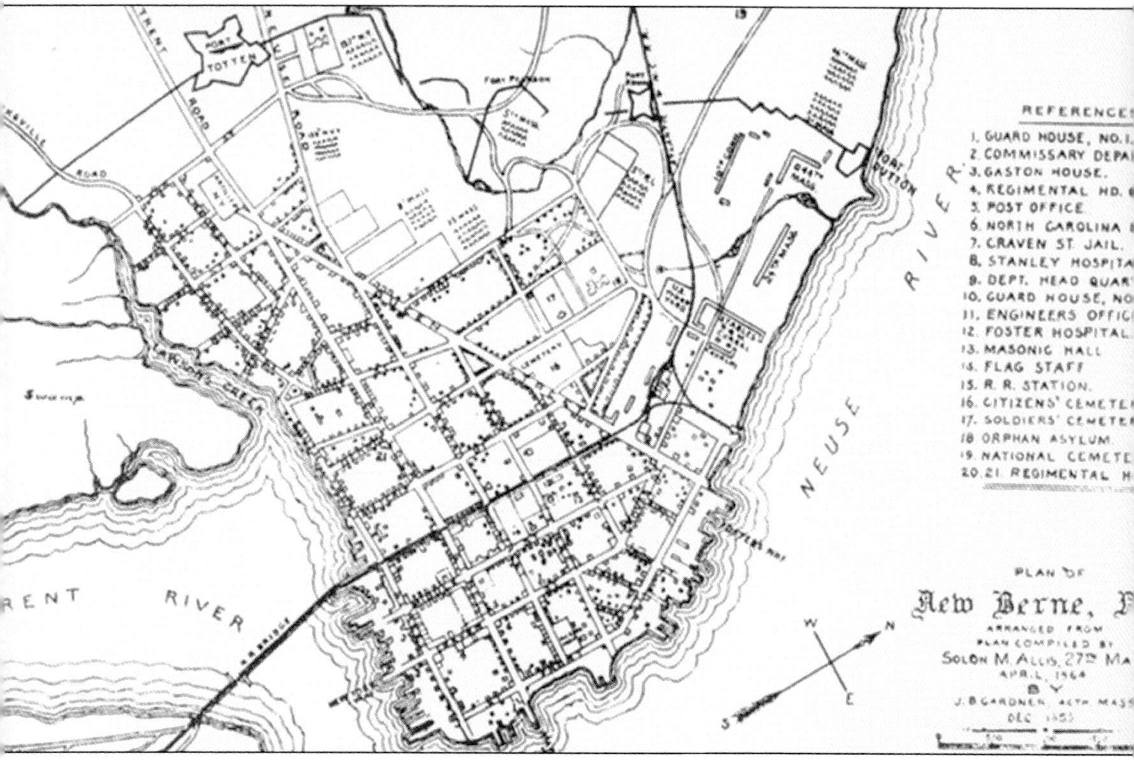

This map showed New Bern as it appeared in 1864. (Courtesy of the New Bern Area Chamber of Commerce.)

Two

FIRES AND DISASTERS

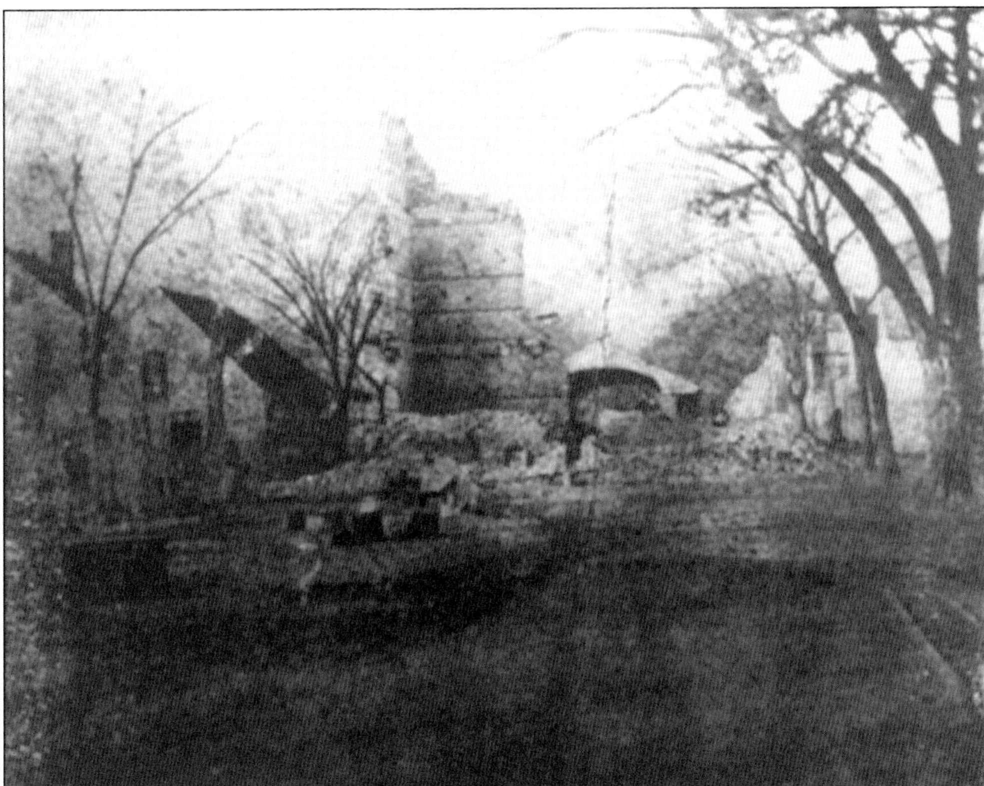

New Bern has faced its fair share of both weather and man-made disasters. This 1861 view depicts part of the ruins of the *c.* 1800 Craven County Courthouse, destroyed by an accidental fire. The courthouse had occupied a site at the center of Broad and Middle Streets. A replacement courthouse was built in 1883 at the northwest corner of Broad and Middle Streets and is still in use today. (Courtesy of New Bern Area Chamber of Commerce.)

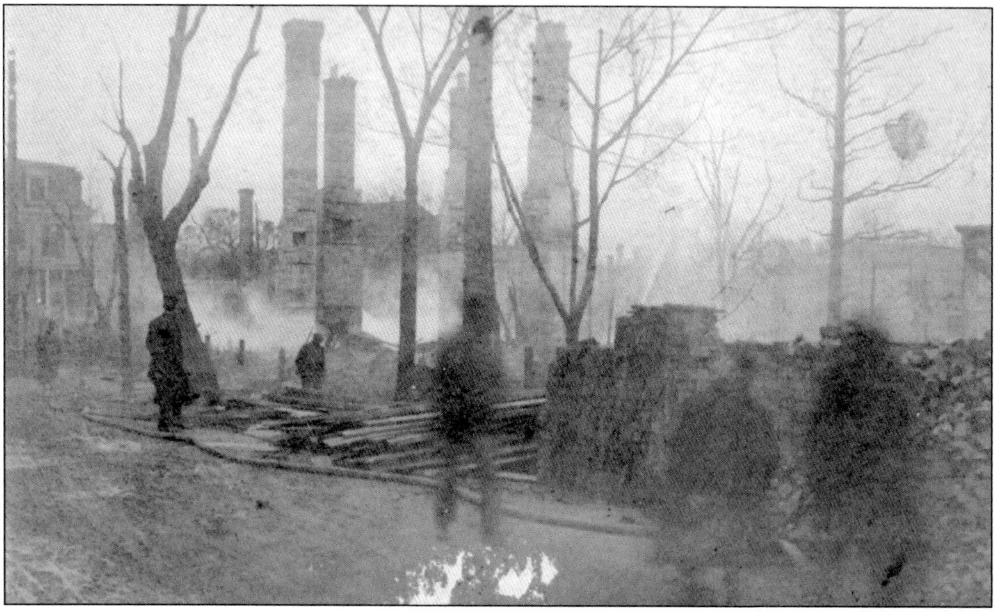

On April 2, 1907, fire destroyed several houses in the Pollock Street area. A newspaper article credited "the magnificent work of the firemen" in containing the blaze. The fire itself was described as "a terrific cyclone of fire sweeping everything before it." (Courtesy of John B. Green III Collection.)

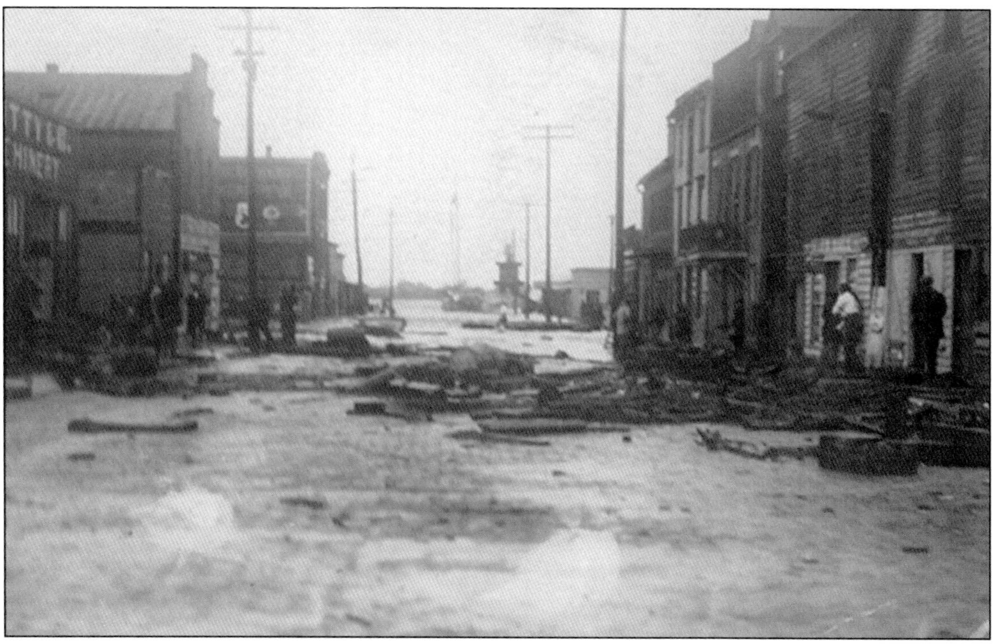

On September 3, 1913, New Bern was struck by a hurricane, which was described at the time as the worst in the town's history. Craven Street (depicted in this postcard) and Middle Street below South Front Street were described as "a scene of desolation" after flood waters rose to a depth of 5 feet. The hurricane also washed away the wooden bridge over the Neuse River. Damages in New Bern totaled $200,000. (Courtesy of John B. Green III Collection.)

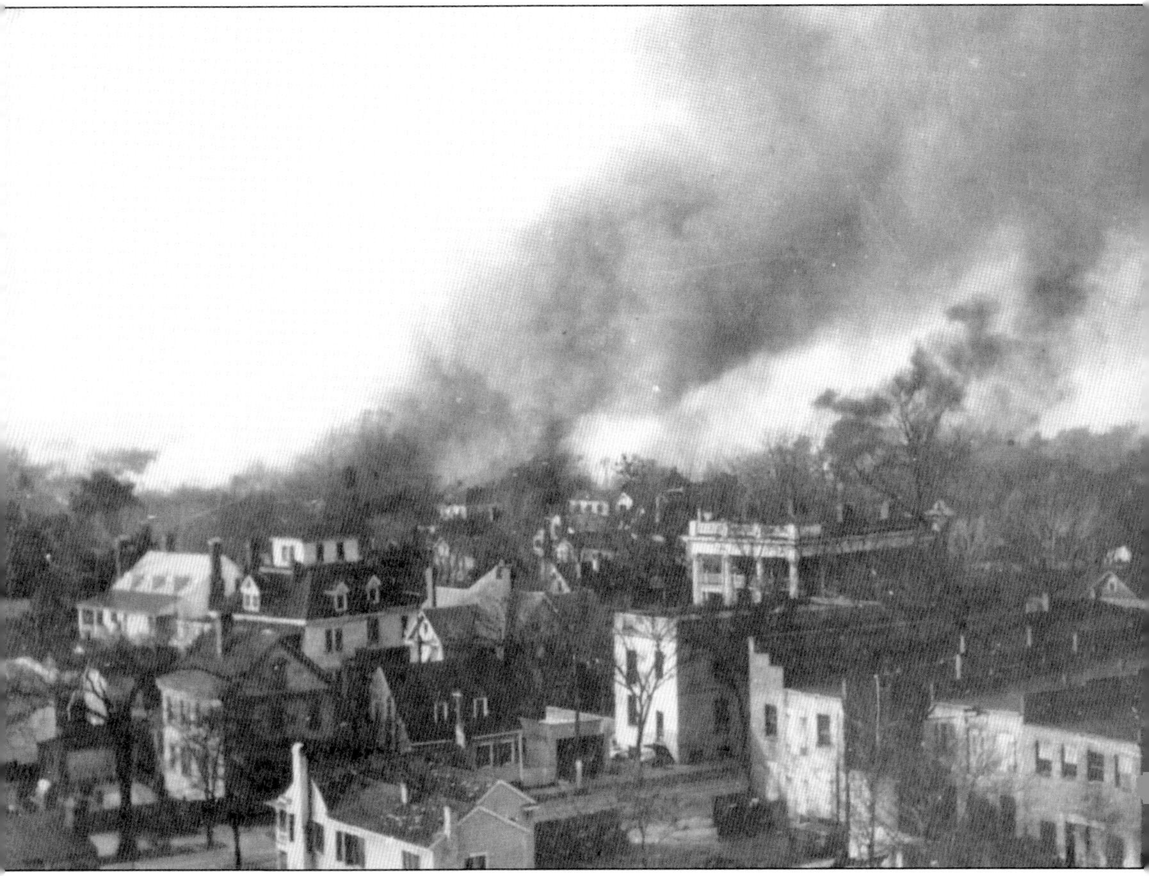

On December 2, 1922, New Bern was struck by a fire of such size and intensity that even today it is still called the Great Fire. Shortly after 8 a.m., a call went out that a fire raged out of control at the Rowland Lumber Company. This first fire was only a sign of things to come. Close to 11 a.m., fire crews were called to another sizable fire in New Bern's African-American community. The fire, fanned by 45-mph winds, quickly consumed three city blocks and steadily moved on as it jumped from house to house, block to block. This view to the northwest shows the fire from the top of the Elks Building at the corner of Middle and Pollock Streets. (Courtesy of New Bern Firemen's Museum.)

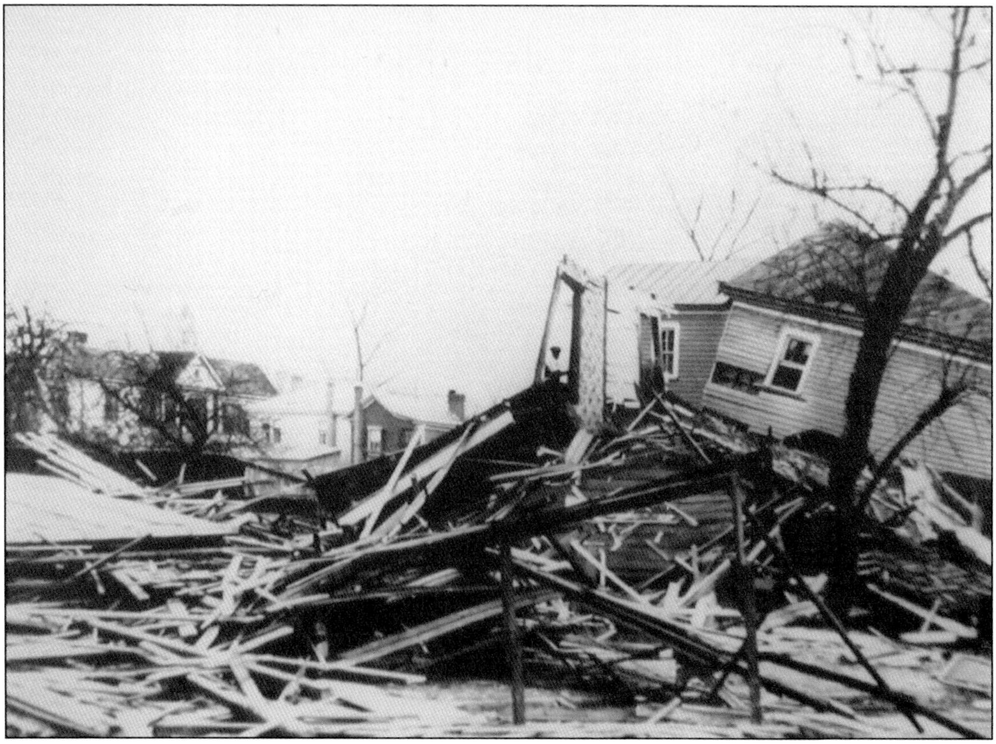

These houses on Queen Street were destroyed by dynamite to create a successful firebreak. Six other houses were pulled down with a cable attached to a railroad switch engine. (Courtesy of New Bern Firemen's Museum.)

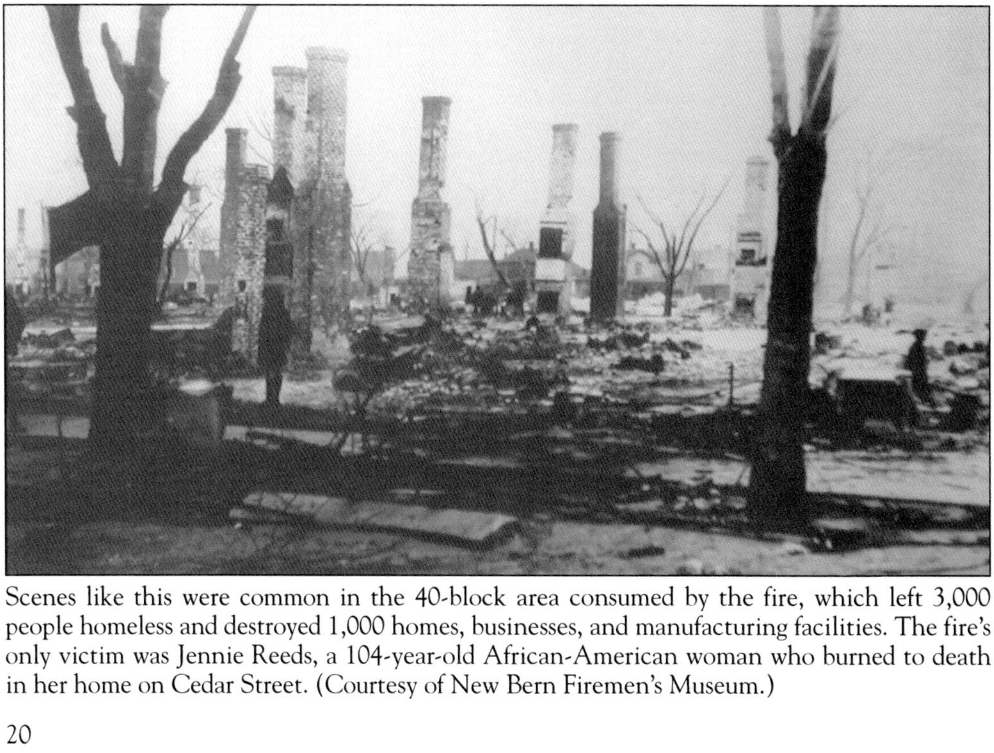

Scenes like this were common in the 40-block area consumed by the fire, which left 3,000 people homeless and destroyed 1,000 homes, businesses, and manufacturing facilities. The fire's only victim was Jennie Reeds, a 104-year-old African-American woman who burned to death in her home on Cedar Street. (Courtesy of New Bern Firemen's Museum.)

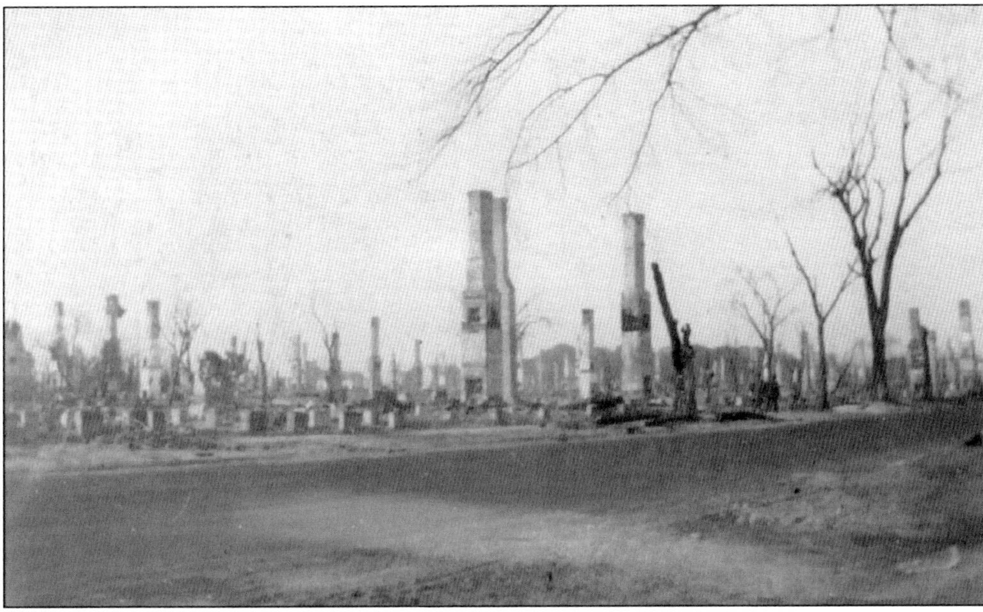

The local newspaper, *The New Bernian*, reported, "Gaunt and stark stood the city of chimneys that marked block upon block of ruins while here and there a brick wall reared its barrier into the air as if to cut off from the sight of further destruction." Financial losses to people and businesses were estimated at $2 million. (Courtesy of John B. Green III Collection.)

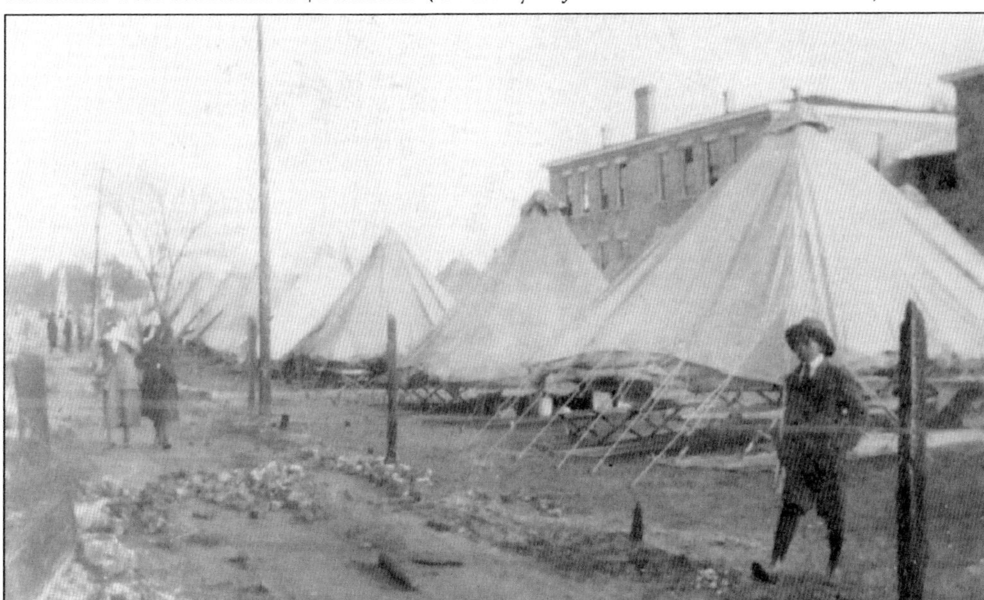

An enormous "Tented City" offered temporary shelter to the thousands left homeless. Thanks to quick action by Senator F.M. Simmons and New Bern Chamber of Commerce president Harry M. Jacobs, tents, cots, and mattresses were provided by the U.S. Army at Fort Bragg, which helped set up food kitchens and arranged for patrols throughout the area to prevent looting. A large food kitchen was also set up in the basement of the West Street colored school to provide sandwiches and coffee. Over 3,000 people were fed on the day following the fire. (Courtesy of John B. Green III Collection.)

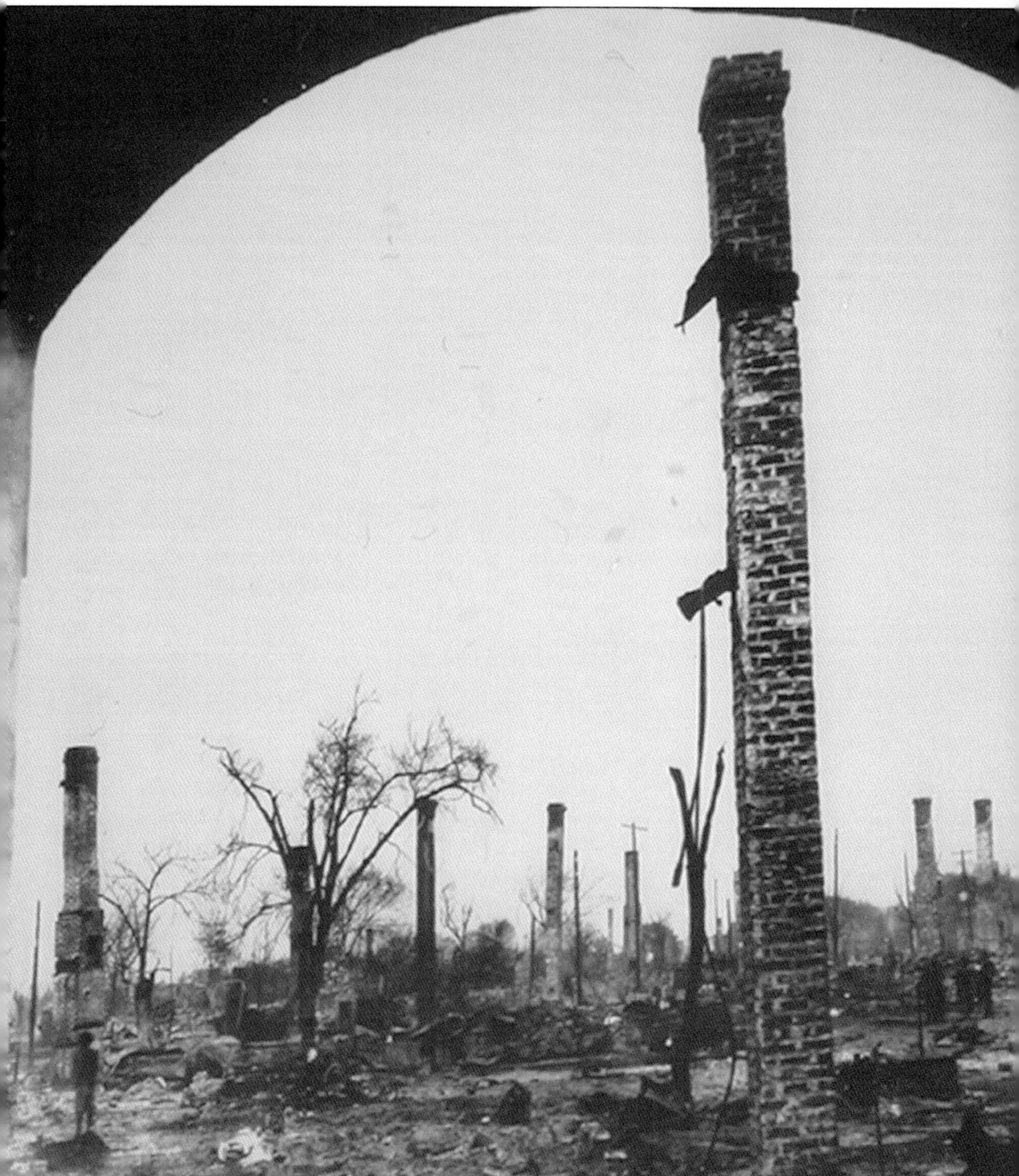

The morning after the fire, New Bern mayor pro tem John S. Holland stated, "We are faced this morning with the most serious and disastrous situation in the history of our city. The fire demon has swooped down upon us and rendered hundreds homeless and penniless. Hundreds are without food, with little clothing, and in many cases nothing except what they have on their backs. It falls upon those of our citizens who have not suffered to give aid to those who are in need." Donations poured in from across the country to help the fire's victims. (Courtesy of New Bern Firemen's Museum.)

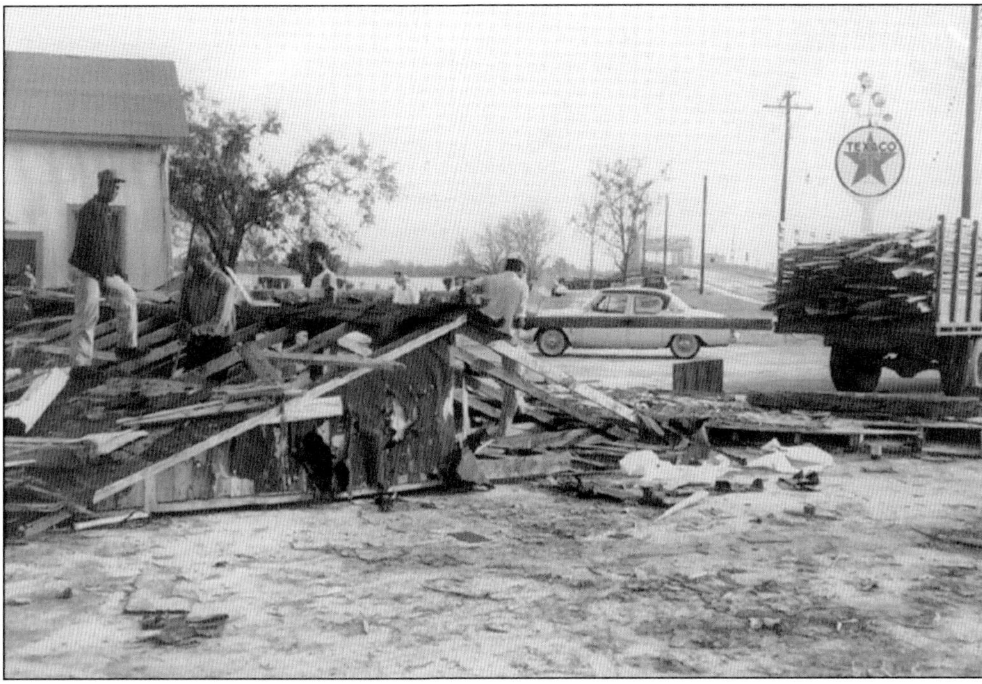

In 1955, New Bern and most of eastern North Carolina faced Hurricanes Connie, Diane, and Ione within five weeks of each other. Connie made landfall on August 12, Diane on August 17, and Ione on September 19. This picture shows the destruction left behind at the corner of South Front and George Streets, which faced the Trent River. These pictures are all dated 1955 but it is not known which hurricane caused the damage shown. All three hurricanes caused wind and flood damage in New Bern. (Courtesy of John B. Green III Collection.)

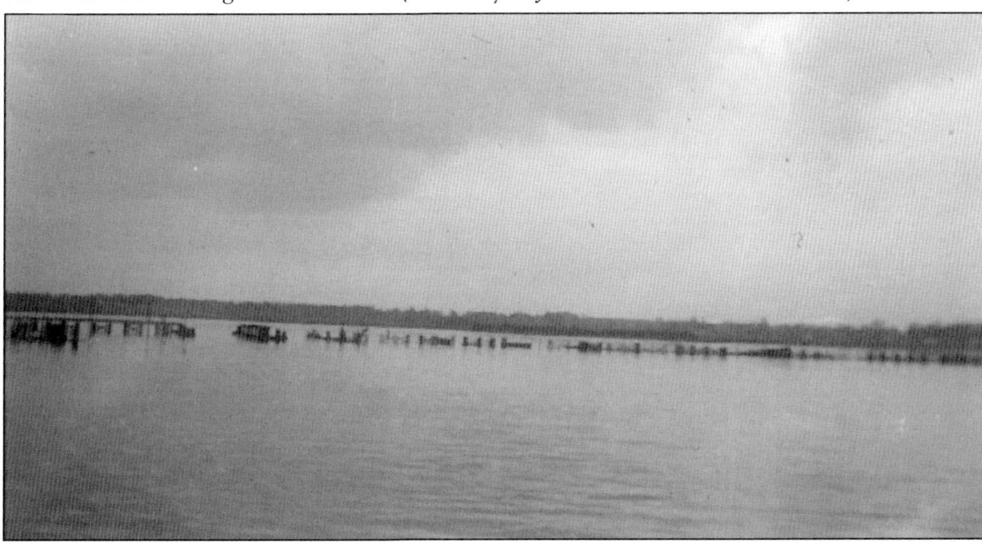

Rapidly rising flood waters caused by one of the 1955 hurricanes washed away the railroad bridge over the Trent River that connected New Bern to James City. The overall wind destruction of Hurricane Connie, which struck in mid-August, was light but the storm's slow movement combined with heavy rainfall and unusually high tides led to the flooding of thousands of acres in eastern North Carolina. (Courtesy of John B. Green III Collection.)

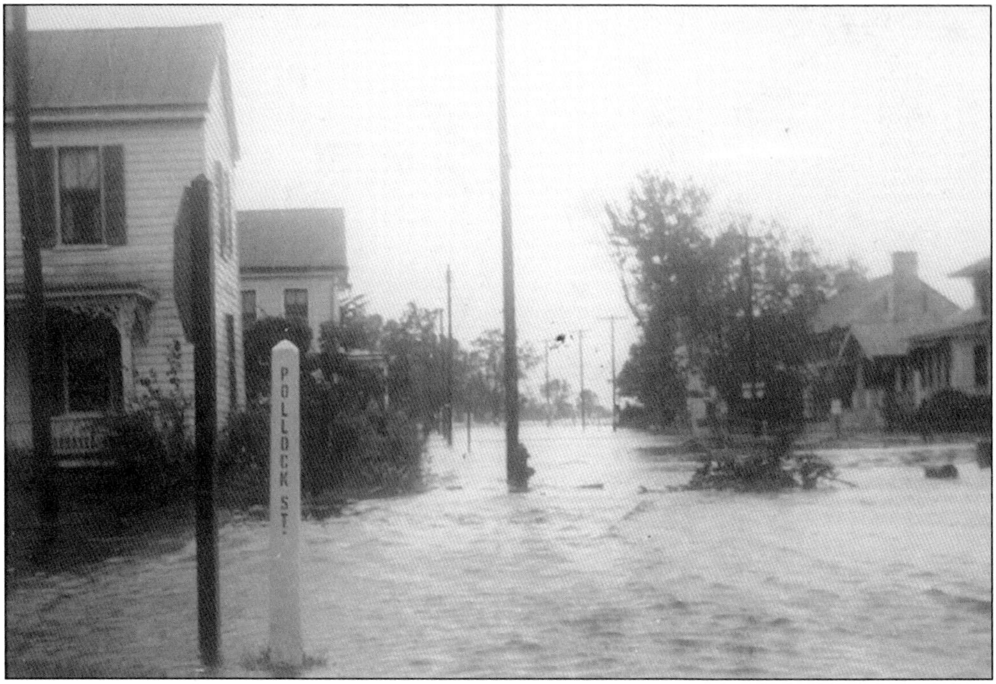

Flooding, shown here at the corner of Pollock and East Front Streets looking toward the northwest, was and is a common occurrence in New Bern after hurricanes. Hurricane Diane, which hit New Bern five days after Connie, caused waist-deep flooding in downtown New Bern. (Courtesy of John B. Green III Collection.)

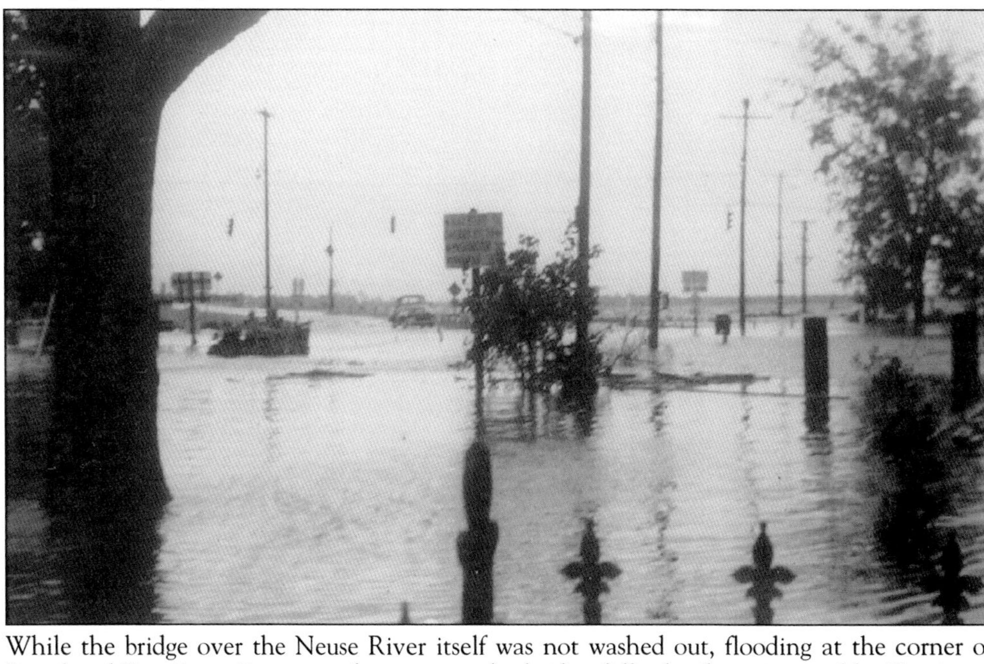

While the bridge over the Neuse River itself was not washed out, flooding at the corner of Broad and East Front Streets made access to the bridge difficult, if not impossible. Hurricane Ione in September 1955 caused flooding over 40 city blocks in New Bern—on some streets even the parking meters were submerged (Courtesy of John B. Green III Collection.)

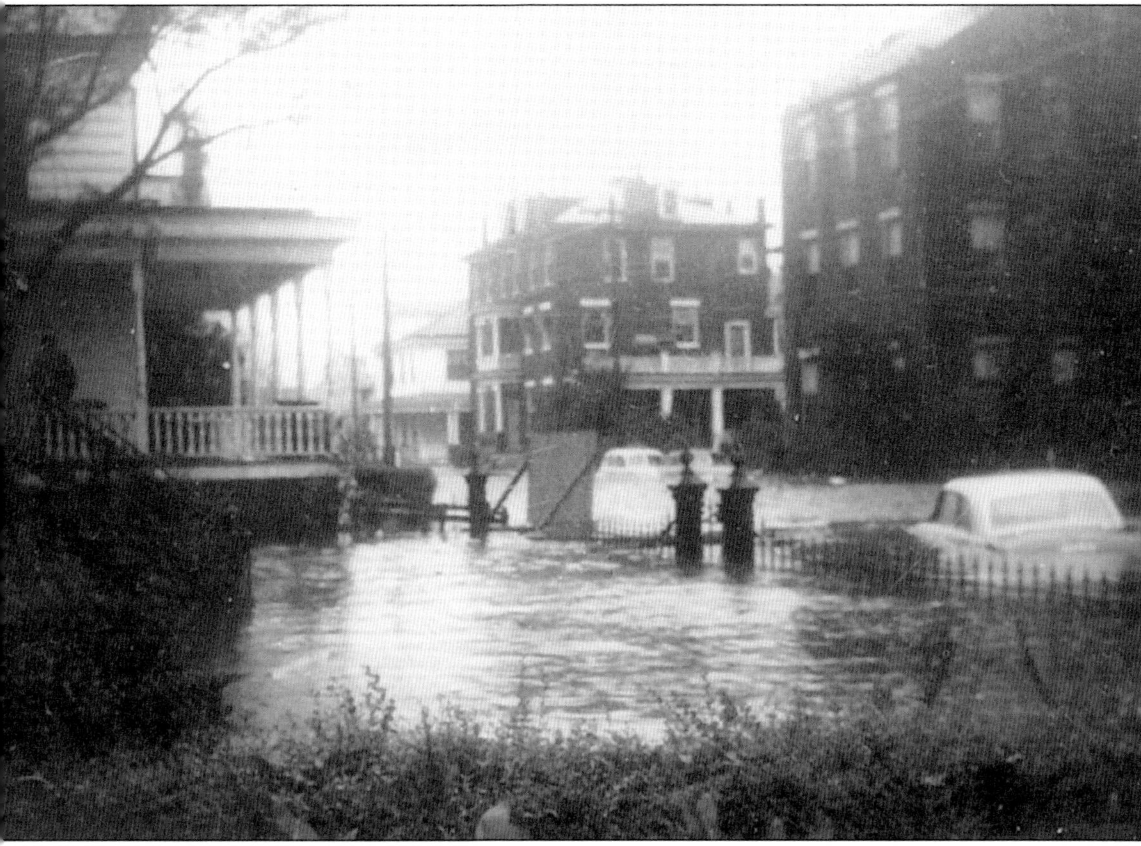

Property and agricultural damage by Connie, Diane, and Ione was estimated at $170 million. Scenes such as the flooding along East Front Street near Pollock Street were common ones. Less than ten days after Ione ravaged eastern North Carolina, New Bernians and other residents of the region breathed a sigh of relief as Hurricane Helene skirted the coast. (Courtesy of John B. Green III Collection.)

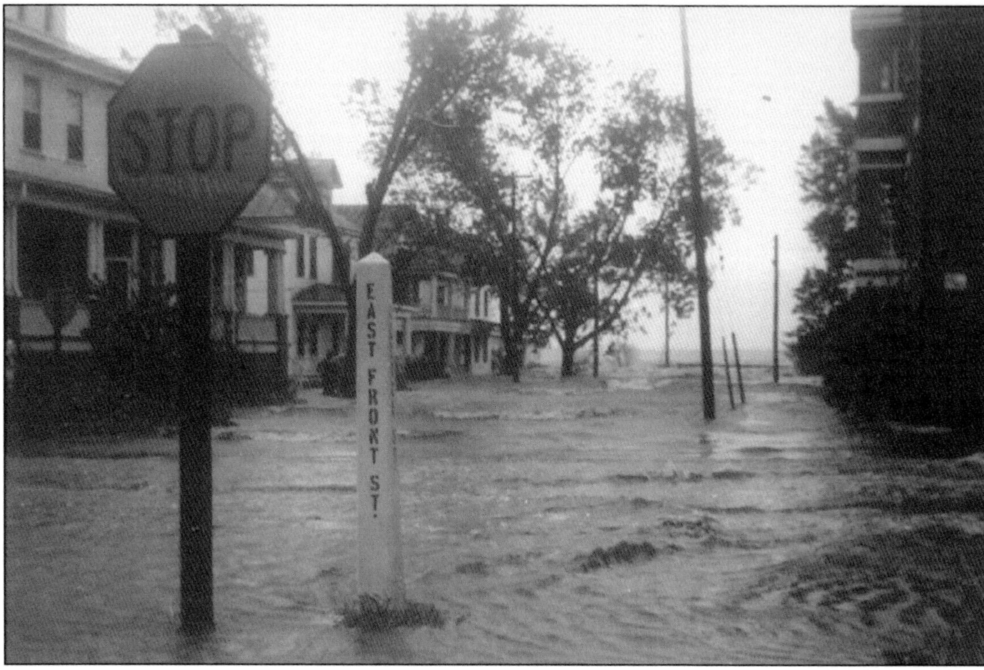

In many neighborhoods, such as the 200 block of Pollock Street looking toward East Front Street and the Neuse River, families sometimes had to be rescued by rowboats. No lives were lost in the area during either Connie or Diane, but two people drowned in New Bern due to flooding caused by Ione. (Courtesy of John B. Green III Collection.)

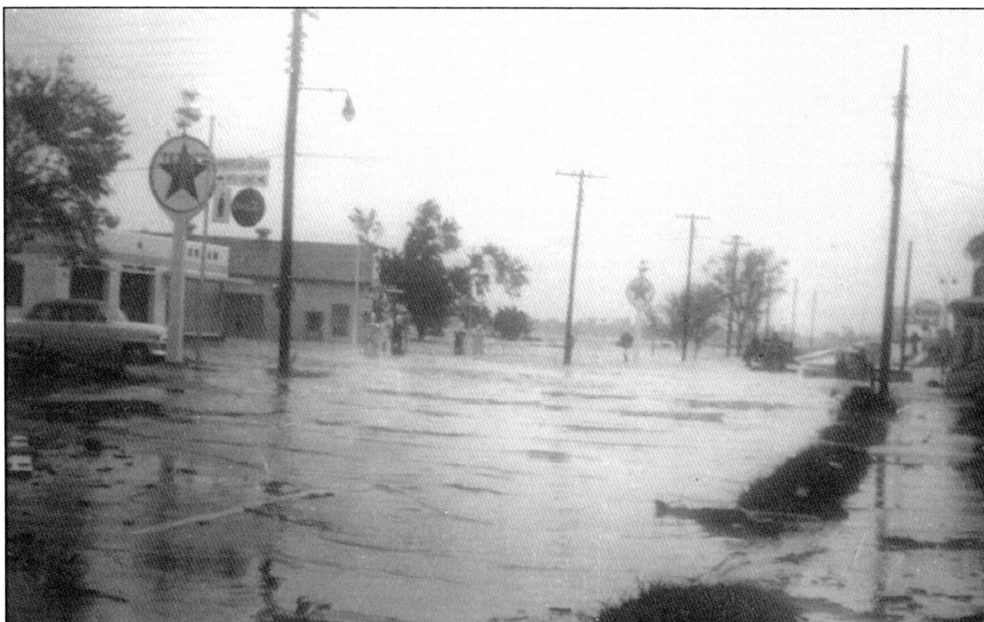

Flooding scenes like this one at the corner of South Front and George Streets—the site of the future South Lawn of the reconstructed Tryon Palace—inspired the Tryon Palace Commission to fill in the garden area with an additional 14 feet of dirt to raise the lawn's level above the highest known flood stage. (Courtesy of John B. Green III Collection.)

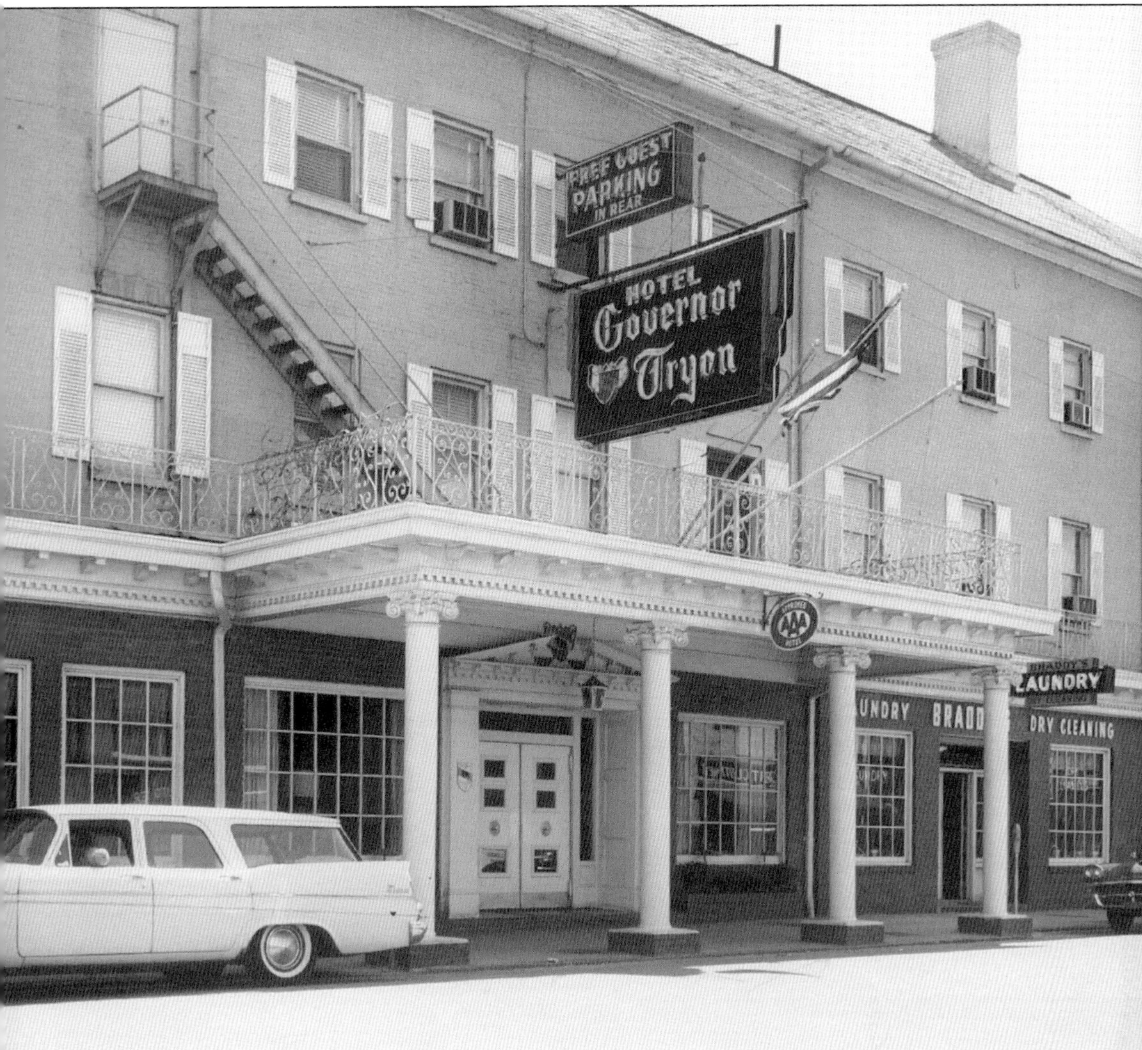

The building that housed the Governor Tryon Hotel was originally built c. 1795–1800 as a combination dwelling and mercantile office. In the 1840s, owners of the Gaston Hotel enlarged the building. The Colonial Hotel Corporation purchased the building in 1954, and they refurbished and reopened it in the mid-1950s as the Hotel Governor Tryon, shown in this 1959 photograph. Advertisements of the day billed the Governor Tryon as "historic New Bern's showplace of the South." (Courtesy of Tryon Palace Historic Sites and Gardens.)

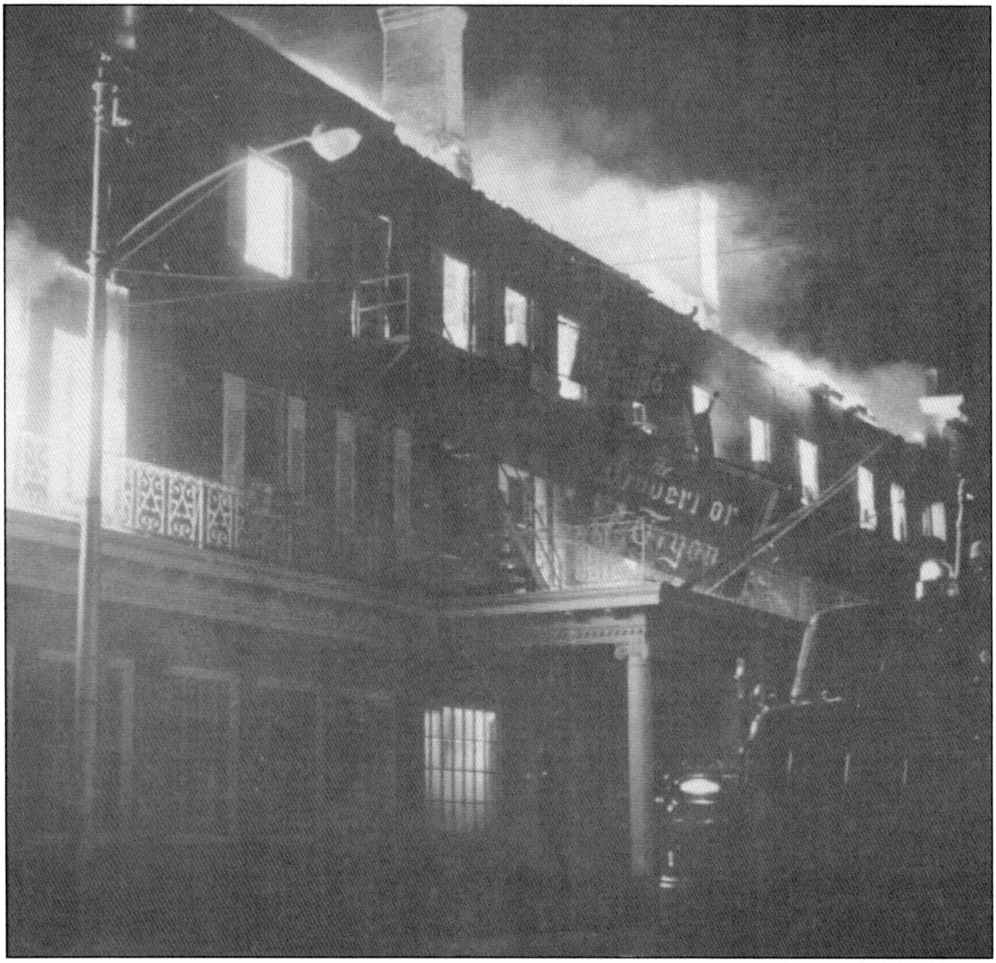

On November 2, 1965, a guest of the hotel smelled smoke and alerted hotel officials. The alarm was sounded at 1:10 a.m. All 37 guests were evacuated safely; however, the blaze intensified until it could be seen for several miles. A bystander at the scene called it New Bern's worst disaster since the Great Fire of 1922. (Courtesy of New Bern Firemen's Museum.)

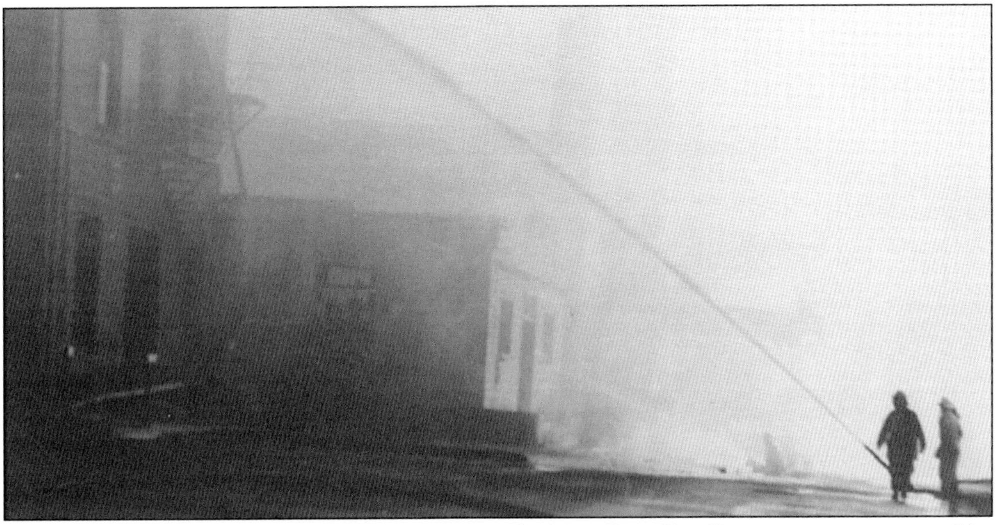

By morning, the building was in smoking ruins. The New Bern Fire Department was assisted by firefighters from Kinston, Cherry Point, Vanceboro, Bridgeton, and Township 7 in containing the blaze. In all, over 100 men and 11 pieces of equipment were used to contain the blaze. Other businesses destroyed by the fire included the A&P Food Store, Craven Bakery, Lady Tryon Beauty Shop, Barker Studios, Liberty Loans, J.W. Smith Insurance Agency, Morgan Glassman Insurance Adjusters, and Coastal Contractors. Damages were estimated at $1 million. (Courtesy of New Bern Firemen's Museum.)

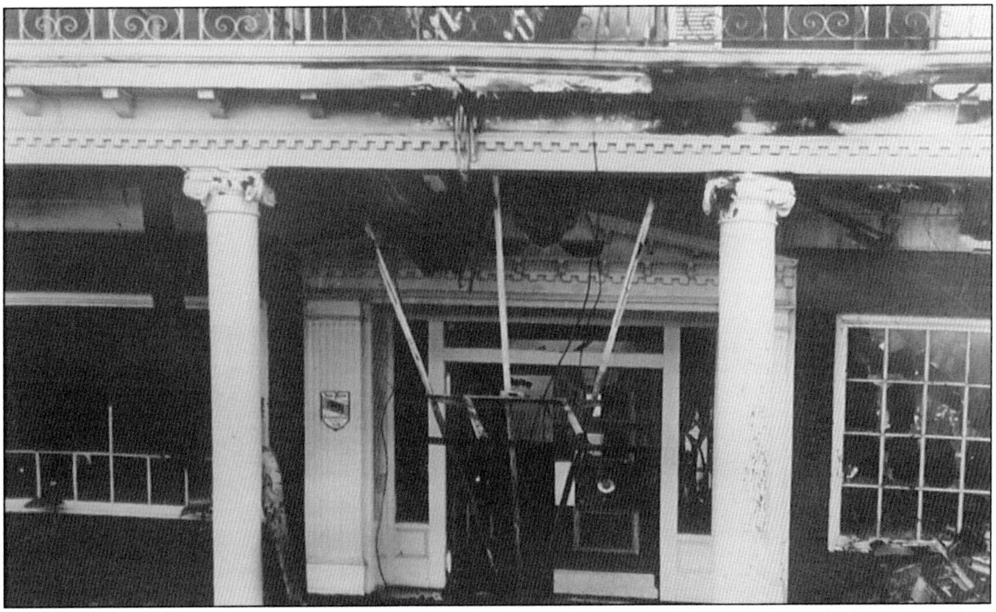

The Hotel Governor Tryon and its predecessor, the Gaston Hotel, were both long noted as prominent city landmarks. The fire of November 1965 ended the building's long reign over the downtown waterfront. Also lost in the blaze was a 250-year-old chandelier and a 150-year-old Italian sofa, among other antiques. That week, the hotel was scheduled to host events celebrating the 20th anniversary of the Tryon Palace Commission. The Sudan Shrine Temple, located in the corner of Broad and East Front Streets, graciously opened its doors to the celebration. (Courtesy of New Bern Firemen's Museum.)

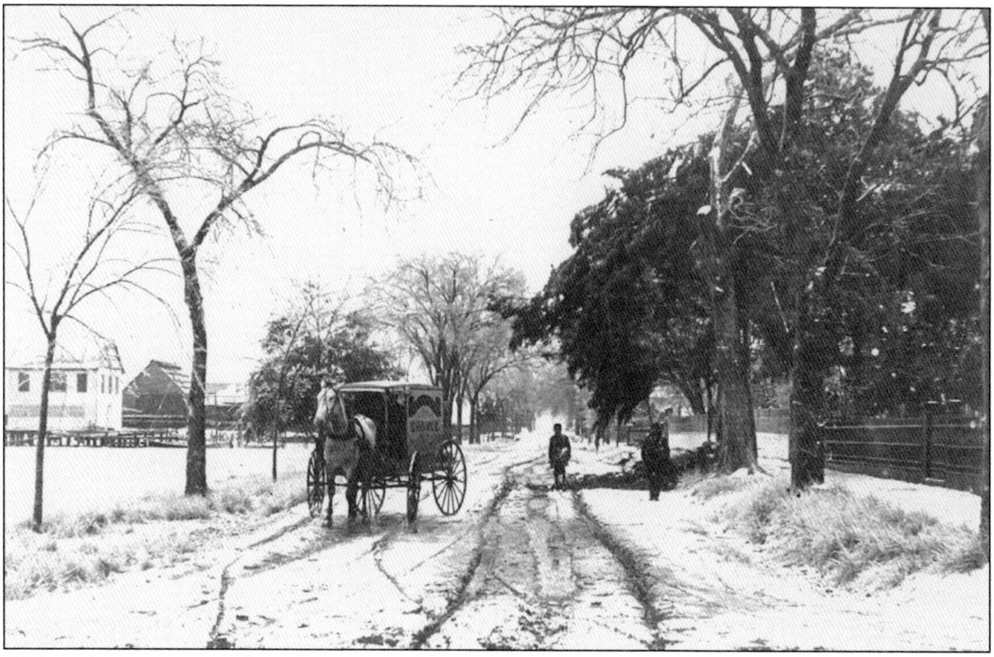

Although not necessarily a disaster on the scale of others depicted in this chapter, snowstorms are rare enough in the New Bern area to warrant a great deal of attention. A c. 1910 snowstorm made the 400 block of East Front Street very picturesque. (Courtesy of Sadie Whitehurst Collection, New Bern-Craven County Public Library.)

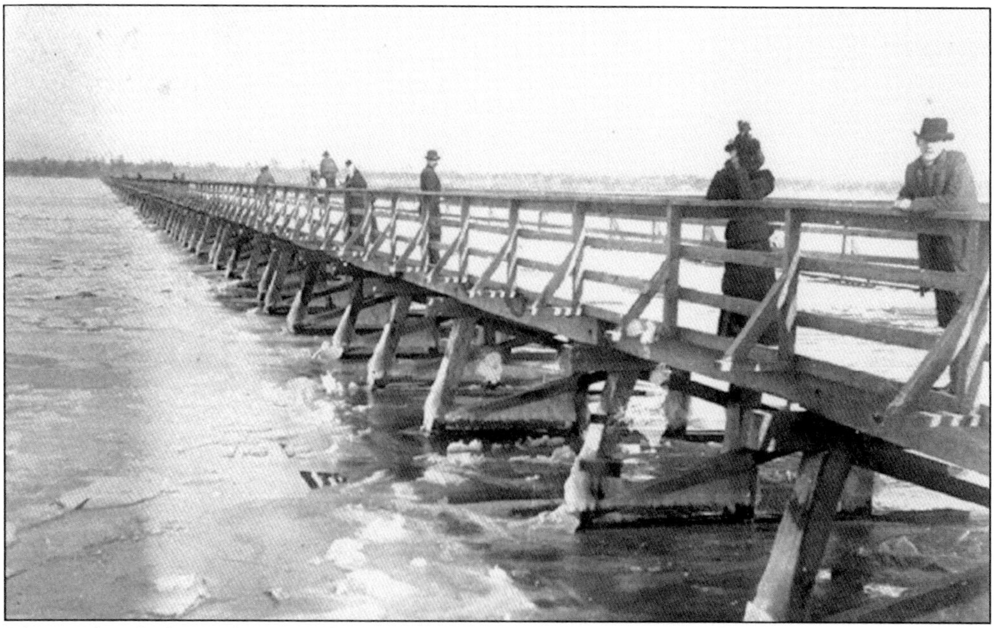

This undated photo depicts a frozen Neuse River. In 1916, a newspaper article in the *Daily Journal* appealed to residents for donations to help purchase clothing and firewood for the city's poor after a prolonged period of colder than normal winter weather. This picture may have been taken around that time. (Courtesy of Sadie Whitehurst Collection, New Bern-Craven County Public Library.)

Three

PLACES OF NEW BERN

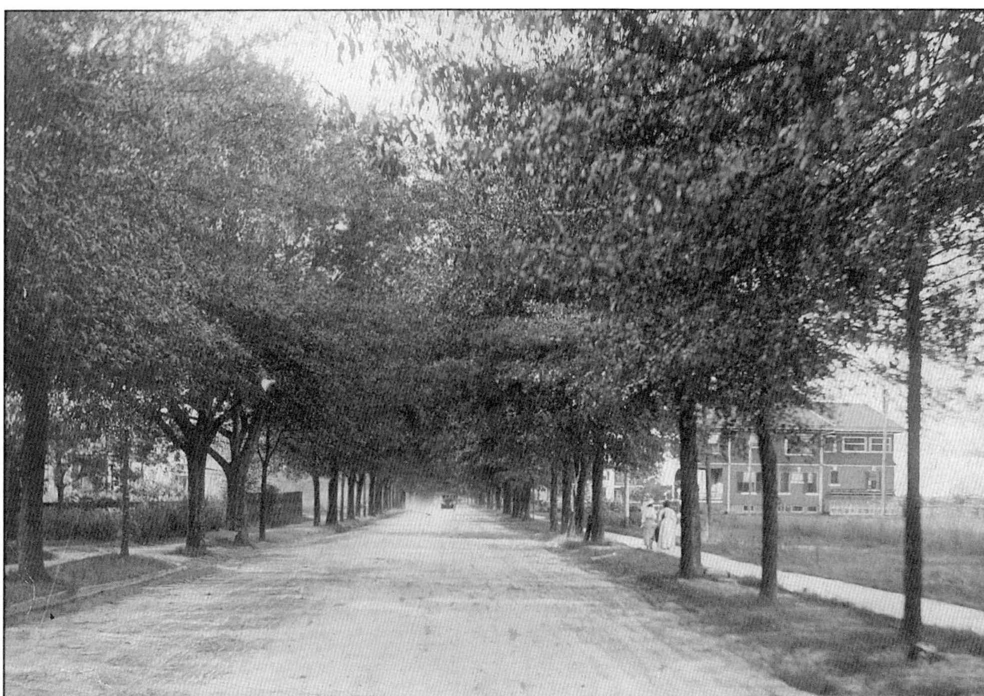

Several women are shown here strolling along dusty National Avenue, *c.* 1900. At that time, New Bern was a quiet, small town. Much was to change over the course of the next hundred years. (Courtesy of Tom Faulkenberry Collection.)

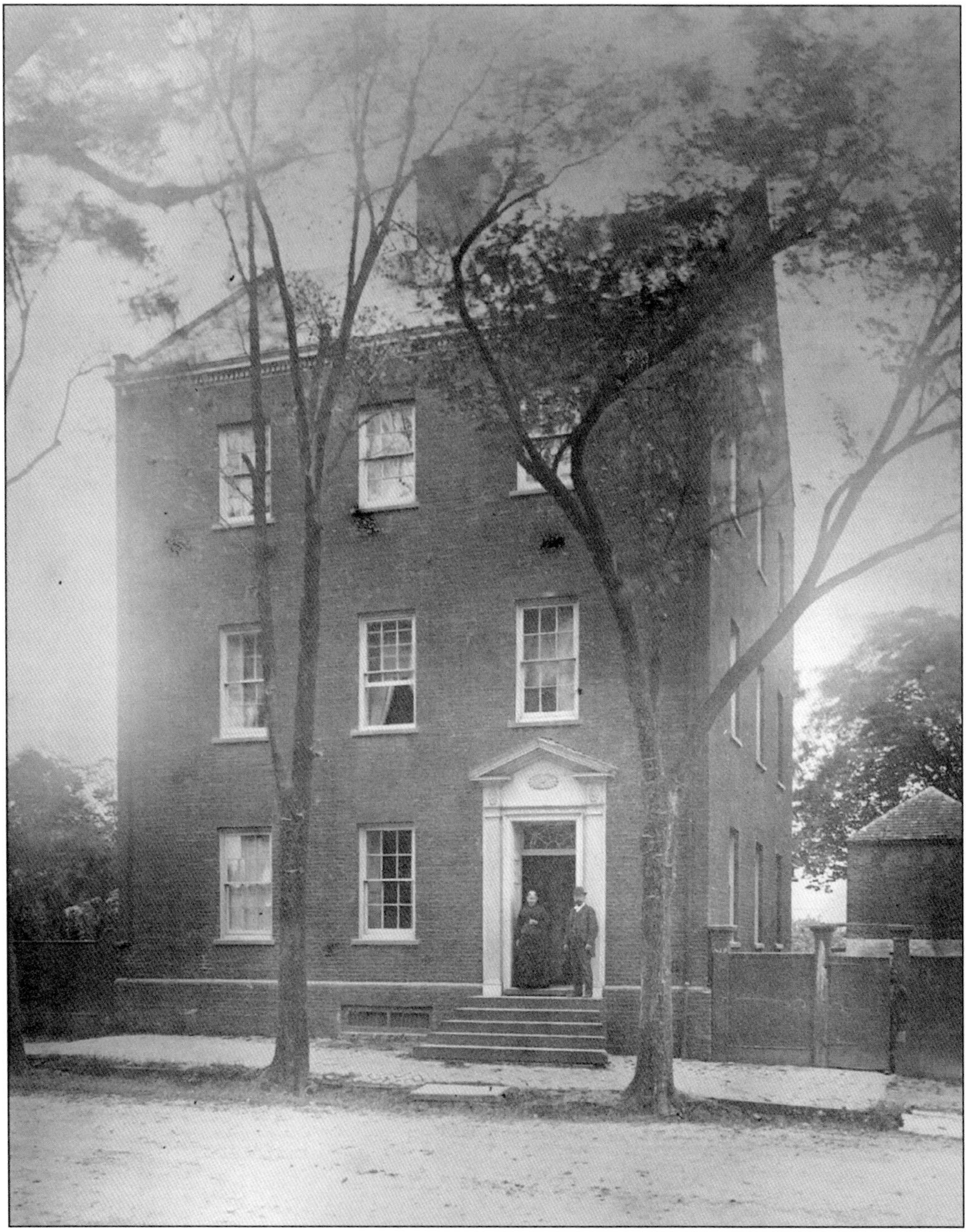

This is an 1880s view of the Isaac Taylor House, originally built *c.* 1792 for that successful merchant, ship owner, and planter. Located at 228 Craven Street, the house today has been fully restored and houses an art gallery (Courtesy of Tryon Palace Historic Sites and Gardens.)

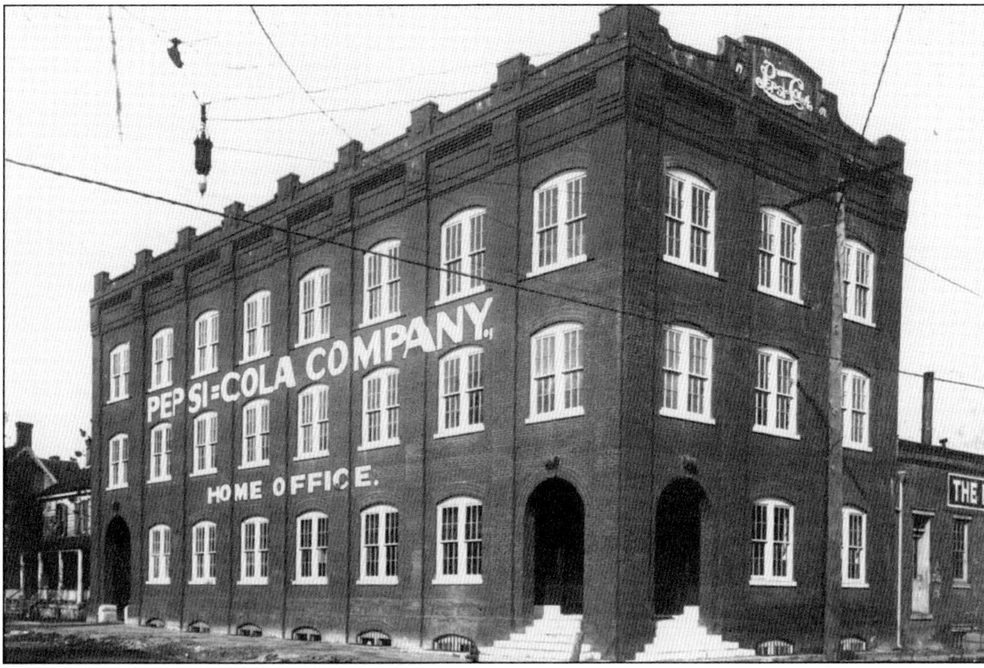

Designed by architect Herbert W. Simpson, the Pepsi-Cola Home Office, constructed in 1902 and shown in this 1908 view, was located at the northwest corner of Johnson and Hancock Streets. Local pharmacist Caleb Bradham, who invented Pepsi, lost the business to bankruptcy in 1923. The home office was connected to the building at the right, known as Bishop's Mill, an older building that was used as a coffin factory during the Civil War. Both buildings were torn down in the 1970s. (Courtesy of Pepsi-Cola Bottling Company Collection, New Bern-Craven County Public Library.)

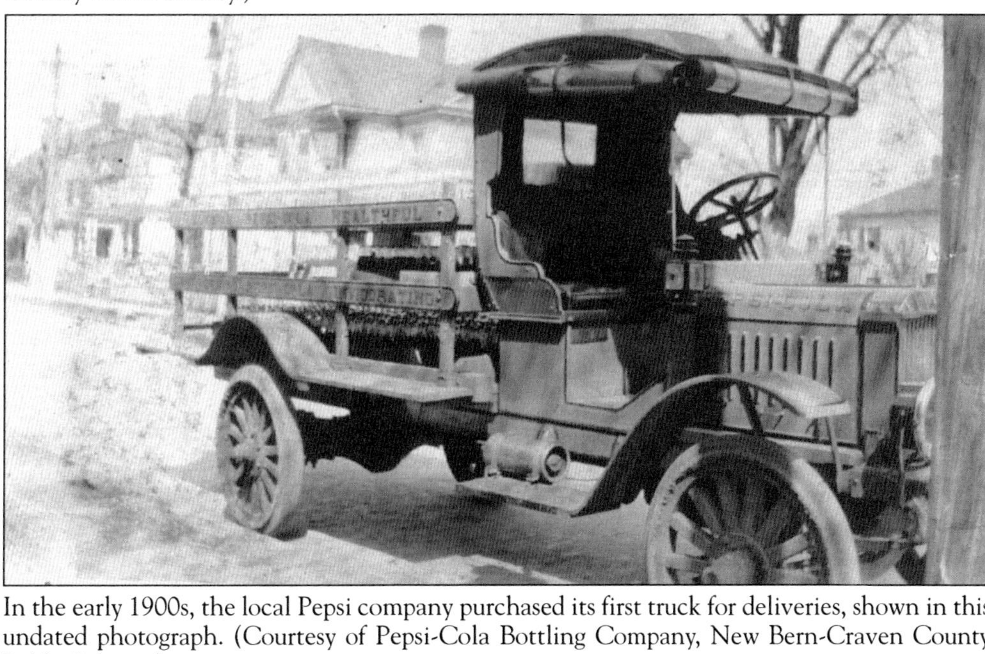

In the early 1900s, the local Pepsi company purchased its first truck for deliveries, shown in this undated photograph. (Courtesy of Pepsi-Cola Bottling Company, New Bern-Craven County Public Library.)

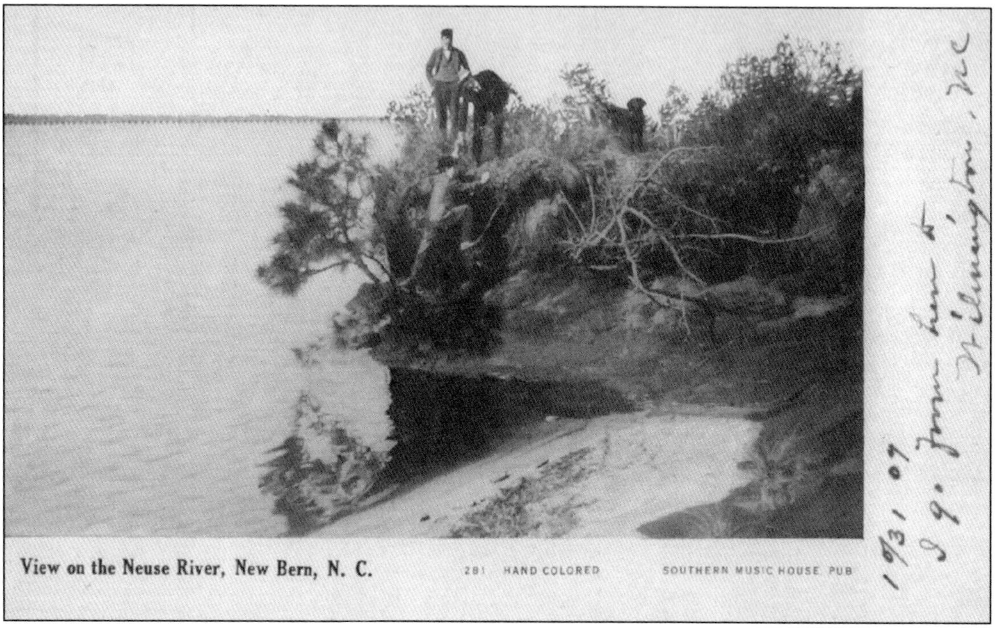

This postcard view of the Neuse River, dating from approximately 1910, was hand-colored. (Courtesy of John B. Green III Collection.)

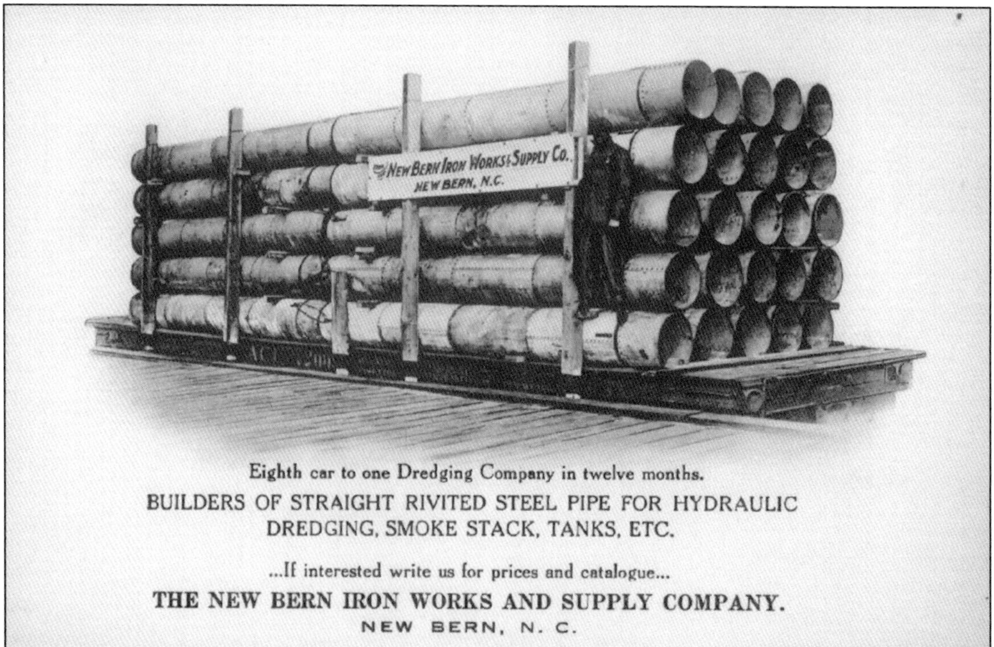

Postcards also were a popular way to advertise local businesses. The New Bern Iron Works and Supply Company offered this *c.* 1910 postcard, inviting prospective customers to "write us for prices and catalogue." (Courtesy of John B. Green III Collection.)

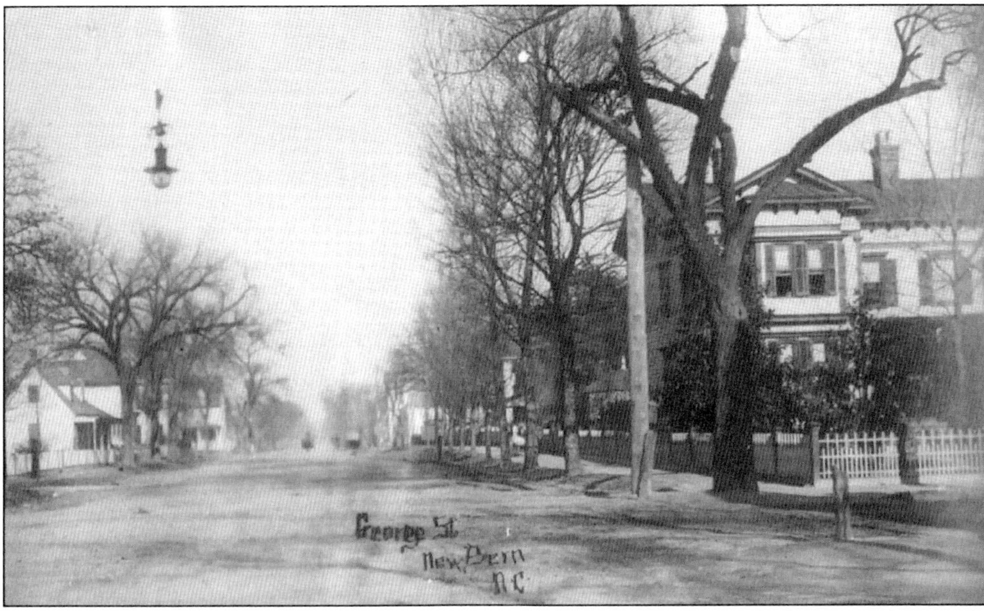

This c. 1910 view shows the intersection of George and Pollock looking to the north. The house at the right, known as the Commission House, is today part of the Tryon Palace Historic Sites and Gardens complex and serves as administrative offices. (Courtesy of John B. Green III Collection.)

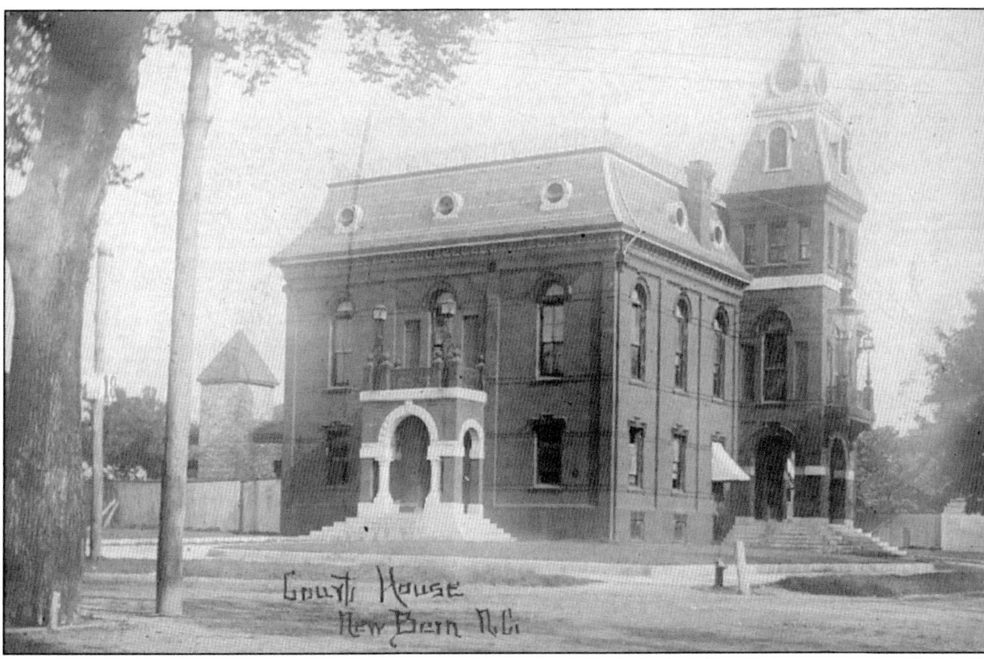

A c. 1910 view of the Craven County Courthouse included the "hanging tower" to the left, where executions by hanging took place. The courthouse was constructed in the 1880s and is still in use today, but the hanging tower is gone. (Courtesy of John B. Green III Collection.)

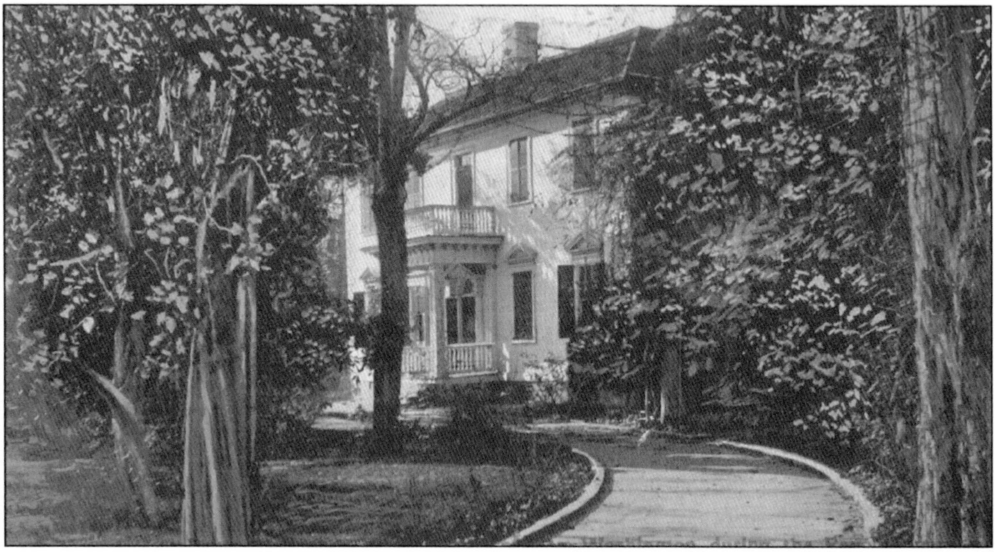

These two views are of the John Wright Stanly home (top postcard, c. 1910), constructed in the late 1700s, which later became the home of James A. Bryan (bottom postcard, c. 1910.) The home was first located at the corner of Middle and New Street and was moved around the corner to a lot on New Street in 1932 to make way for the new federal post office. The Bryan heirs at that time sold the house to the library association, and it was remodeled and used as a library for three decades. In the 1960s, a new regional library building was constructed at Johnson and Middle Streets, and the library board donated the house to the Tryon Palace complex with the proviso that the house be restored. Tryon Palace removed the oldest part of the house to a lot at 307 George Street in 1966, and restored the home to its appearance in the lifetime of John Wright Stanly. George Washington spent two nights in this house during his southern tour in 1791; the house had been empty since Stanly and his wife died of yellow fever in 1789. Occupied and then sold by Stanly heirs, the house changed hands a number of times before Bryan purchased it in 1884. (Courtesy of John B. Green III Collection.)

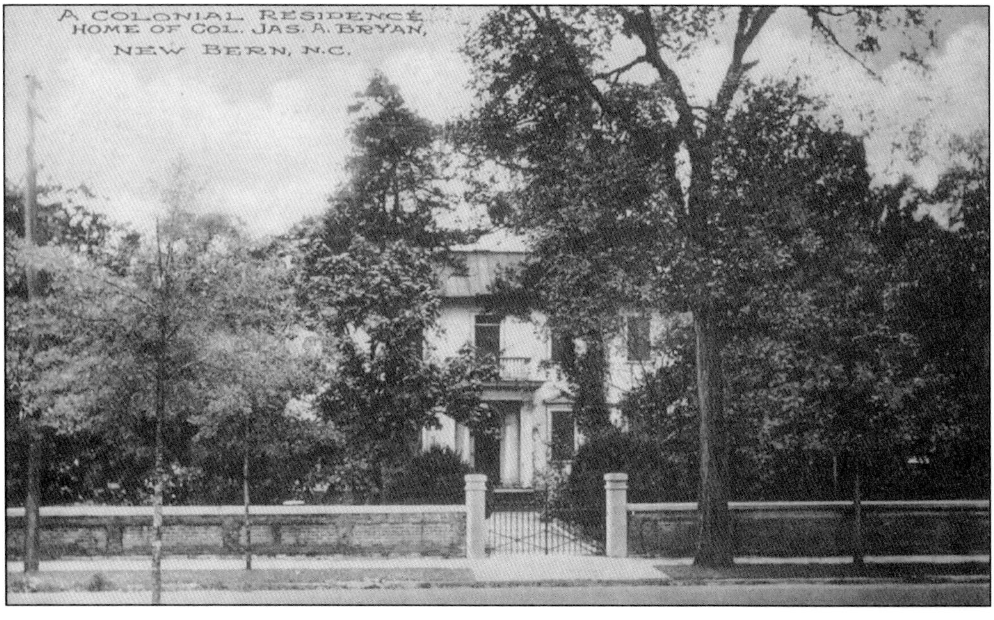

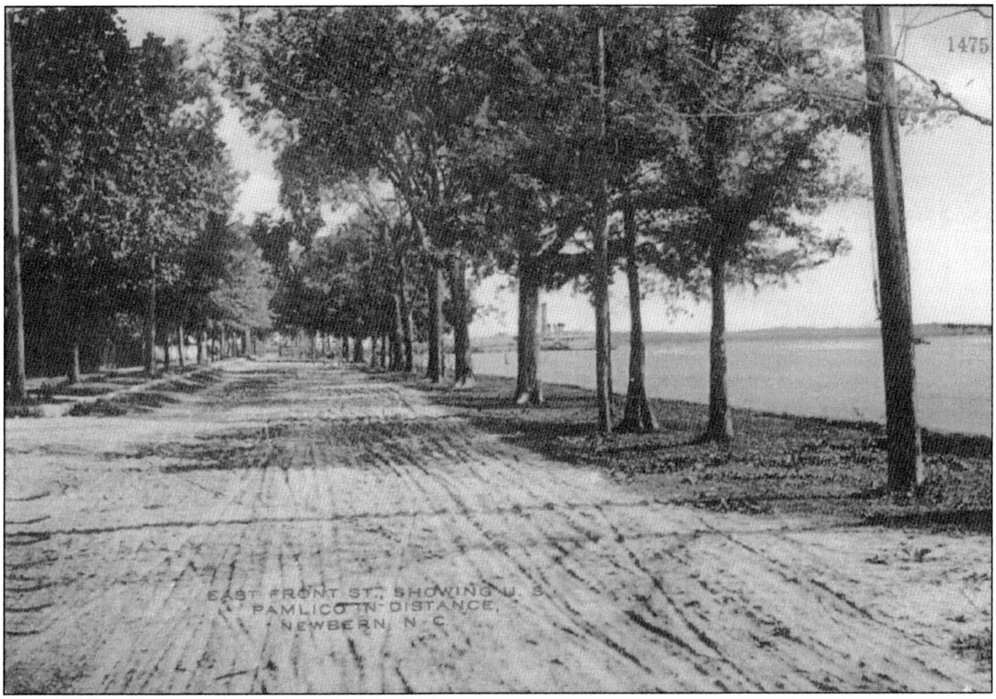

This *c.* 1910 postcard view of East Front Street (top postcard) depicts the Coast Guard cutter *Pamlico* in the distance. Built in 1907, it patrolled the waters of eastern North Carolina and often docked at the foot of Pollock Street (bottom postcard) until it was decommissioned in 1947. The hull of the *Pamlico* was painted gray during World War II. (Courtesy of John B. Green III Collection.)

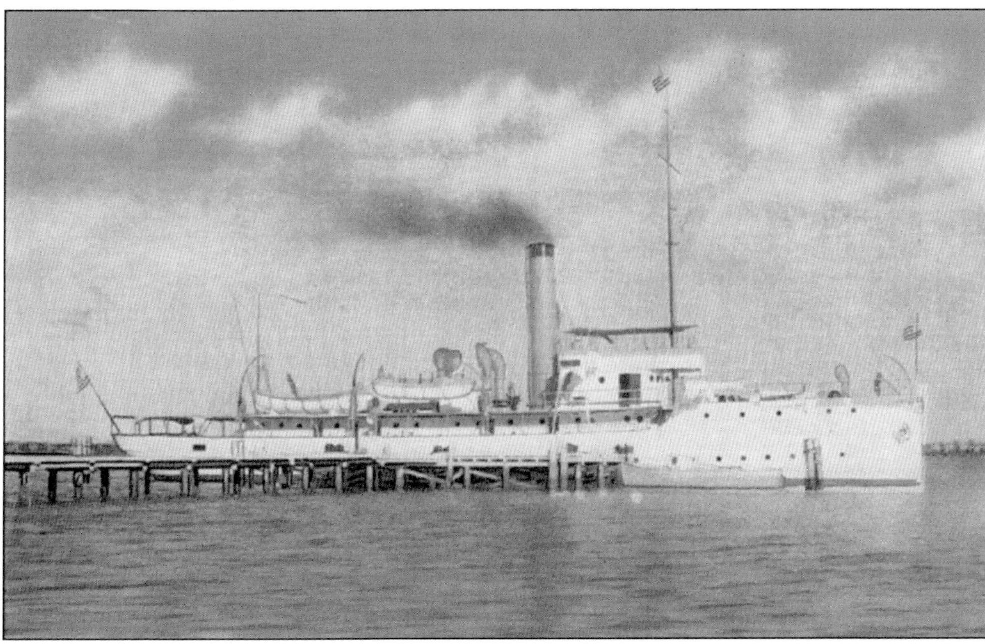

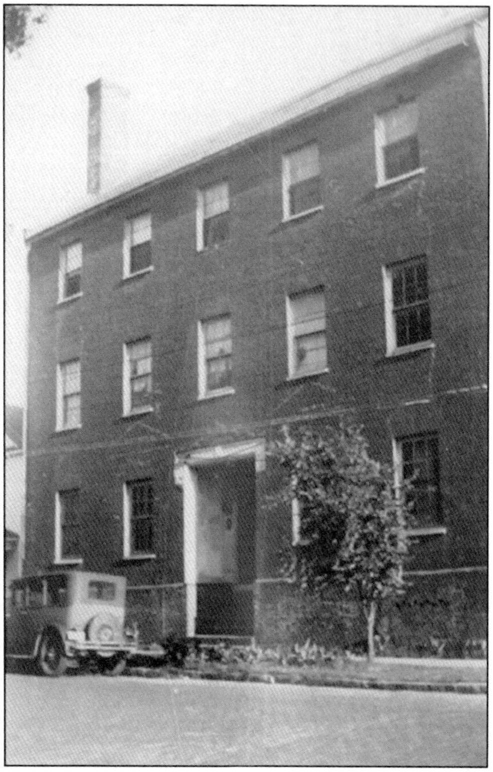

The Harvey Mansion, 219 South Front Street, was originally constructed in 1798 for John Harvey as a combination residence, business, and warehouse. Shown in this 1922 photograph, the building has been used for a number of purposes, including a boardinghouse, an academy, an apartment building, and a community college before it was restored as a bed-and-breakfast inn. (Courtesy of John B. Green III Collection.)

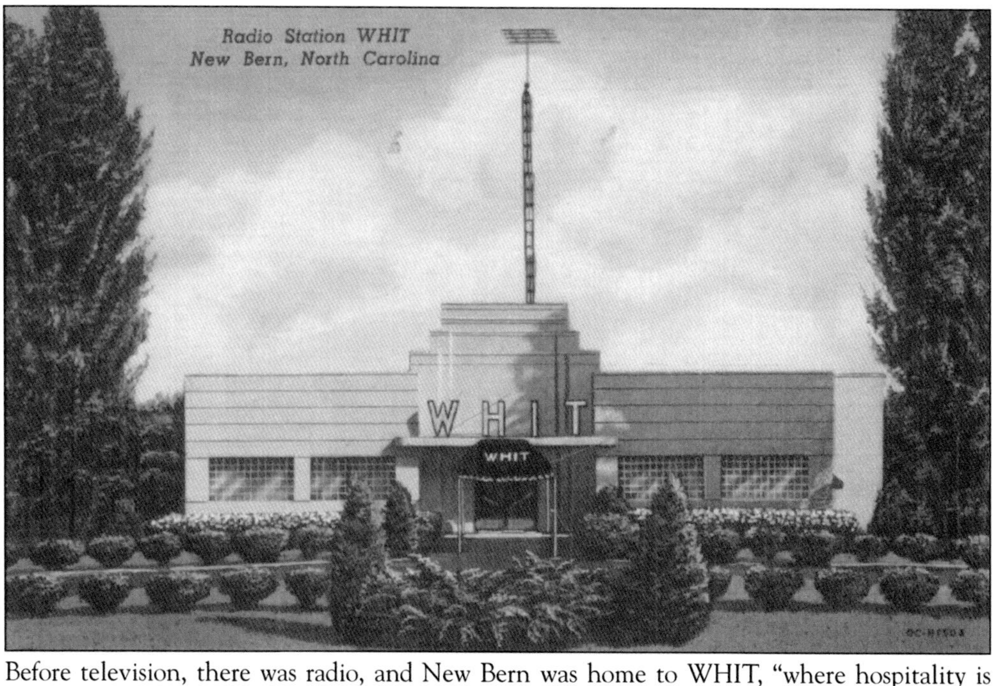

Before television, there was radio, and New Bern was home to WHIT, "where hospitality is traditional." The station, shown in this c. 1940s postcard, was established in 1942. (Courtesy of John B. Green III Collection.)

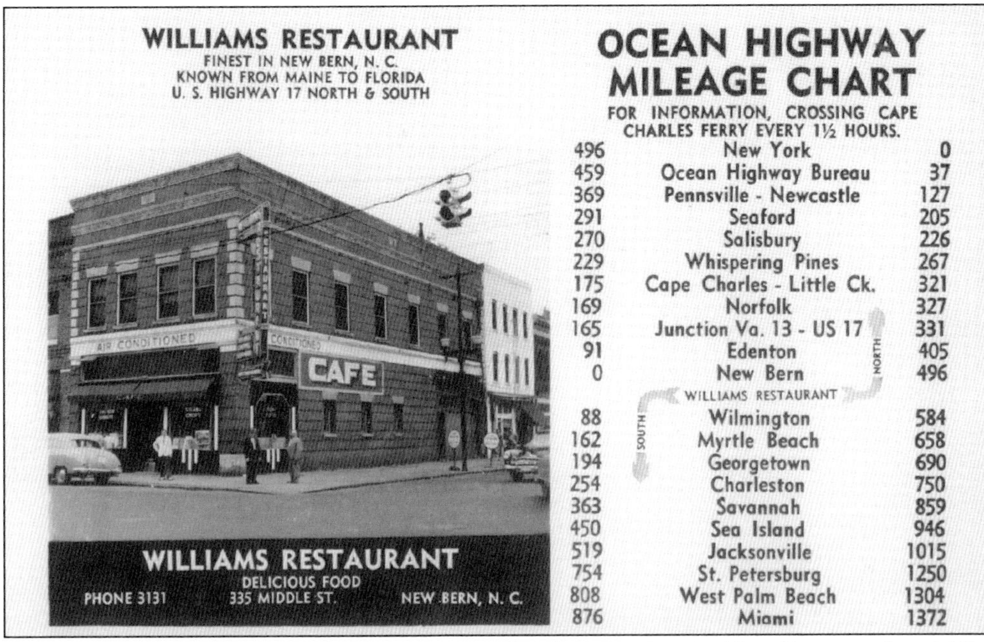

Locally owned restaurants and cafes were popular dining spots for New Bern residents. The Williams Restaurant, located on the corner of Broad and Middle Streets in the old site of Caleb Bradham's second pharmacy, boasted of its delicious food "known from Maine to Florida." (Courtesy of John B. Green III Collection.)

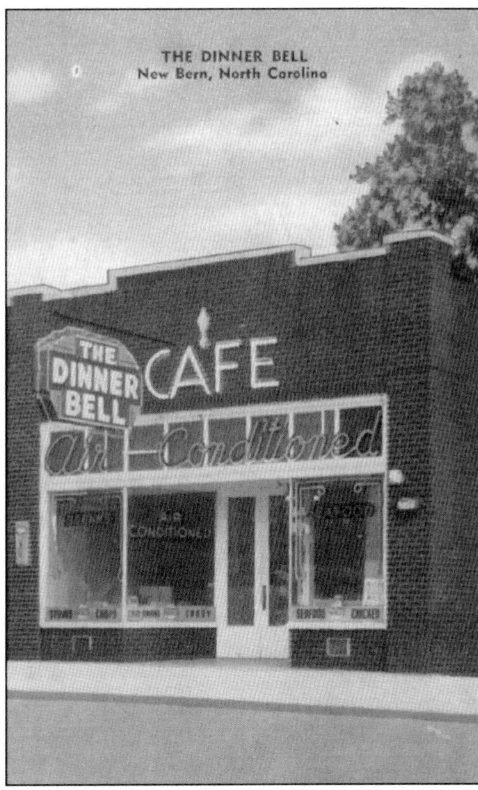

The Dinner Bell (c. 1930s), obviously proud of its air conditioning, a new novelty of the time, was located at 413 Broad Street and served "home cooked foods." (Courtesy of John B. Green III Collection.)

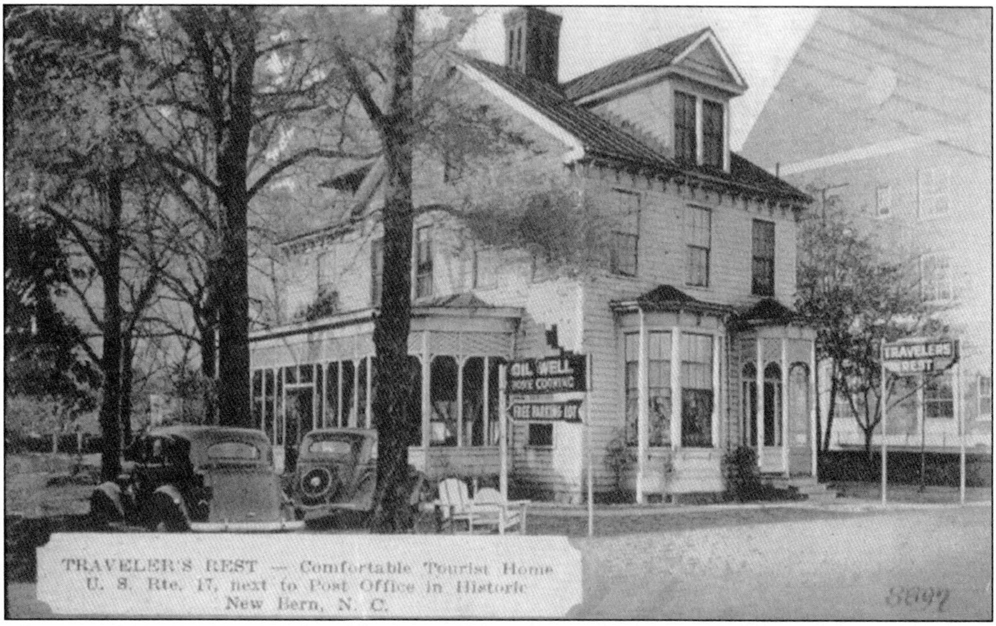

The Traveler's Rest, a "comfortable tourist home," was located on Middle Street next to the lavish federal post office. These postcards often provided guests with a quick way to write home. (Courtesy of John B. Green III Collection.)

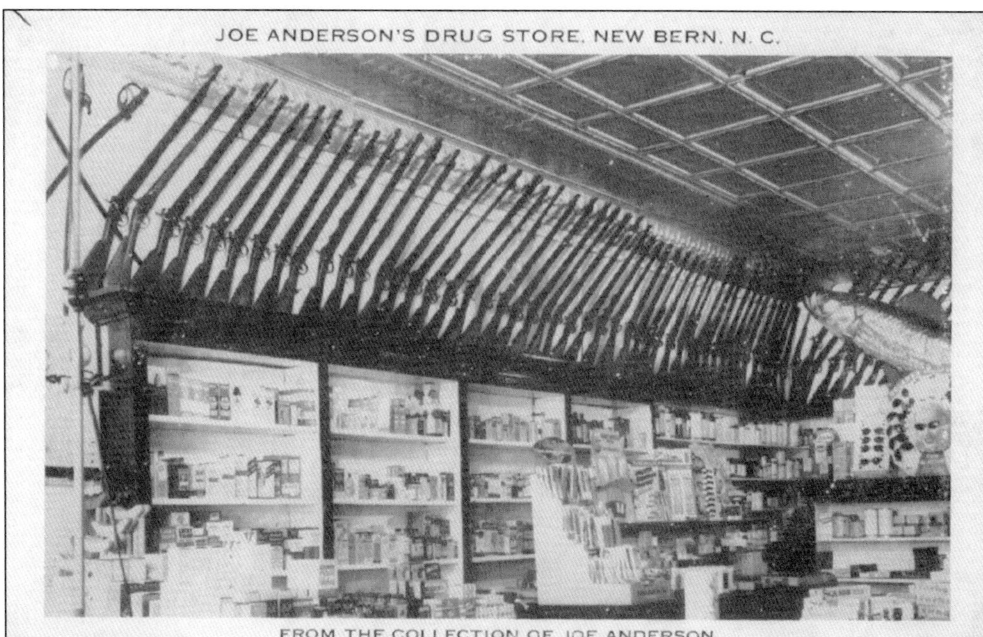

Joe Anderson's Drug Store, located on the southwest corner of Fleet and Broad Streets in New Bern, housed part of his collection of historic firearms, dating back to the pre-Revolutionary days. He also had some 16th-century Chinese pieces on display. (Courtesy of John B. Green III Collection.)

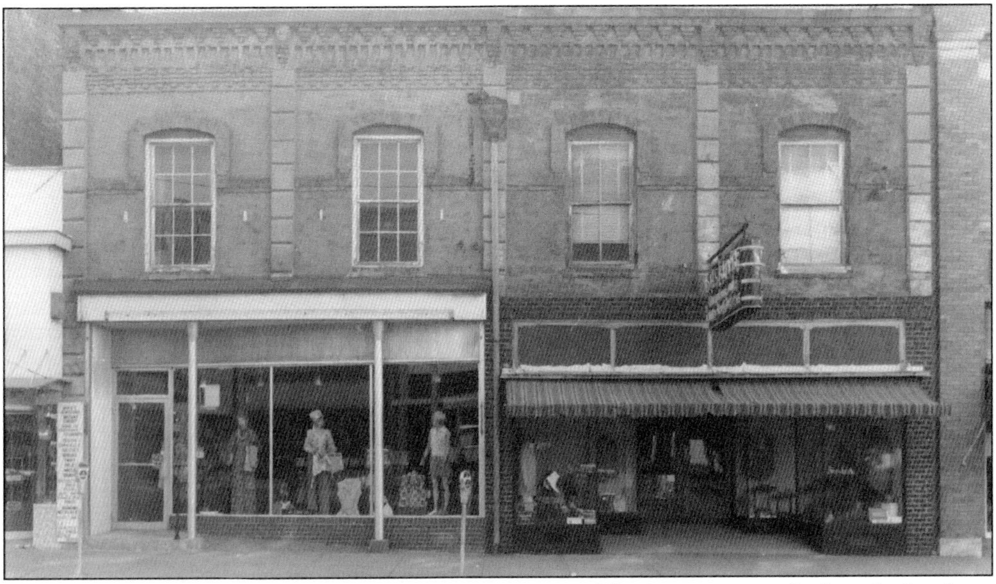

This c. 1970 view of the Windley Building, 220–222 Middle Street, certainly dates before later improvements were made. Constructed for Ernest Windley in 1885 for use as rental properties, the building over the years has housed such businesses as a saloon and billiards parlor, a clothing store, a dry goods operation, and a furniture store. (Courtesy of Tryon Palace Historic Sites and Gardens.)

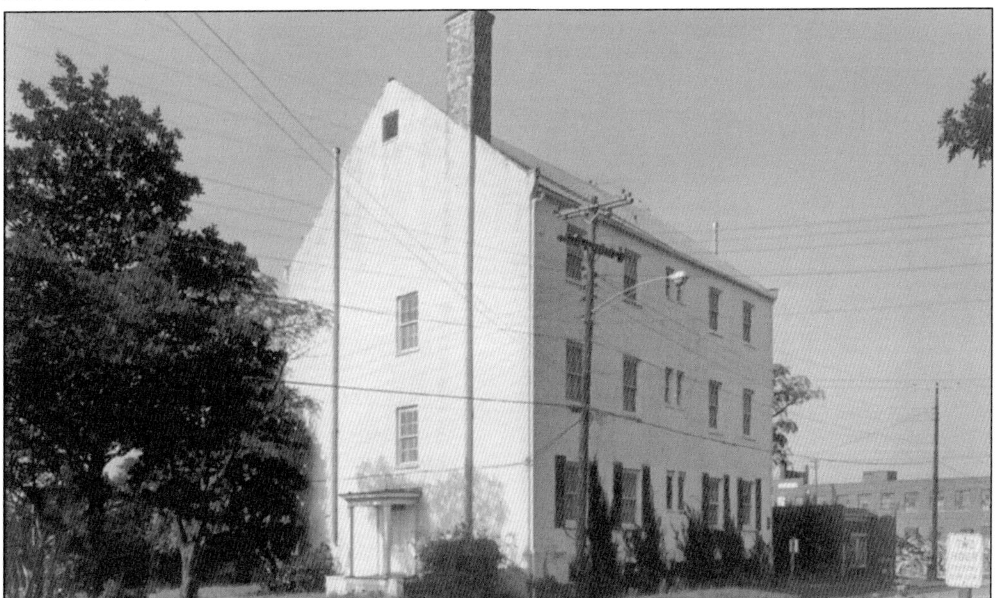

A 1971 view of the Harvey Mansion on South Front Street (at that time called Tryon Palace Drive) shows it to be a survivor of "progress." From 1969, the year the waterfront area became the target of the federally funded Central Waterfront Urban Renewal Project, until 1978, properties in the area were purchased and nearly all demolished. The Harvey Mansion, which had been sold to the federal government, was auctioned in 1979, and subsequent owners have since worked hard to restore and keep up the building. Today it houses a restaurant and bed-and-breakfast inn. (Courtesy of Tryon Palace Historic Sites and Gardens.)

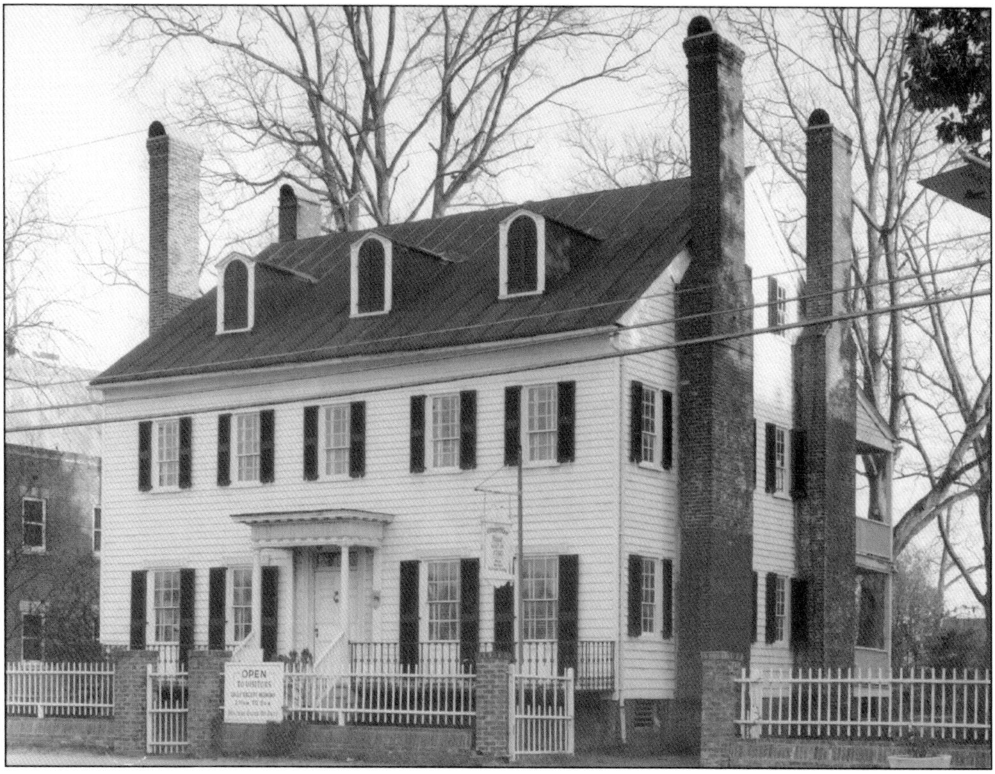

The 1790 Attmore-Oliver House, shown here in 1971, is owned by the New Bern Historical Society, which purchased the building in 1953. Constructed *c.* 1790 and enlarged in 1834, the house was originally owned by Isaac Taylor, who in all likelihood gave the house to his daughter Mary when she married George Attmore. They later left the house to their daughter Hannah Oliver. Located at 513 Broad Street, the house is open for public tours. (Courtesy of Tryon Palace Historic Sites and Gardens.)

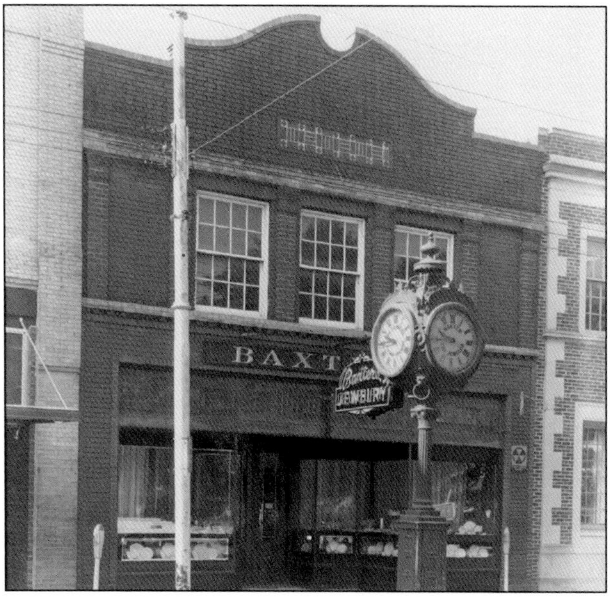

This view of Baxter's Jewelry Store at 323 Pollock Street, with its ornate four-faced Seth Thomas clock, was taken in 1972. The Baxter family, which had been in business since the 1890s, purchased this building in 1917, and the jewelry store remains in business at this site today. The clock was hit by an automobile in 1977 and rendered inoperable, but was later restored by Swiss Bear, the downtown development agency. (Courtesy of Tryon Palace Historic Sites and Gardens.)

Four

Community Celebrations

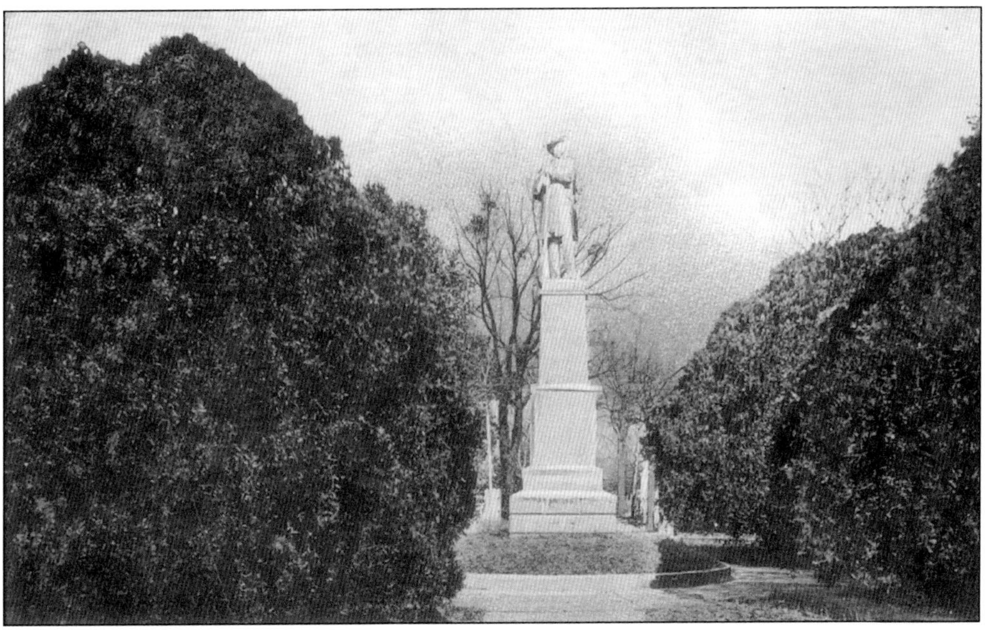

This Confederate memorial, a project started in 1878 by the Ladies Memorial Association of New Bern, was dedicated in 1885 in Cedar Grove Cemetery. This postcard view dates from the turn of the 20th century. (Courtesy of John B. Green III Collection.)

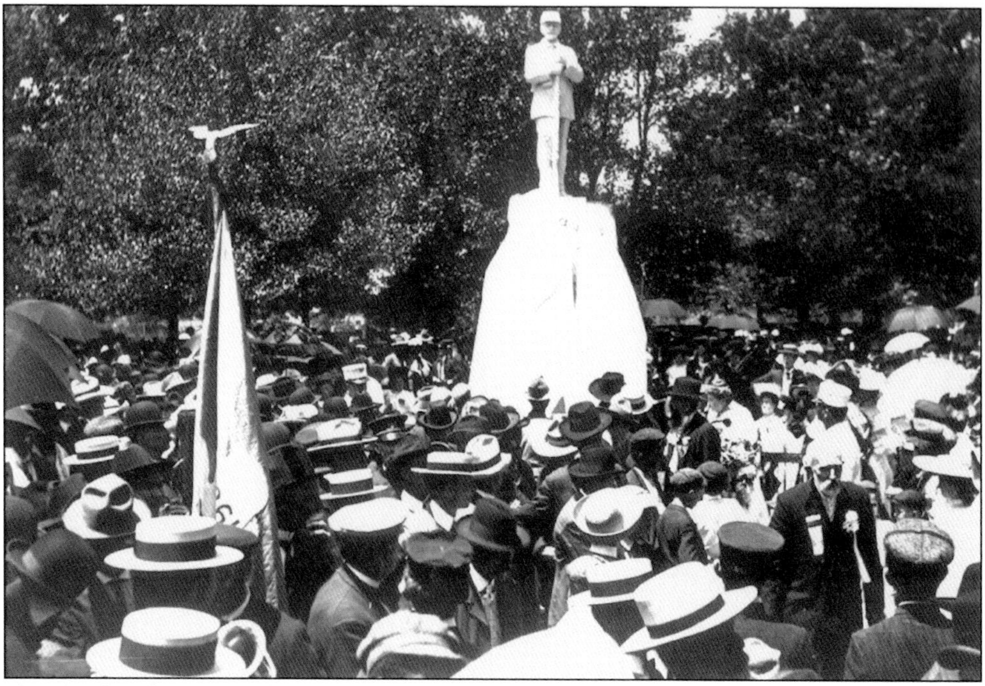

Shortly after the turn of the 20th century, several northern states erected tributes to remember their great deeds and fallen comrades. Veterans of the 9th New Jersey Infantry, whose first appearance in New Bern in March 1862 evoked panic and terror, received a much more jovial welcome when they returned to New Bern in May 1905 for a two-day celebration. New Bern residents welcomed the returning soldiers with parties, receptions, speeches, and banquets. (Courtesy of New Bern Historical Society Collection, New Bern-Craven County Public Library.)

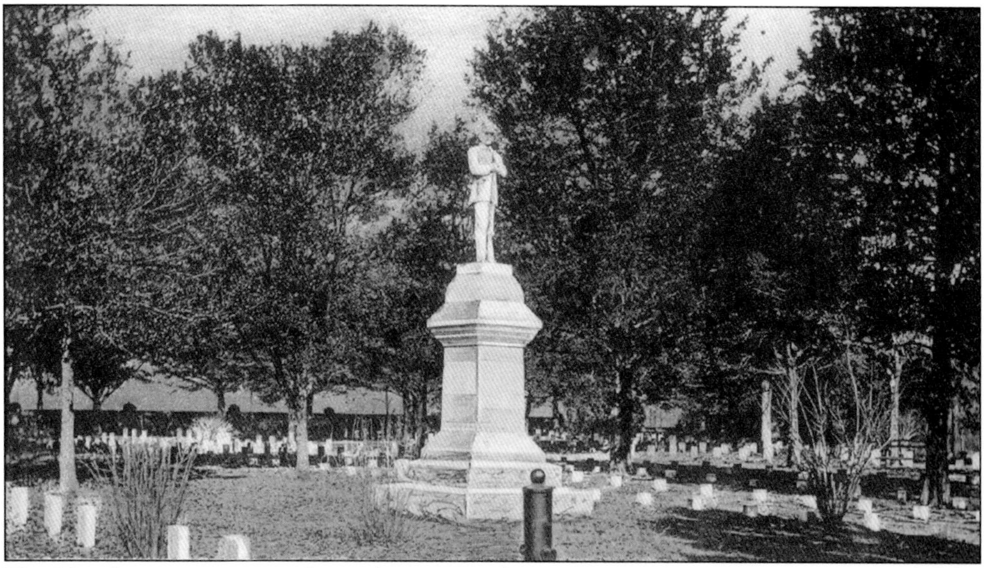

The New Jersey monument, located in National Cemetery, is shown in this *c.* 1907 postcard. National Cemetery was established by the federal government in 1867. Many of the veterans' graves were moved there from other locations. (Courtesy of John B. Green III Collection.)

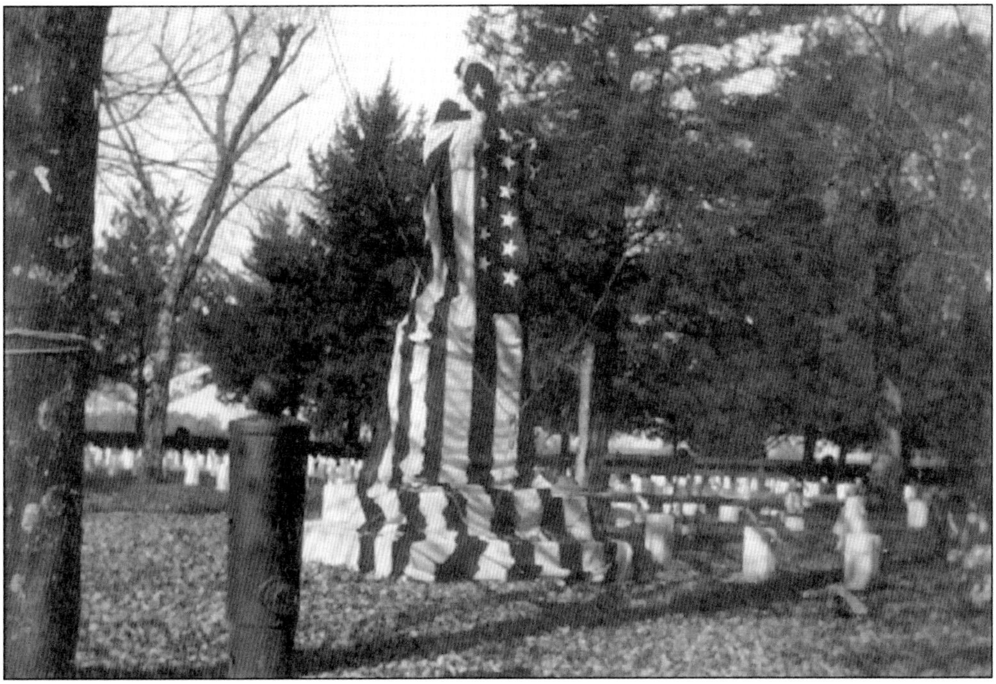

Similarly, veterans from Massachusetts also came to New Bern in November 1908 for the dedication of their monument in National Cemetery. Prior to its unveiling, the monument was veiled by the American flag. (Courtesy of Frances T. Bowden Balma Collection, New Bern-Craven County Public Library.)

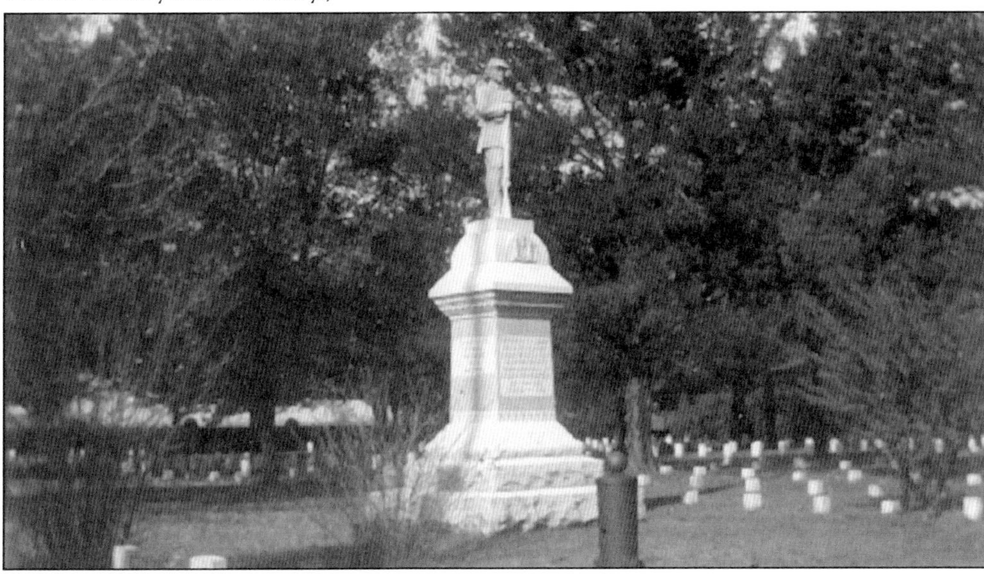

The white stones surrounding the Massachusetts monument and located throughout the graveyard were standard government issue. The graveyard itself was located on part of the site where Union troops conducted drills during their occupation of New Bern, 1861–65. These photographs were taken by William Bowden, a Union veteran who returned to New Bern for the monument's dedication. (Courtesy of Frances T. Bowden Balma Collection, New Bern-Craven County Public Library.)

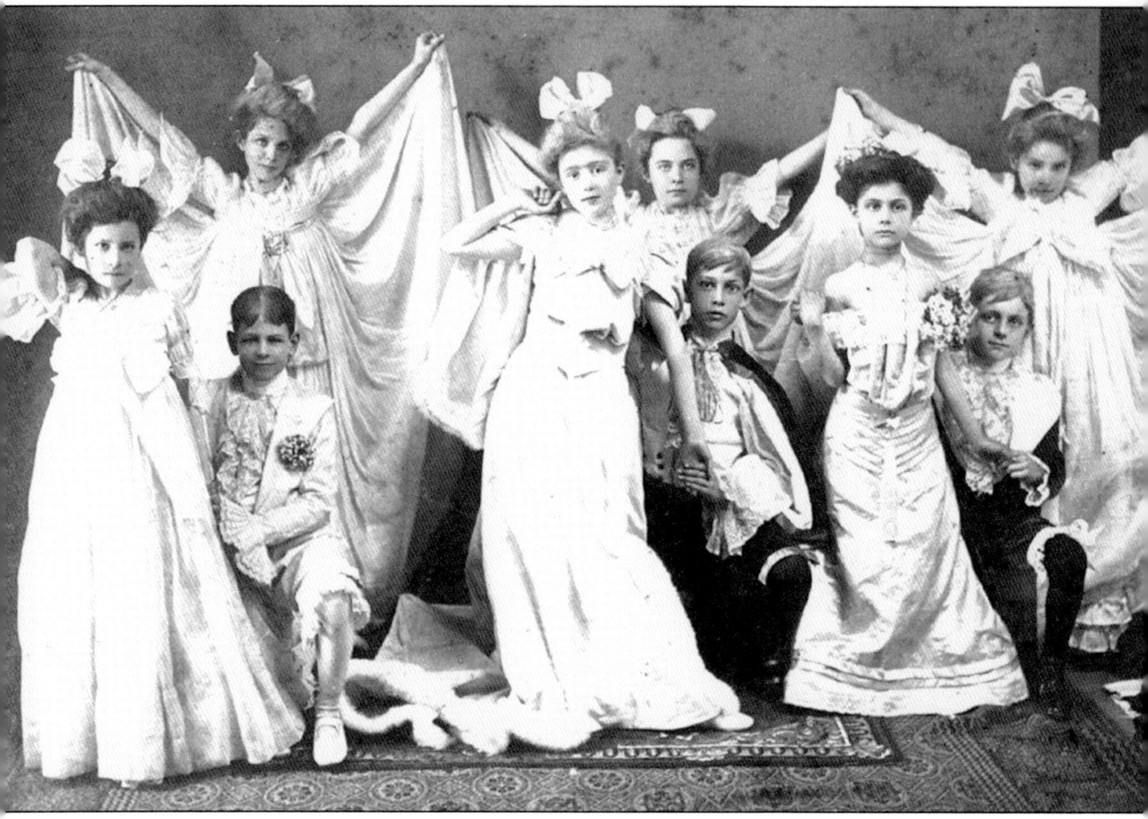

Young actors of the *Cinderella Pantomime*, who performed at the New Bern Opera House, posed in this 1904 photograph. Before movies and television, events such as musicals, plays, operas, and balls, as well as community festivals and church gatherings, provided social outlets for New Bern residents. (Courtesy of Mrs. Nettie Pinnix Collection, New Bern-Craven County Public Library.)

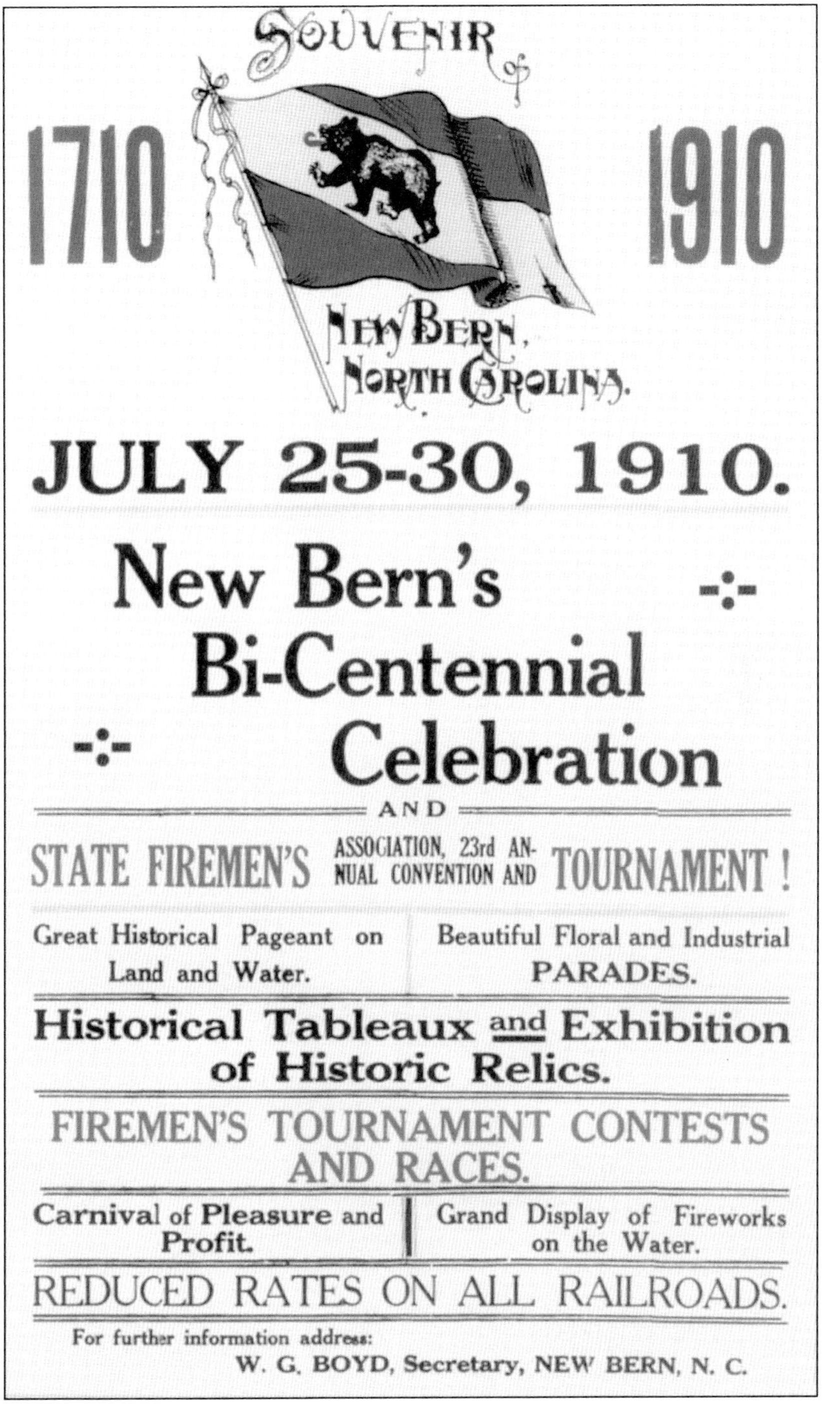

This poster of 1910 advertises the New Bern Bicentennial Celebration, held July 25–30. The events of the week coincided with the State Firemen's Association's annual convention and tournament. So many visitors came to New Bern for the celebration that a special train ran those who could not find accommodations in New Bern to Morehead City's Atlantic Hotel. (Courtesy of New Bern Area Chamber of Commerce.)

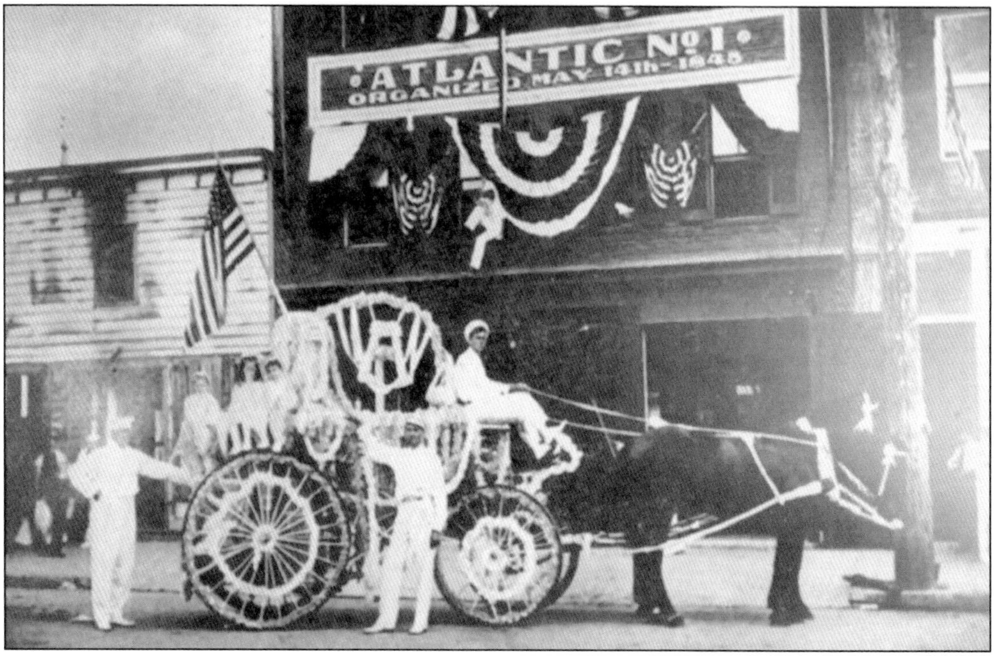

Firemen decorated the Sibley fire engine for the big parade. In addition to the bicentennial celebration, 67 fire companies from 32 towns and cities across North Carolina came to New Bern for the firemen's convention. (Courtesy of New Bern Area Chamber of Commerce.)

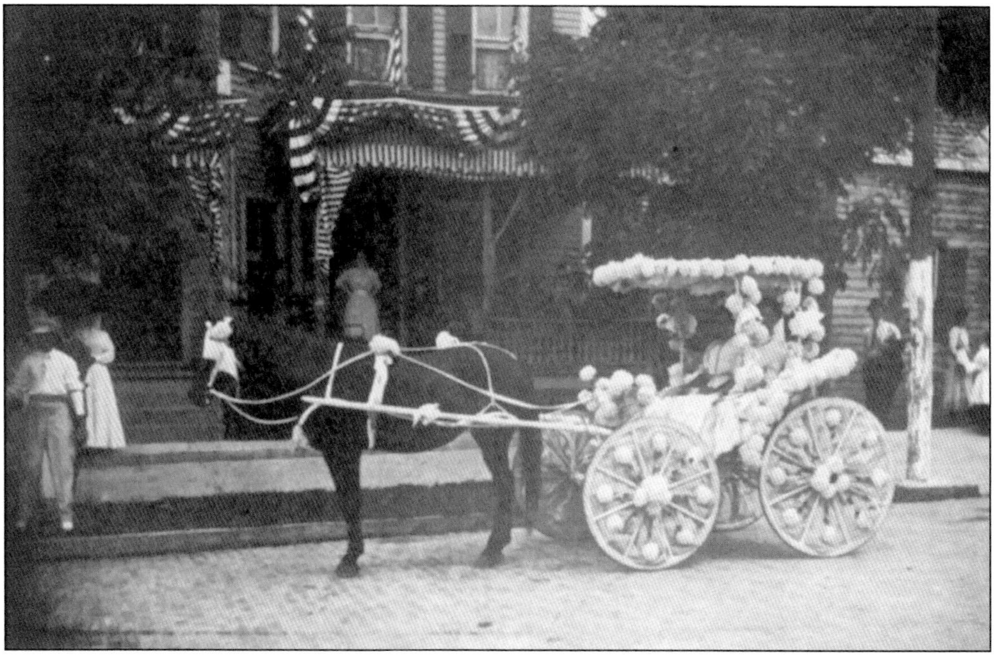
Many local residents, clubs, and businesses decorated carriages and vehicles to demonstrate their pride in New Bern's historical heritage. This carriage is shown in the 400 block of Broad Street. (Courtesy of New Bern Area Chamber of Commerce.)

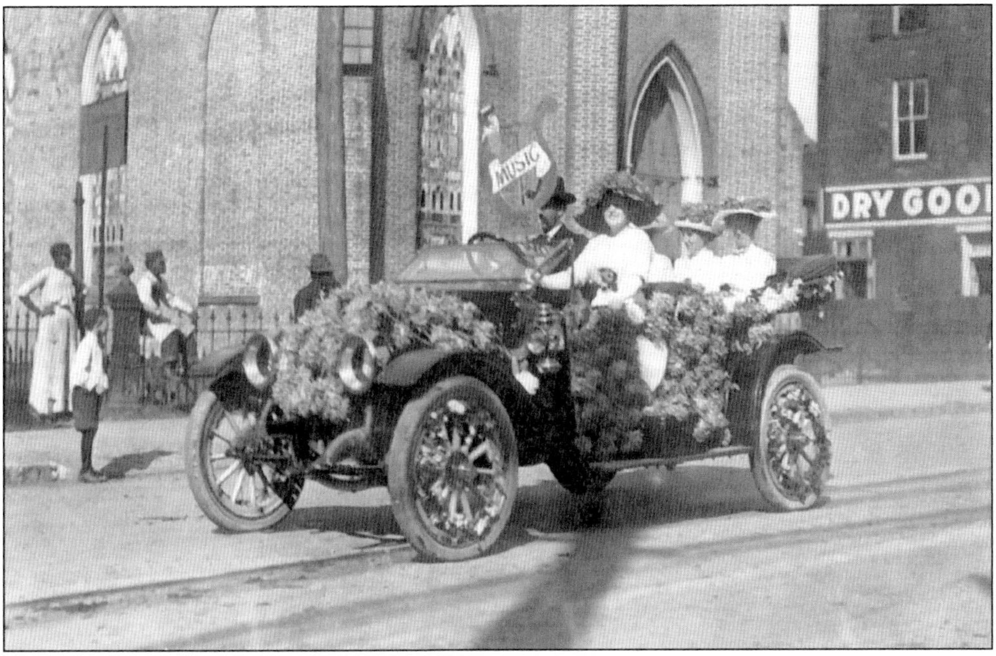

These three ladies of the music club proudly drove their decorated Ford convertible along Middle Street. The church seen in the background is the First Baptist Church, a Middle Street landmark since its construction in 1848. (Courtesy of John B. Green III Collection.)

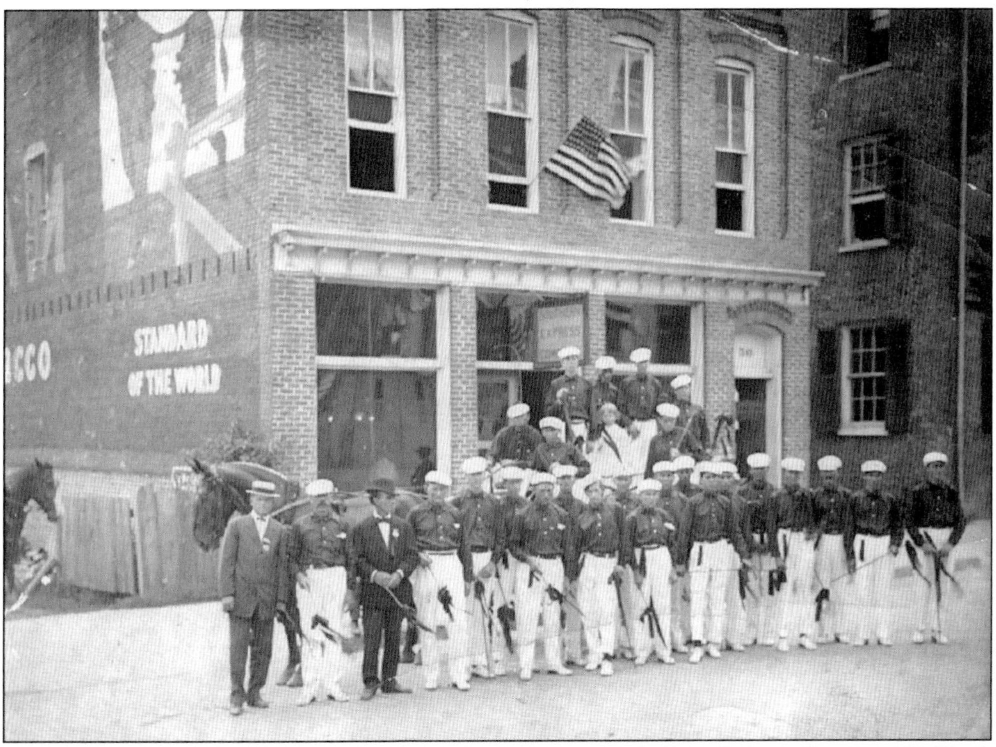

Another company of New Bern firefighters participating in the parade paused in the 200 block of Craven Street for this photograph. (Courtesy of John B. Green III Collection.)

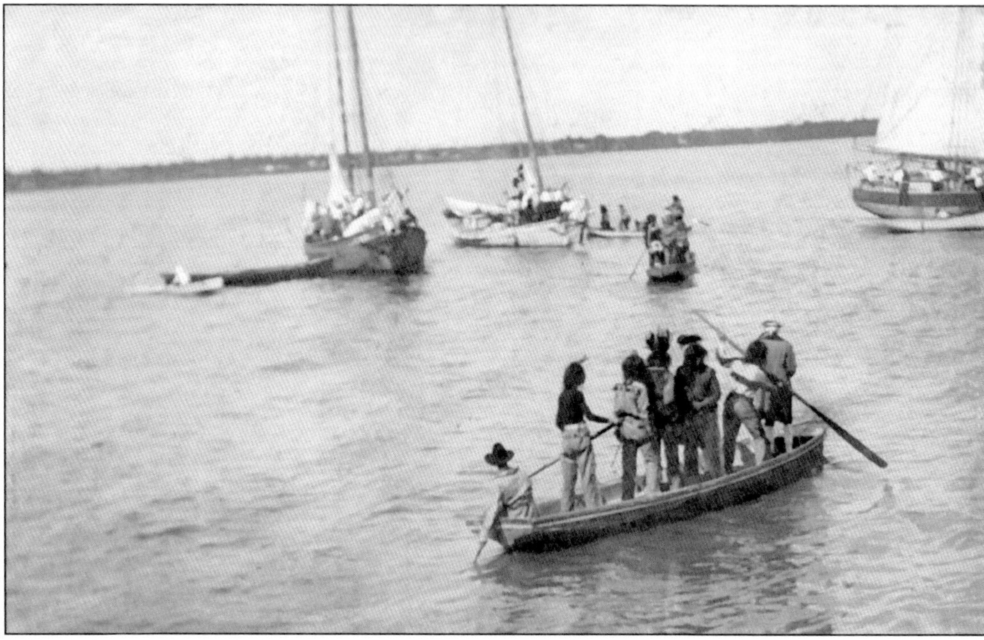

Included in the bicentennial celebration was a re-enactment of Baron de Graffenried's landing on the banks of the Neuse River and his first meeting with area Native Americans, as shown on this *c.* 1910 postcard. (Courtesy of John B. Green III Collection.)

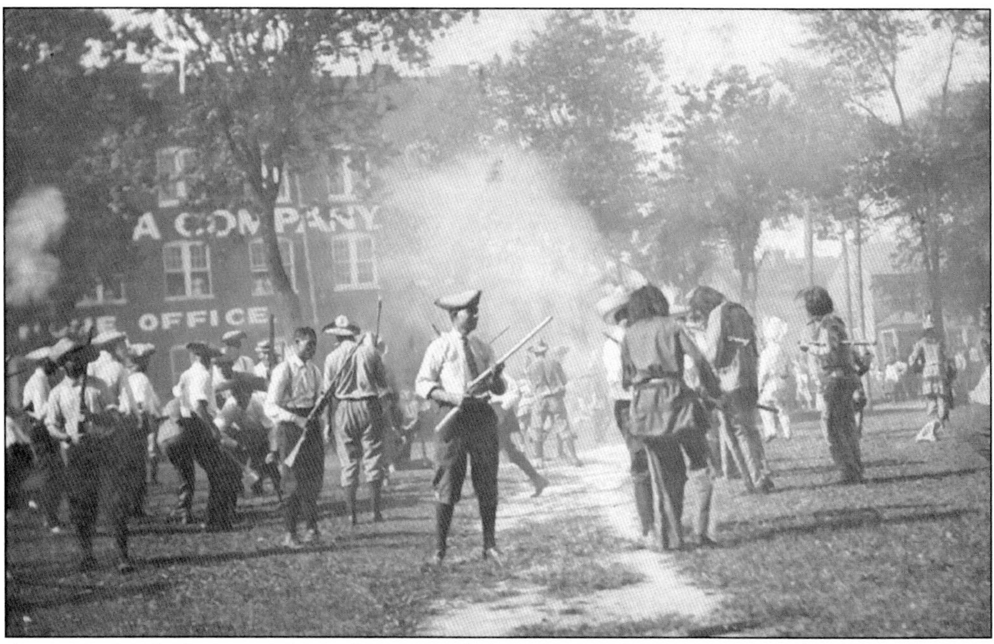

An early battle between the colonists and the Native Americans was also re-enacted on the Academy Green lawn. This resulted in some minor injuries, unlike the real battle itself. The building in the background is the Pepsi-Cola home office. (Courtesy of John B. Green III Collection.)

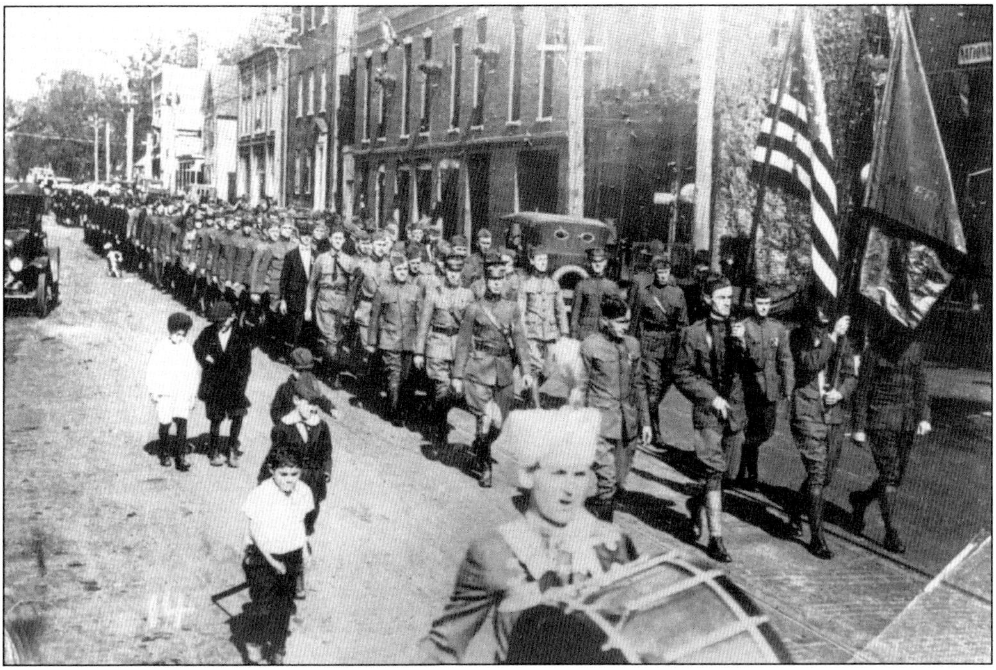

This undated photograph of a parade along Craven Street possibly depicts doughboys of World War I. (Courtesy of New Bern Historical Society Collection, New Bern-Craven County Public Library.)

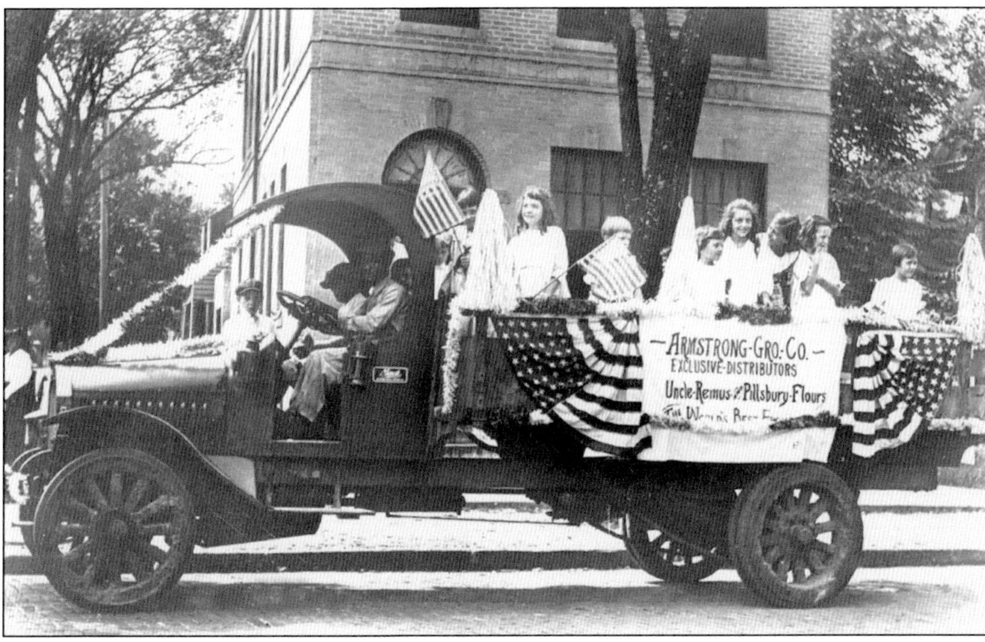

New Bern residents decided again to celebrate the town's historical legacy with historical celebrations and a pageant in June 1929. Proceeds from the pageant totaling $3,500 were donated toward the restoration of Tryon Palace. The pageant, of course, featured a parade. Armstrong Grocery Company decorated its truck, shown here at the corner of Hancock and Broad Streets. (Courtesy of Wernike Collection, New Bern-Craven County Public Library.)

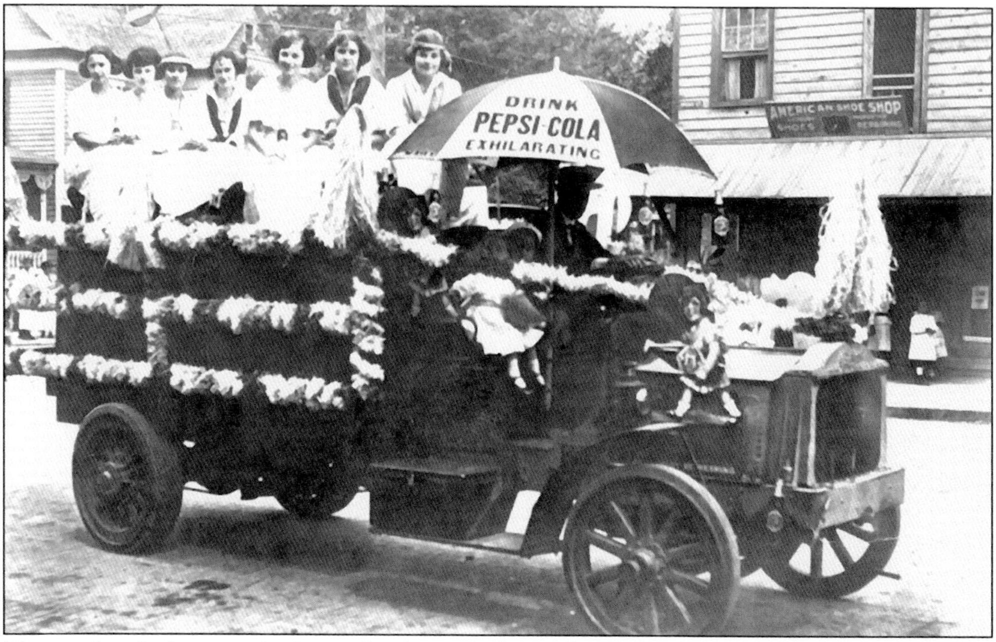

This undated photograph shows the Pepsi-Cola truck, driven by E.W. Paul Sr. in a parade along Broad Street. (Courtesy of Pepsi-Cola Bottling Company Collection, New Bern-Craven County Public Library.)

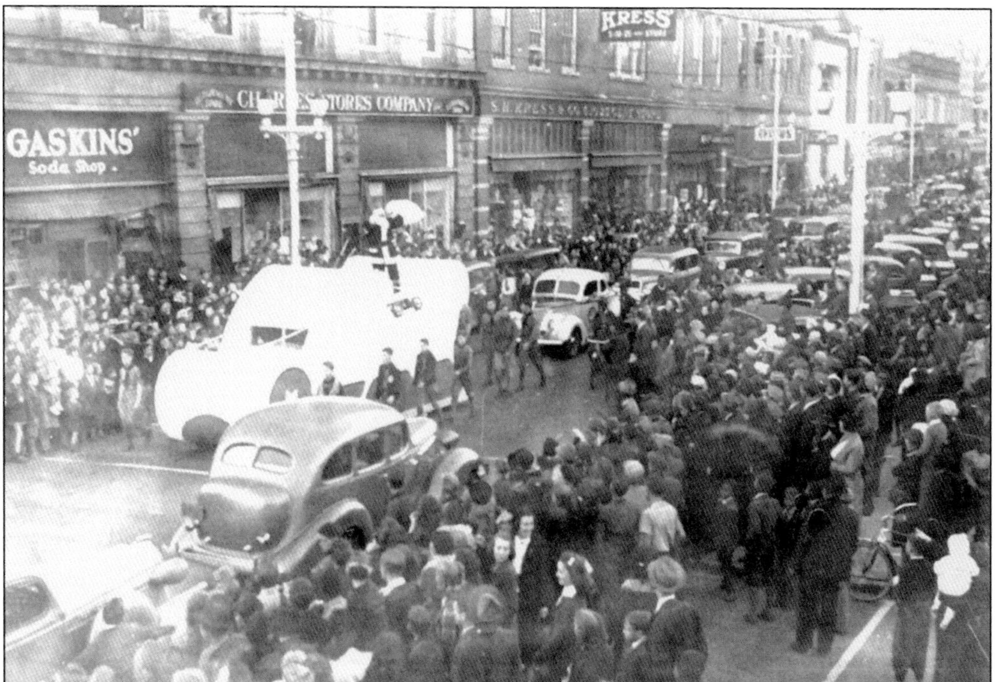

What excitement is generated then and now when Santa Claus comes to town! From his sleigh, Santa waved to the crowds in the 300 block of Middle Street in the 1950s Christmas Parade. (Courtesy of New Bern Area Chamber of Commerce Collection, New Bern-Craven County Public Library.)

Five

Downtown

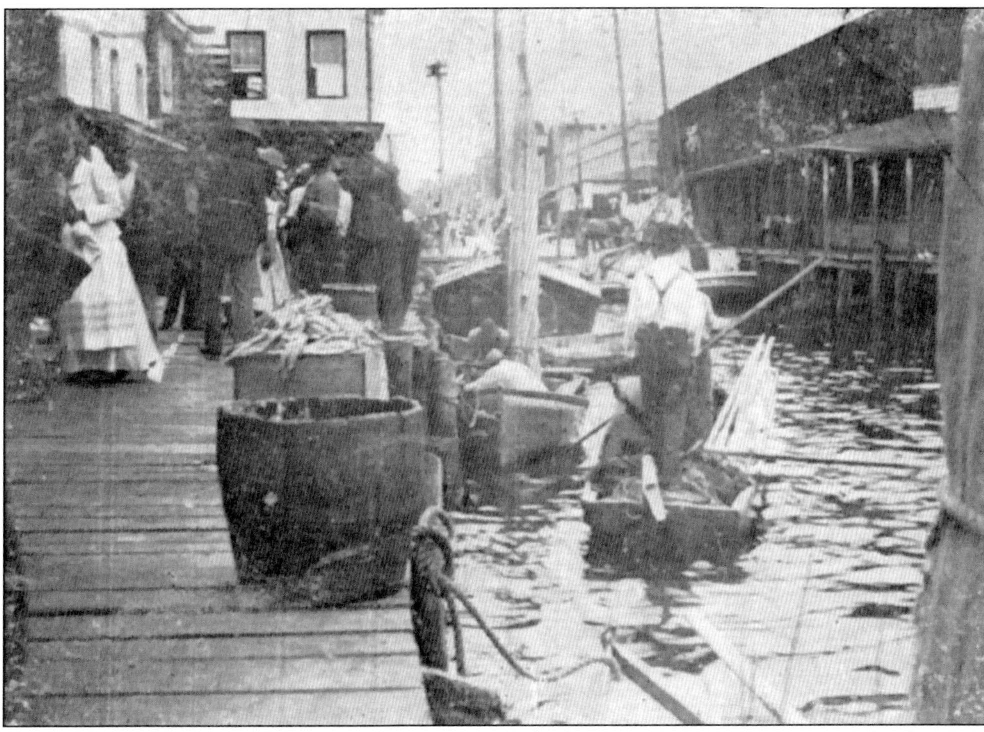

From New Bern's beginning, its prosperity was linked to its success as a port city. Its location at the confluence of the Neuse and Trent Rivers, was no small factor in this success. Before rail and motor transportation became common, people depended on waterways for quick transportation and shipment of goods. This *c.* 1900 postcard depicts the Market Dock downtown on the Trent River. Fish and oysters were an important part of New Bern's thriving economy at the turn of the 20th century—and a staple in most local residents' diets. (Courtesy of John B. Green III Collection.)

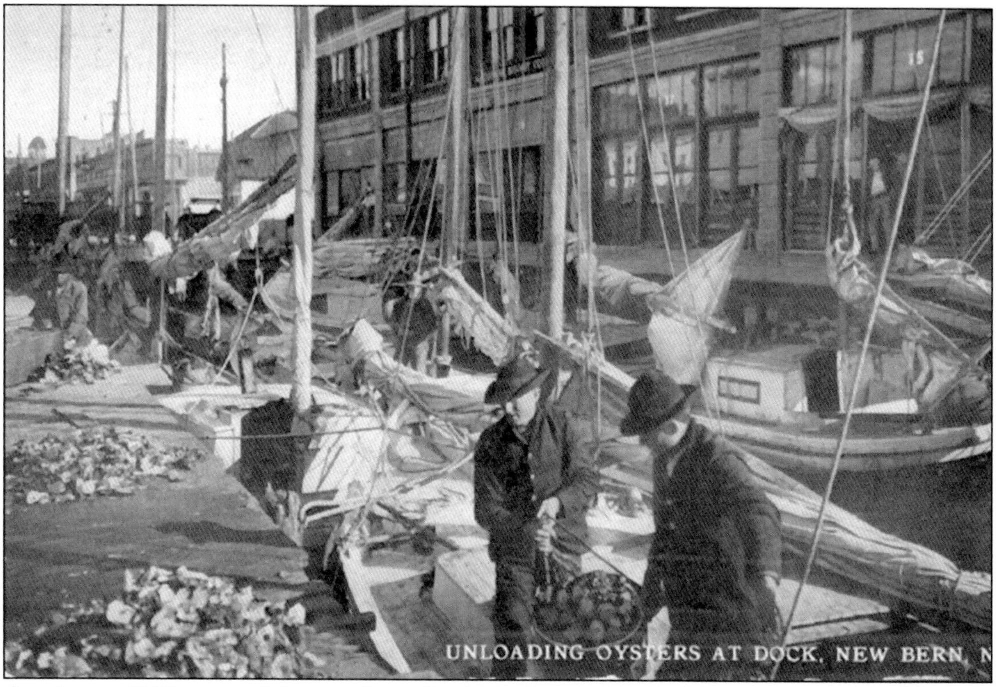

Another c. 1910 postcard depicts the unloading of oysters at New Bern's Market Dock. By the mid-1920s, undependable rail services and high shipping charges had led to a great decline in New Bern's fishing industry. (Courtesy of John B. Green III Collection.)

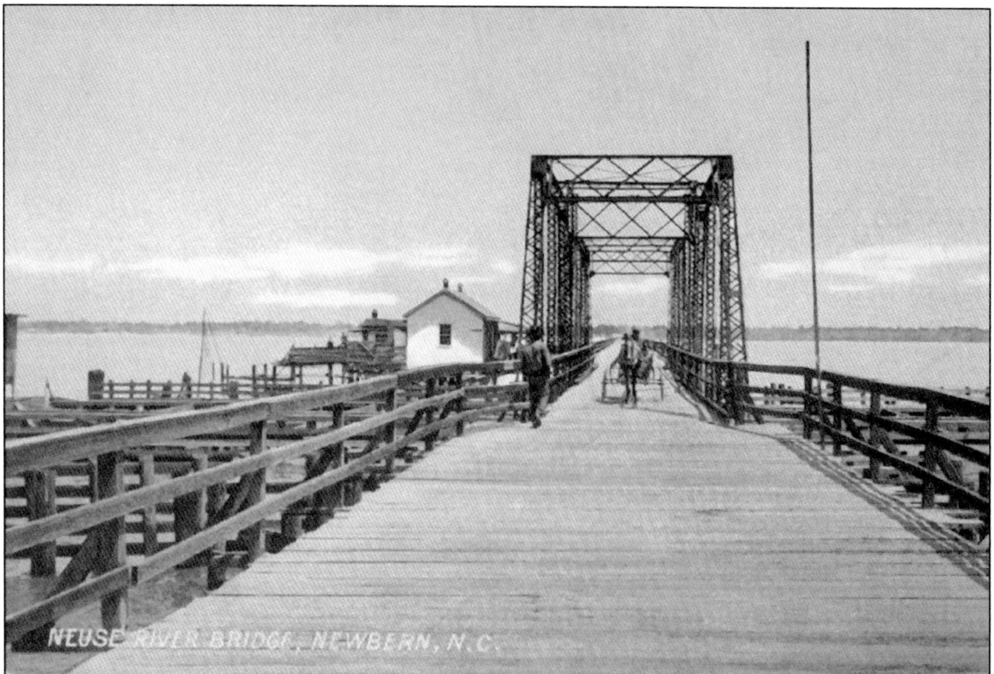

This c. 1900 postcard shows the first wooden bridge in 1896–98, built to span the Neuse River. It was destroyed by the 1913 hurricane. (Courtesy of John B. Green III Collection.)

The *New Bern Daily Journal* was founded in 1882 and at first located in the 200 block of Middle Street, next to the First Baptist Church, as shown in this undated photograph. (Courtesy of Margaret Harper Collection, New Bern-Craven County Public Library.)

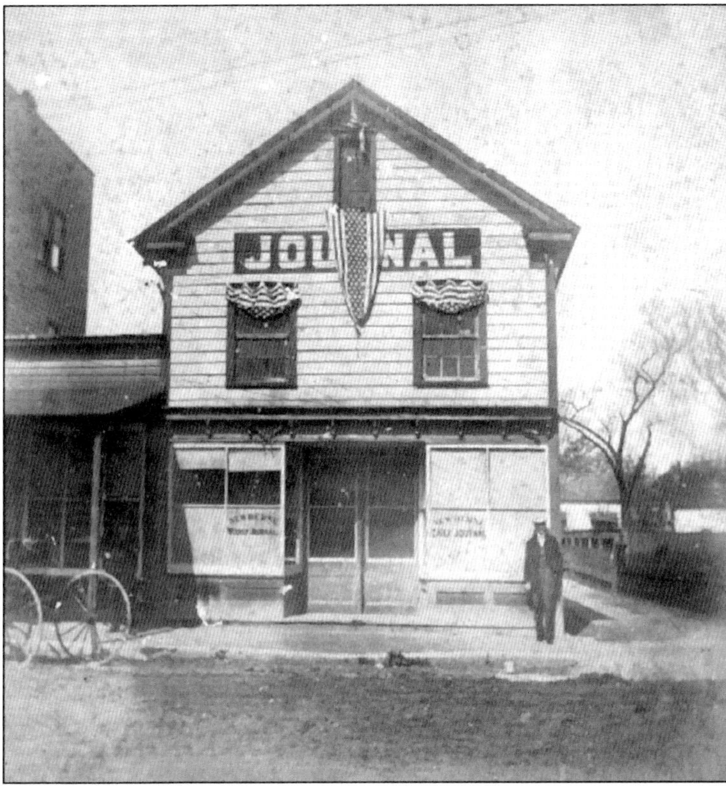

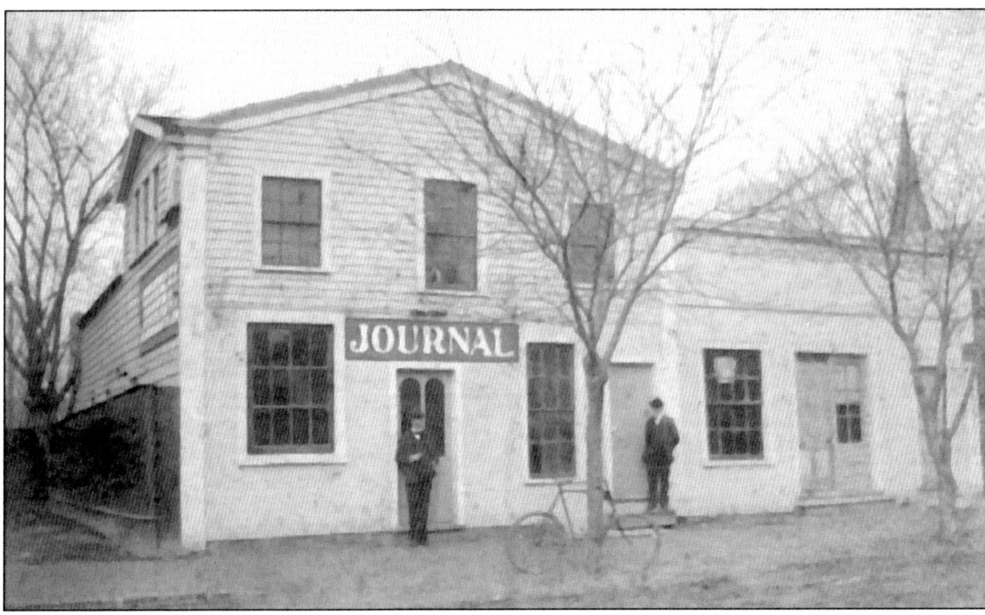

The *Journal* by February 1904 had moved to this office in the 200 block of Craven Street. In 1914, the *Journal* and the *Sun*, founded in 1907 by Owen G. Dunn, merged to form the *Sun Journal*. The *Sun Journal*, which was owned by various local newspapermen before its purchase in 1978 by Freedom Communications, still serves as New Bern's daily newspaper. (Courtesy of Margaret Harper Collection, New Bern-Craven County Public Library.)

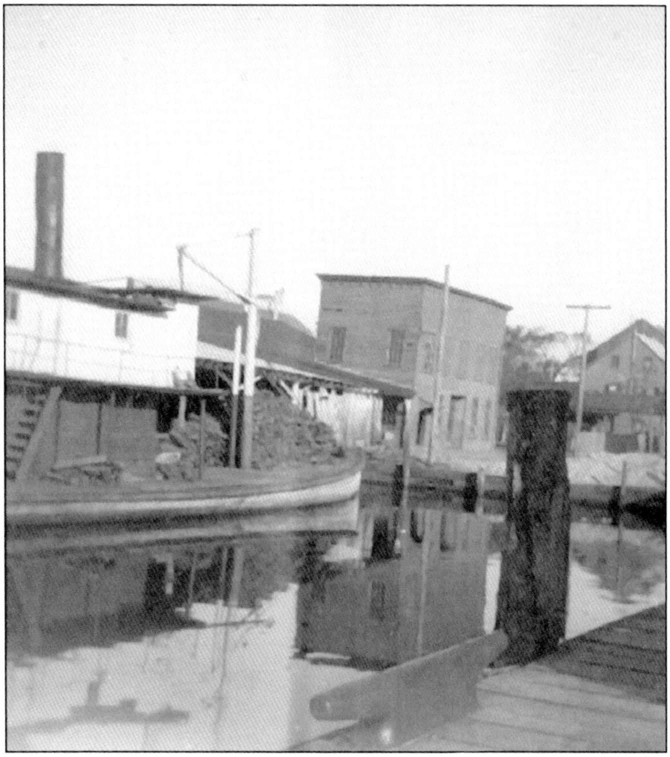

In November 1908, former Union soldier William Scobie Bowden returned to New Bern for the dedication of the Massachusetts monument in New Bern's National Cemetery. The early 20th century saw the return of many Union soldiers who had been stationed in New Bern during the Civil War as monuments were erected to remember those who died during the war. Among Bowden's pictures was a close-up view of New Bern's waterfront docks. (Courtesy of Frances T. Bowden Balma Collection, New Bern-Craven County Public Library.)

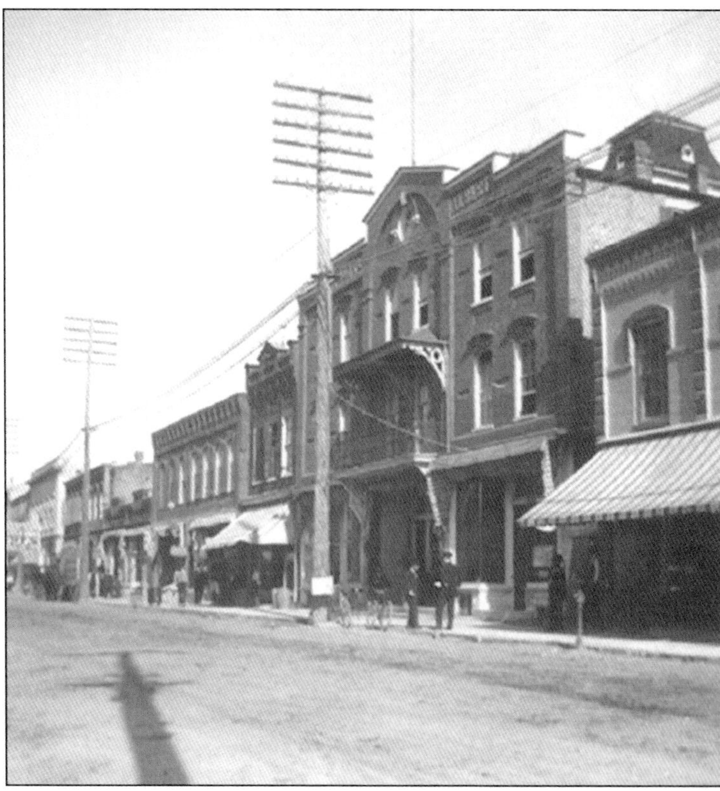

This three-story building was originally constructed as the Hotel Albert in 1887. Located in the 200 block of Middle Street, it replaced the Central Hotel, which was destroyed in an 1885 fire that razed nearly all the east side of Middle Street. The hotel had changed hands and names several times; by the time of Bowden's visit in November 1908, it was known as the Hotel Hazelton. (Courtesy of Frances T. Bowden Balma Collection, New Bern-Craven County Public Library.)

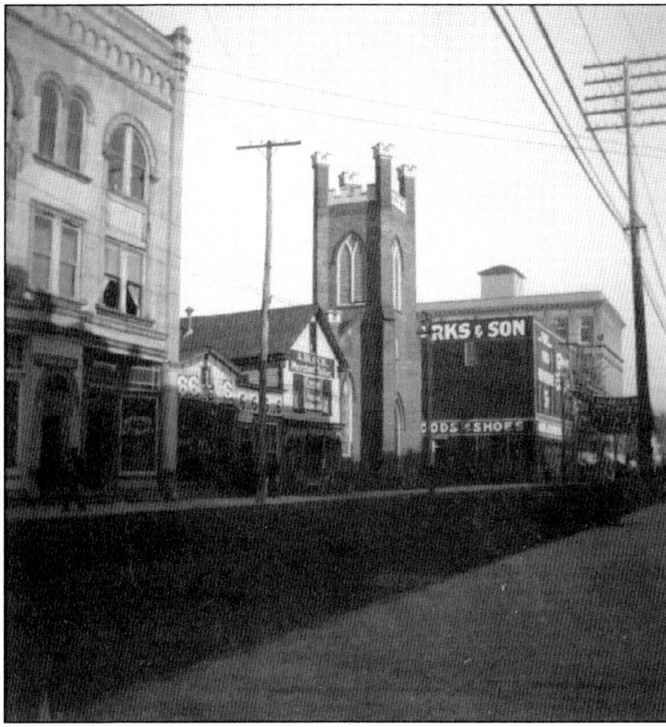

The First Baptist Church, originally constructed in 1848 and still in use today, is shown in this west side view of the 200 block of Middle Street. In the distance can be seen the Elks Building, located on the northwest corner of Pollock and Middle Streets, which was constructed in early 1908. The smaller building located next to the church, which had served as the home of the *New Bern Daily Journal*, housed a tailor's establishment in November 1908. (Courtesy of Frances T. Bowden Balma Collection, New Bern-Craven County Public Library.)

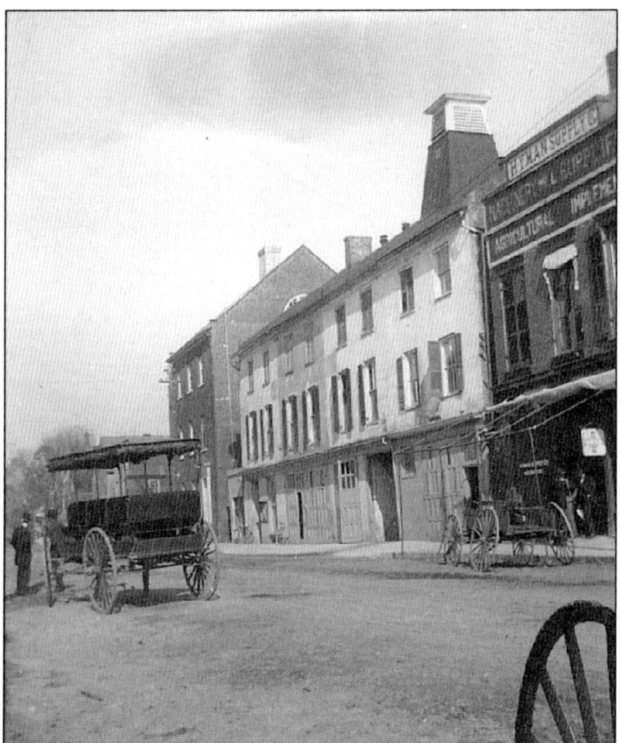

This view of the old city hall, located in the 200 block of Craven Street, was taken by Bowden during his November 1908 visit to New Bern. The building, which was constructed between 1816–18, originally housed a row of individual brick stores. After a bank foreclosure, the bank sold the property individually, and they were each held separately until 1888. That year, the City of New Bern, which had already converted one of the stores to serve as an engine house for the Atlantic Steam Fire Company, purchased the building and used it as city offices until 1935. (Courtesy of Frances T. Bowden Balma Collection, New Bern-Craven County Public Library.)

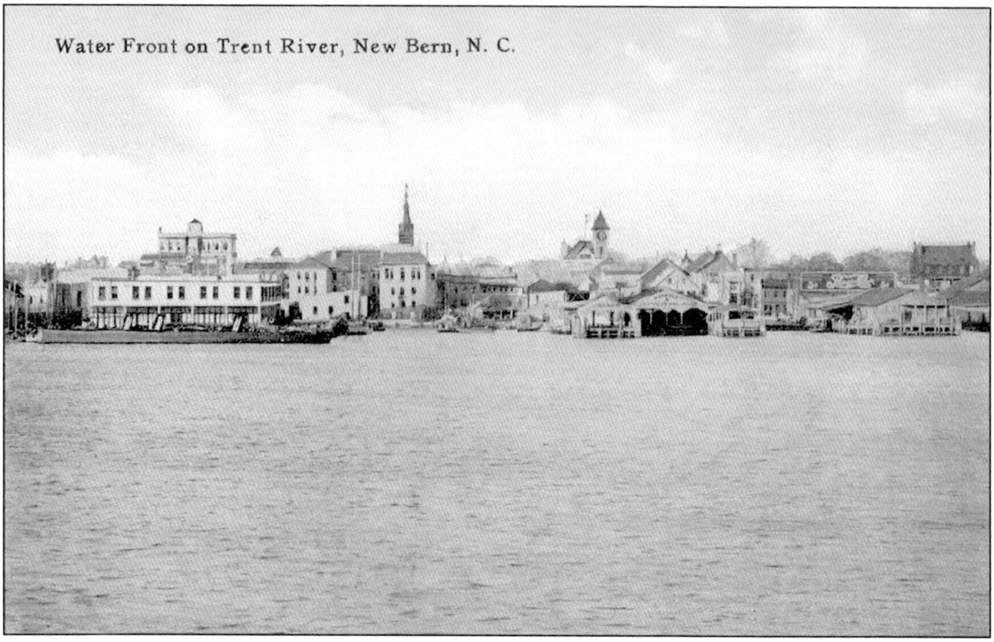

A *c.* 1910 postcard of the Trent River waterfront shows such distinctive landmarks as the federal courthouse clock and the Baptist church steeple. The face of New Bern's waterfront was to change drastically by the 1970s, when urban renewal led to the demolition of many run-down buildings in the waterfront area. (Courtesy of John B. Green III Collection.)

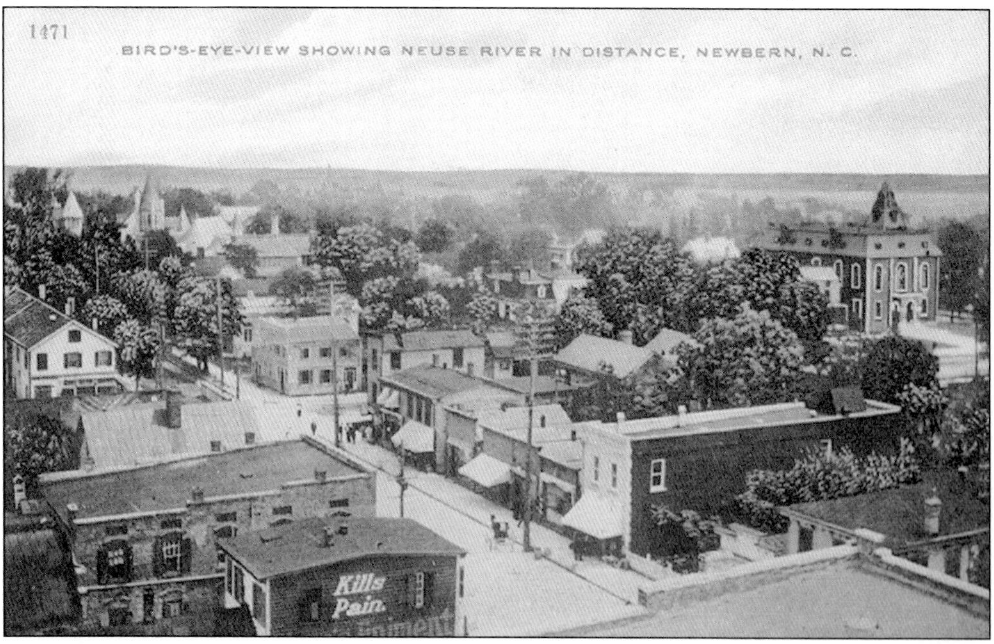

A "bird's-eye view," most likely taken from the Elks Building at the corner at Pollock and Middle Streets, shows a *c.* 1910 look to the northwest of the town and the Neuse River. Buildings shown on this postcard that are still standing today include the Craven County Courthouse, seen to the right, and Centenary Methodist Church, at left. (Courtesy of John B. Green III Collection.)

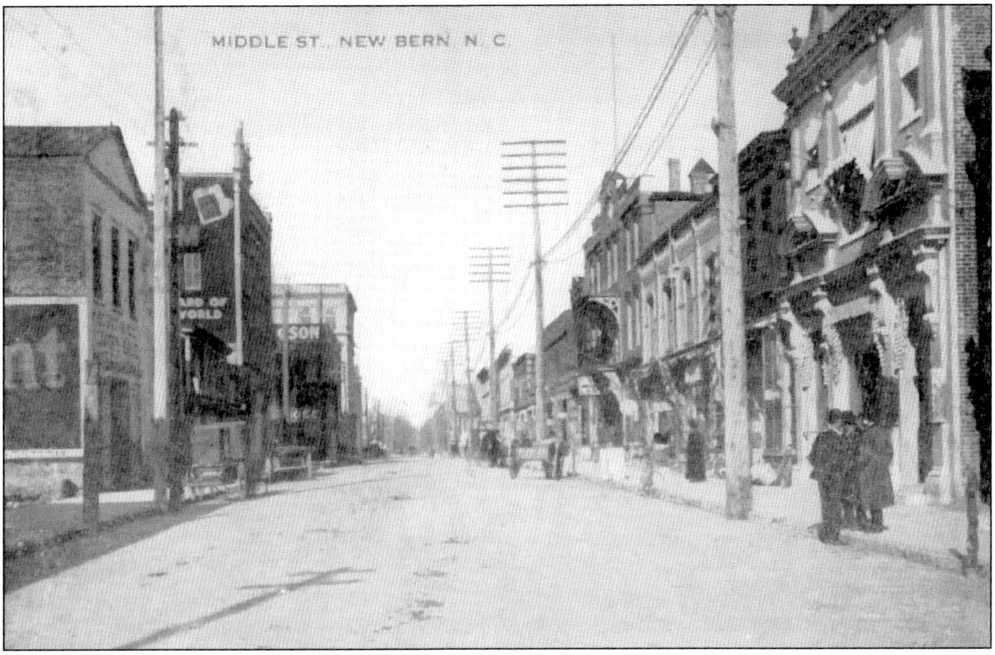

This c. 1910 postcard view of Middle Street looking north shows little change to the downtown area in the two years since Bowden had visited. (Courtesy of John B. Green III Collection.)

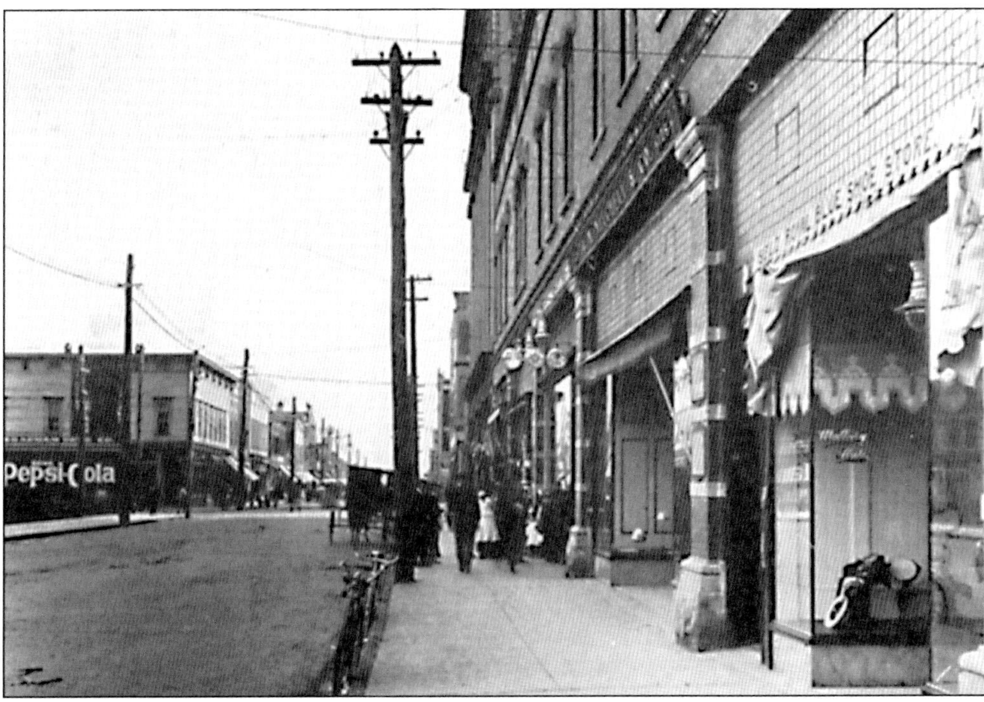

This view of the Middle Street looking south is dated from around 1914 and taken from the *Illustrated City of New Bern*, the city business directory of 1914. The building on the left is Caleb Bradham's original drugstore, where he invented the popular soft drink Pepsi in 1898. (Courtesy of Tom Faulkenberry Collection.)

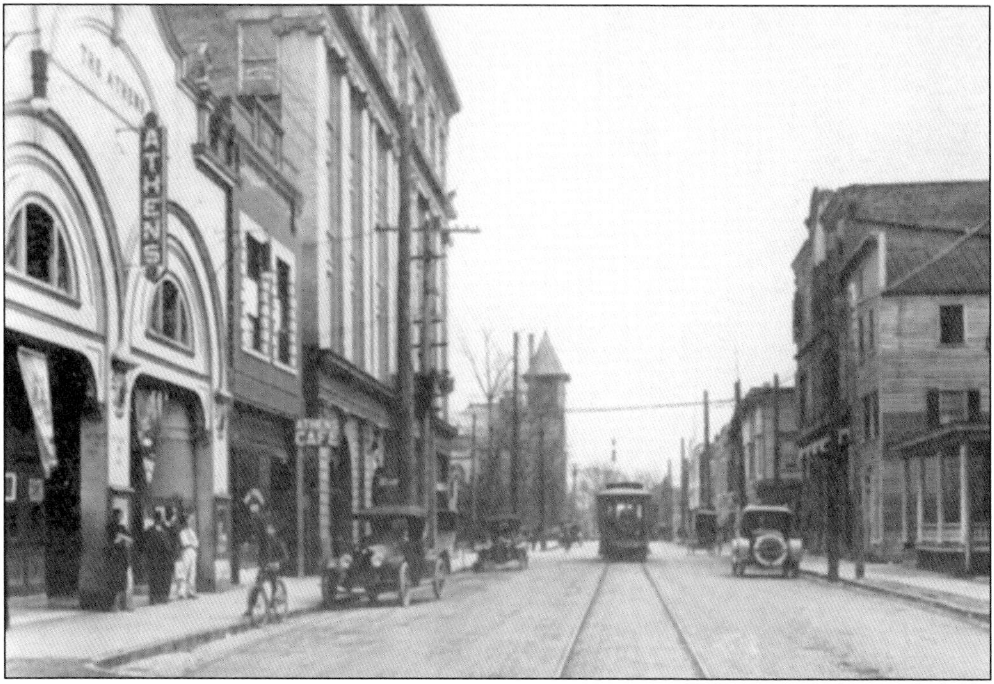

Another view from the 1914 directory depicts the 300 block of Pollock Street looking east. The Athens Theatre, designed by New Bern architect Herbert W. Simpson, opened in 1910. Next door was the Athens Cafe, and just up the street was the Elks Temple, newly constructed in 1908. (Courtesy of Tom Faulkenberry Collection.)

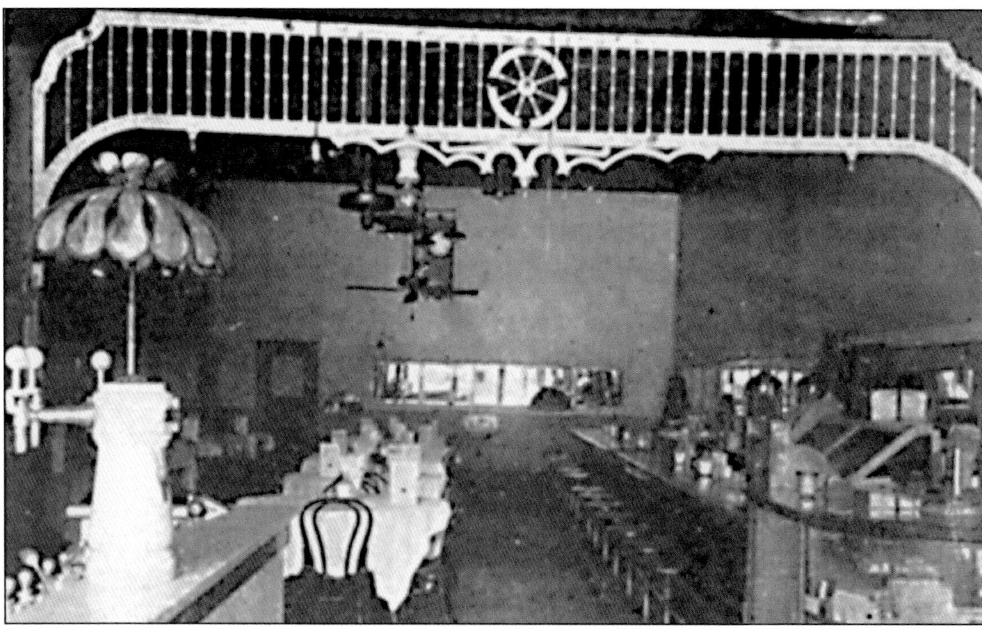

The Athens Cafe was operated by the Raftelis brothers and had a prime location between the Elks Temple and the Athens Cafe. The 1914 directory described the cafe as "beautifully fitted up throughout and [one that] enjoys the reputation of being one of the finest places of its kind in Eastern North Carolina." (Courtesy of Tom Faulkenberry Collection.)

The U.S. Post Office and Courthouse, built 1895–97, was located on the corner of Pollock and Craven Streets. A small clock was constructed atop the building in 1907, but was replaced in 1911 with a large, four-faced clock after citizens complained the original clock was too small to be seen. In 1935, the city of New Bern purchased the building for use as a city hall and that remains its function today. (Courtesy of Tom Faulkenberry Collection.)

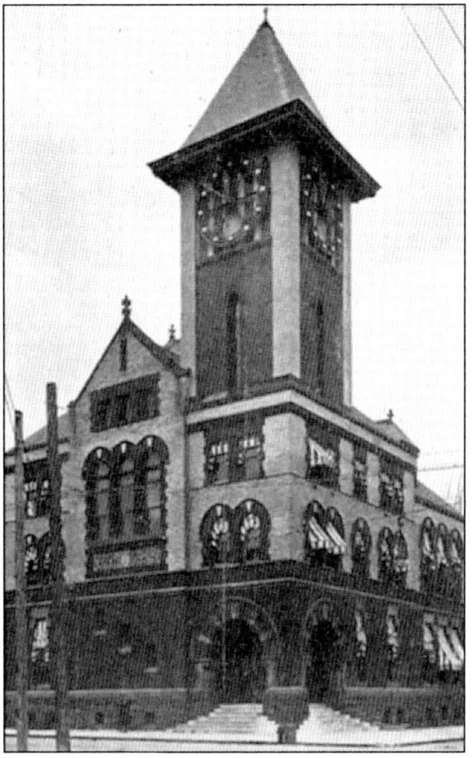

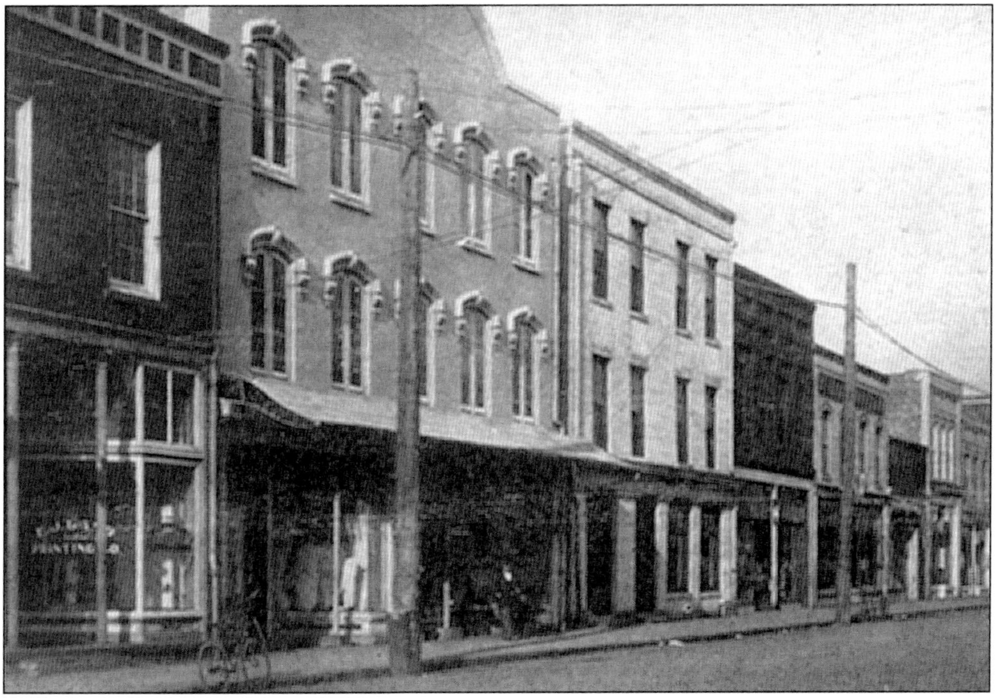

This view of the 200 block of Pollock Street appeared in the 1914 city directory. (Courtesy of Tom Faulkenberry Collection.)

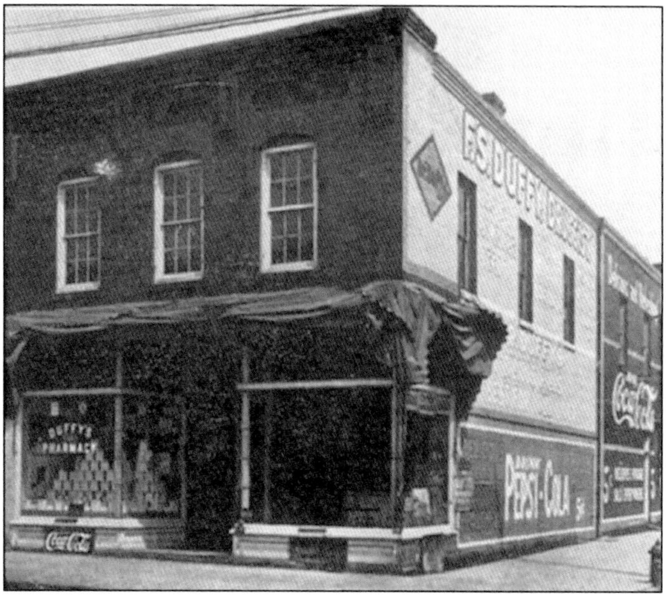

F.S. Duffy continued his uncle's pharmacy and drugstore at the northeast corner of South Front and Middle Streets. Duffy also owned a pharmaceutical manufacturing company, producing such medicinal preparations as Dr. Duffy's Pain Destroyer and Dr. Duffy's Cough Killer. The 1914 directory describes Duffy as "one of the prominent men of affairs of New Bern, (who) stands high in professional, business and social circles." (Courtesy of Tom Faulkenberry Collection.)

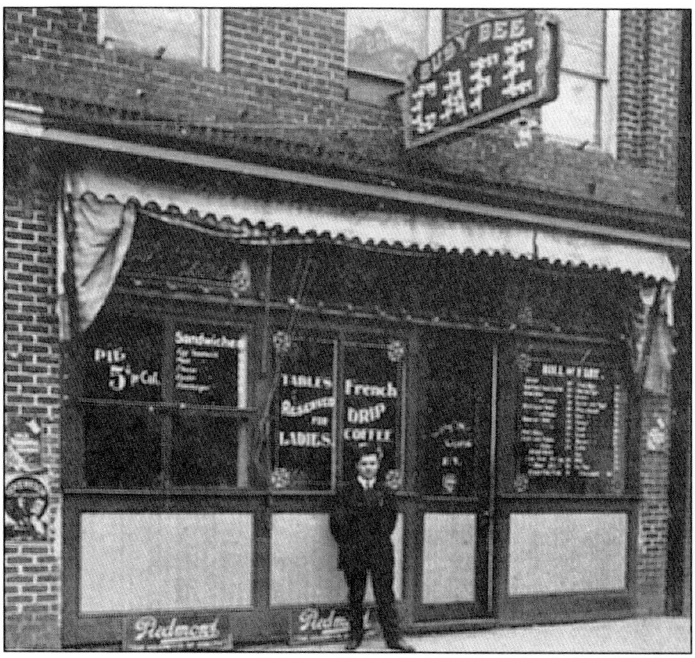

The Busy Bee Cafe was a popular gathering site in the 200 block of Middle Street. The 1914 city directory praised manager George Bambalis for his "reasonable prices and excellent accommodations." (Courtesy of Tom Faulkenberry Collection.)

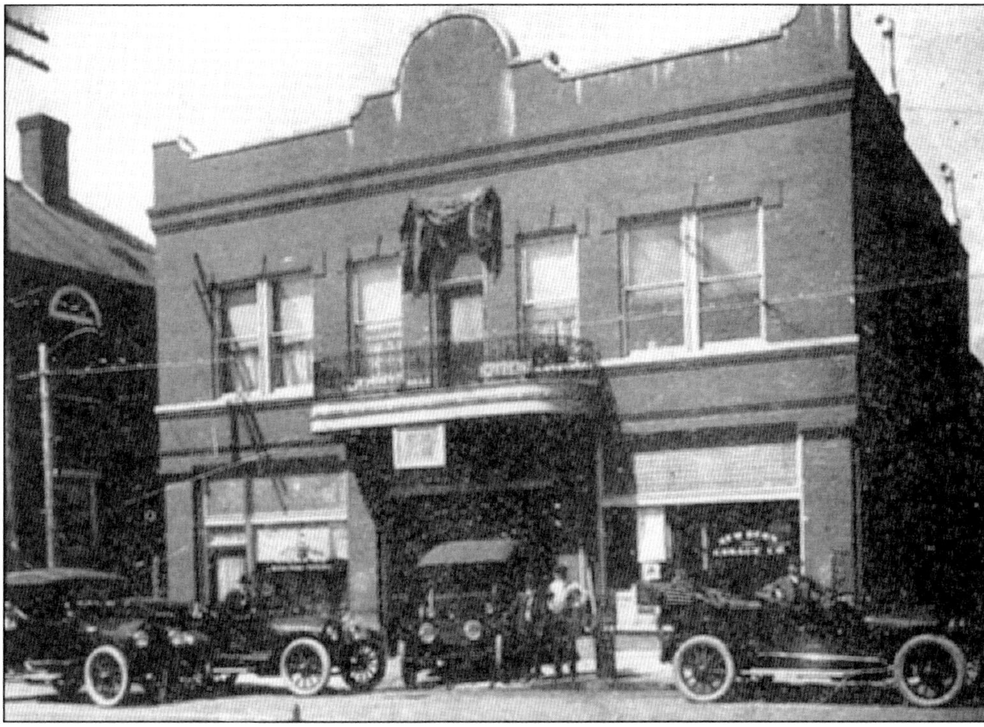

The New Bern Garage Company in the 200 block of Craven Street was incorporated in August 1911. The garage, which performed repair work, also sold Buick and Hudson automobiles and Henderson motorcycles, as well as tires, gas, oils, and greases, according to the 1914 city directory. (Courtesy of Tom Faulkenberry Collection.)

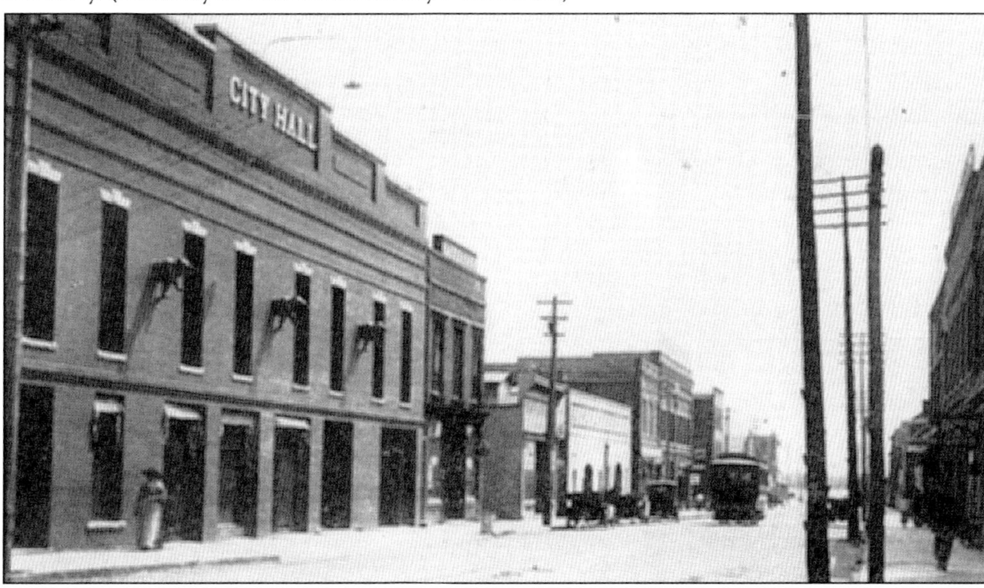

The 1914 city directory included a number of street scenes. This one shows the city hall then located in the 200 block of Craven Street. The city hall building is located diagonally across the street from the New Bern Garage Company; both buildings are still standing today. (Courtesy of Tom Faulkenberry Collection.)

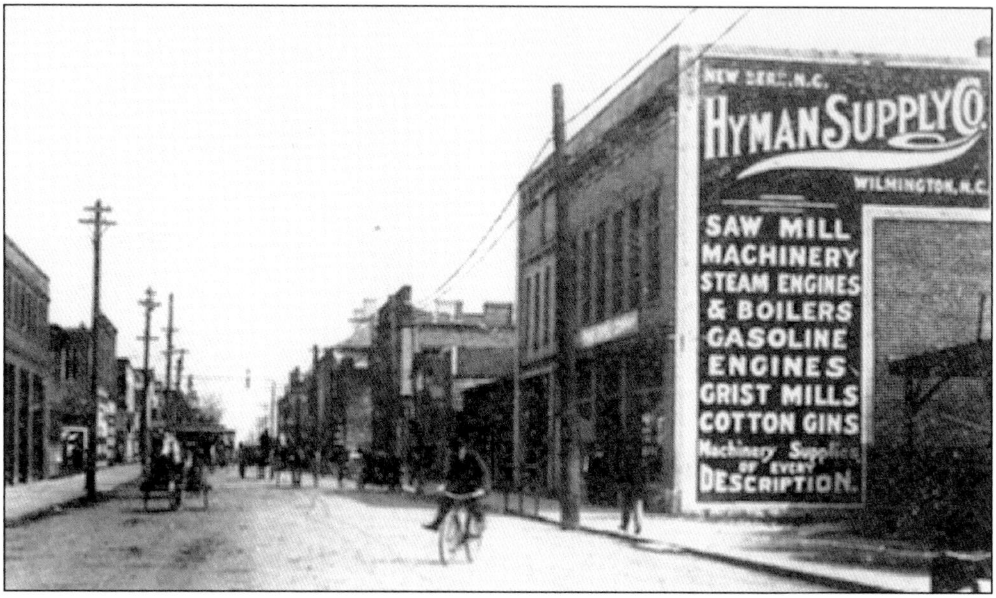

This view of South Front Street includes the Hyman Supply Company, which carried "Everything for the Mill" and operated offices in both New Bern and Wilmington according to the 1914 city directory. (Courtesy of Tom Faulkenberry Collection.)

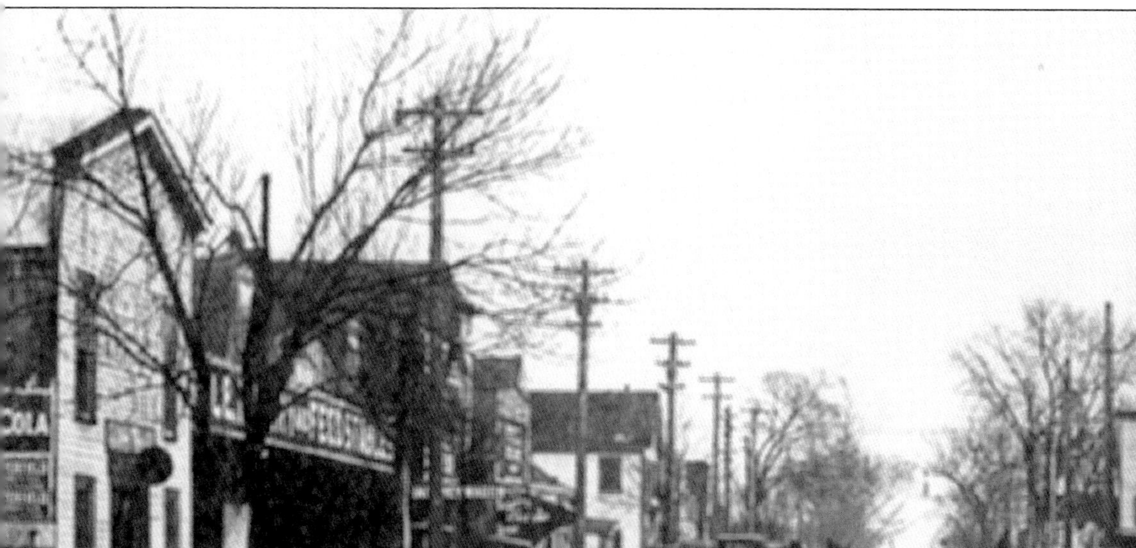

This 1914 photograph of Broad Street was taken from the intersection at Hancock Street,

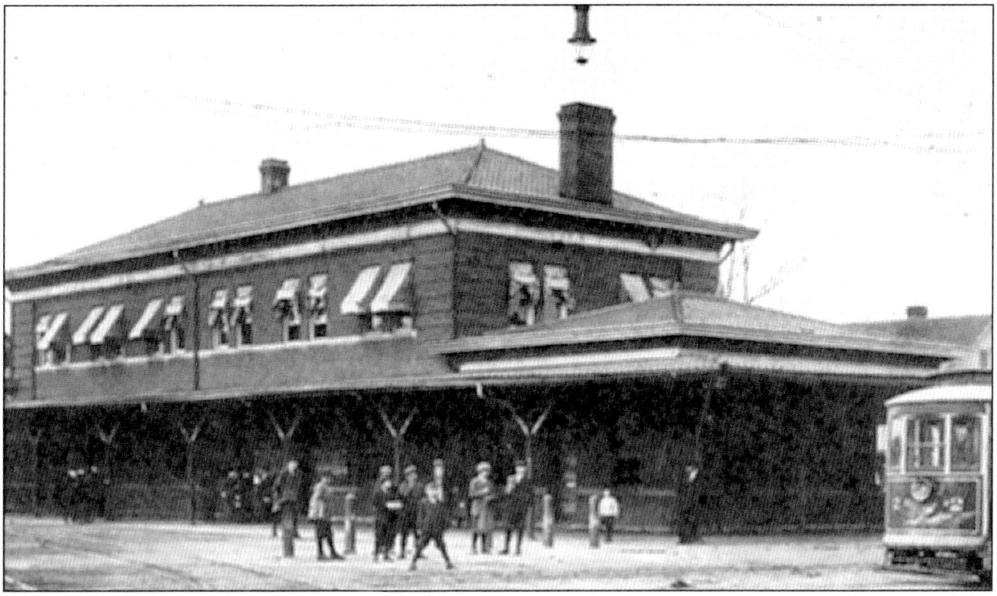

Long distance travel was most often accomplished by railroad, and visitors to New Bern who arrived by railroad made their stop in town at Union Station, located on Queen Street and built in 1910. New Bern was served by three railroads: the Norfolk Southern Railroad, the Atlantic Coast Line Railroad, and the Atlantic and North Carolina Railroad, and it quickly began a hub for passenger and freight service. (Courtesy of Tom Faulkenberry Collection.)

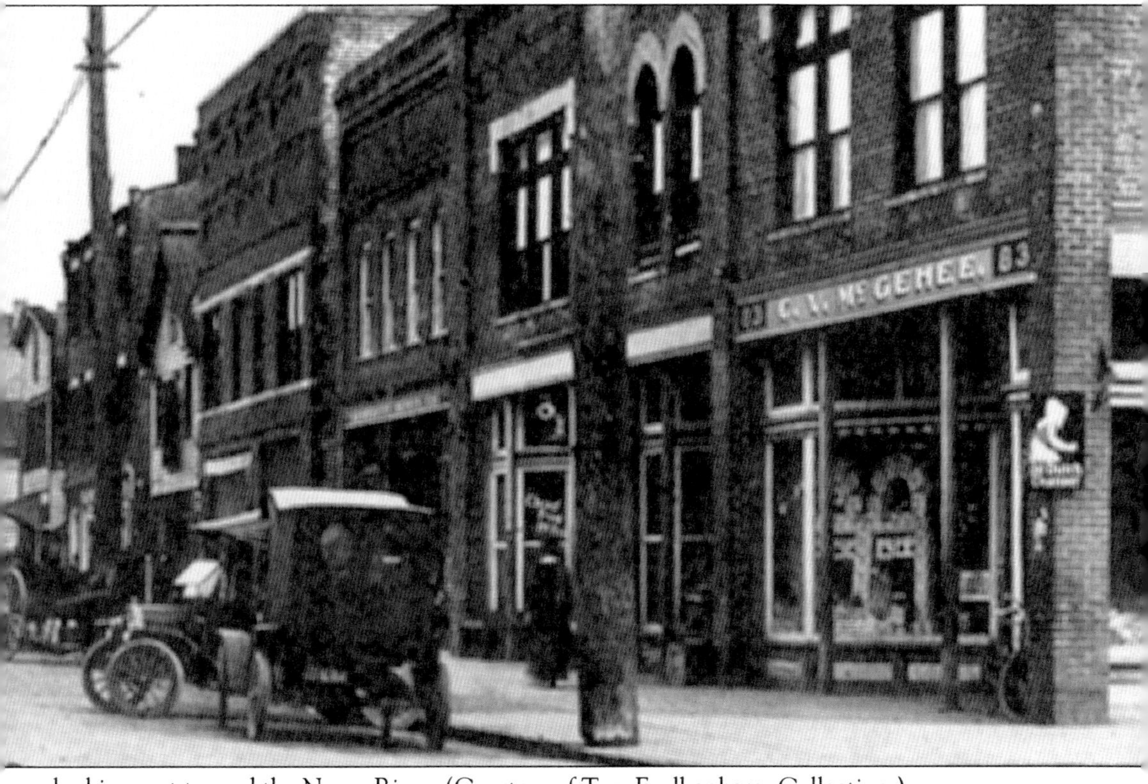

looking east toward the Neuse River. (Courtesy of Tom Faulkenberry Collection.)

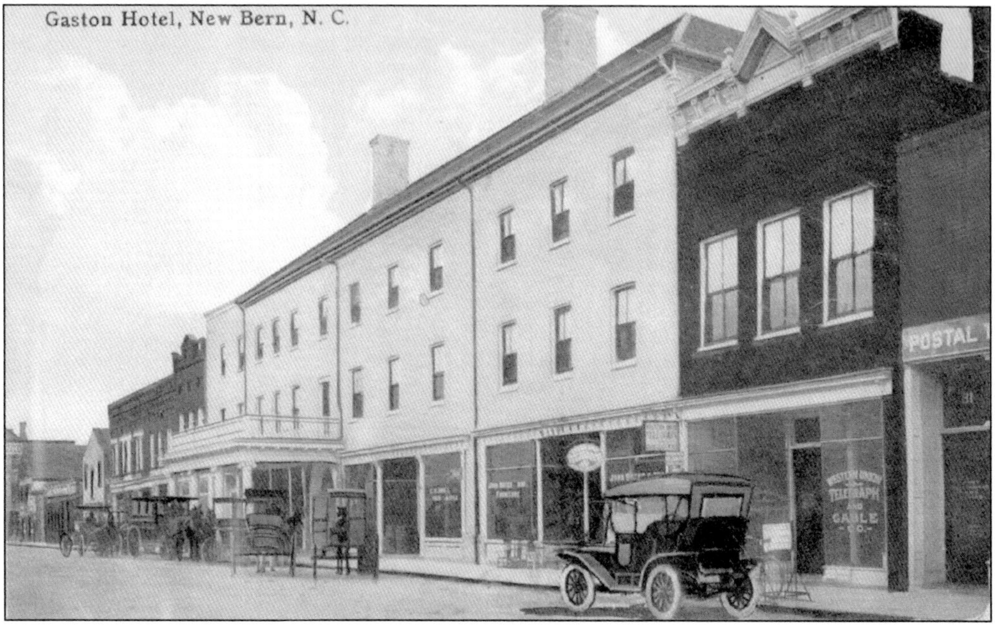

The Gaston Hotel, later refurbished as the Hotel Governor Tryon in the 1950s, opened in the 1840s. The building, located in the 200 block of South Front Street, had earlier served as shipping offices. (Courtesy of John B. Green III Collection.)

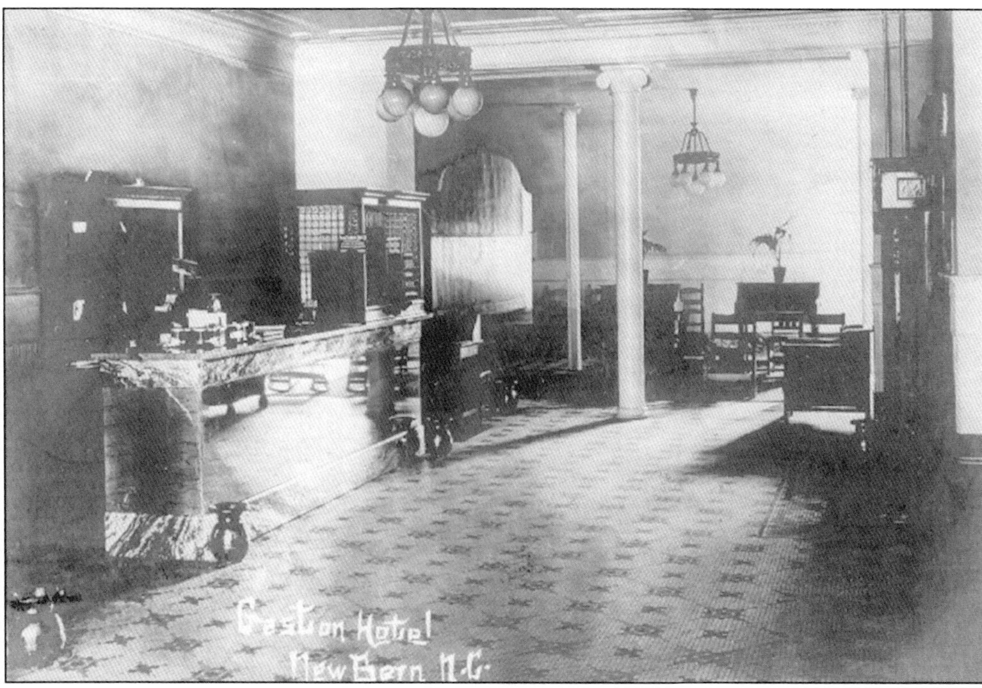

Another postcard view of the Gaston Hotel shows the lobby as it appeared c. 1910. The hotel was noted in the 1914 city directory for having such modern conveniences as electric lights, telephones, and hot and cold running water in all its rooms. (Courtesy of John B. Green III Collection.)

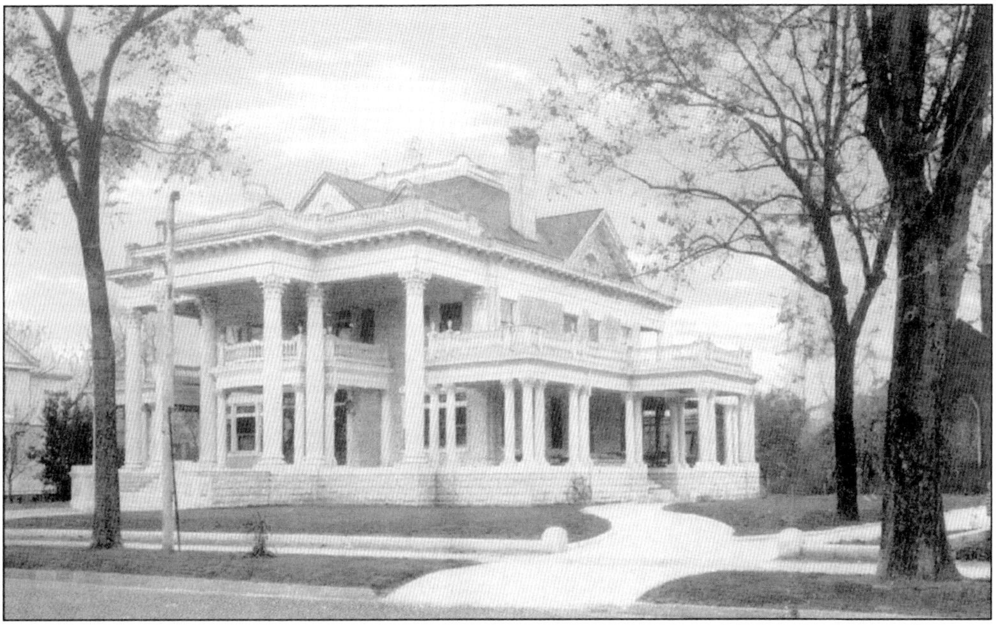

The grand home of James B. Blades on Broad Street was designed by architect Herbert W. Simpson and built in the 300 block of Middle Street. This c. 1930 postcard shows the home before it was enlarged for use as a hotel. Blades and his brother William came to the area in the late 1800s and owned successful timber companies and sawmills. (Courtesy of John B. Green III Collection.)

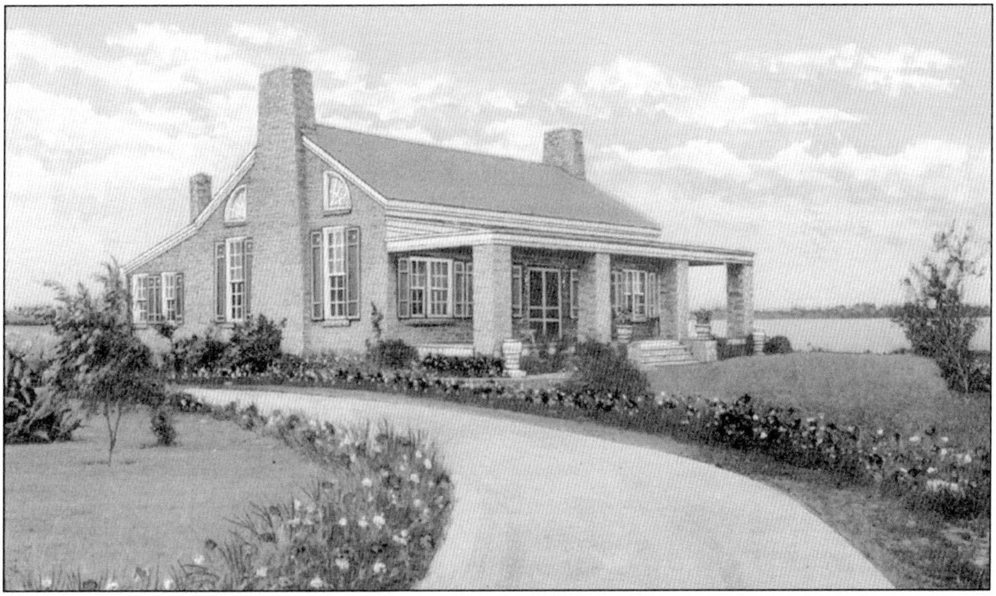

The Women's Club Building, located in Union Point Park and shown in this c. 1930s postcard, was dedicated in April 1933. The Women's Club of New Bern, with the help of local unemployed men and Works Project Administration funds, transformed the area from an unsightly dump to a pleasant park at the confluence of the Neuse and Trent Rivers. The clubhouse itself was constructed of discarded concrete curbing found in the dump. (Courtesy of John B. Green III Collection.)

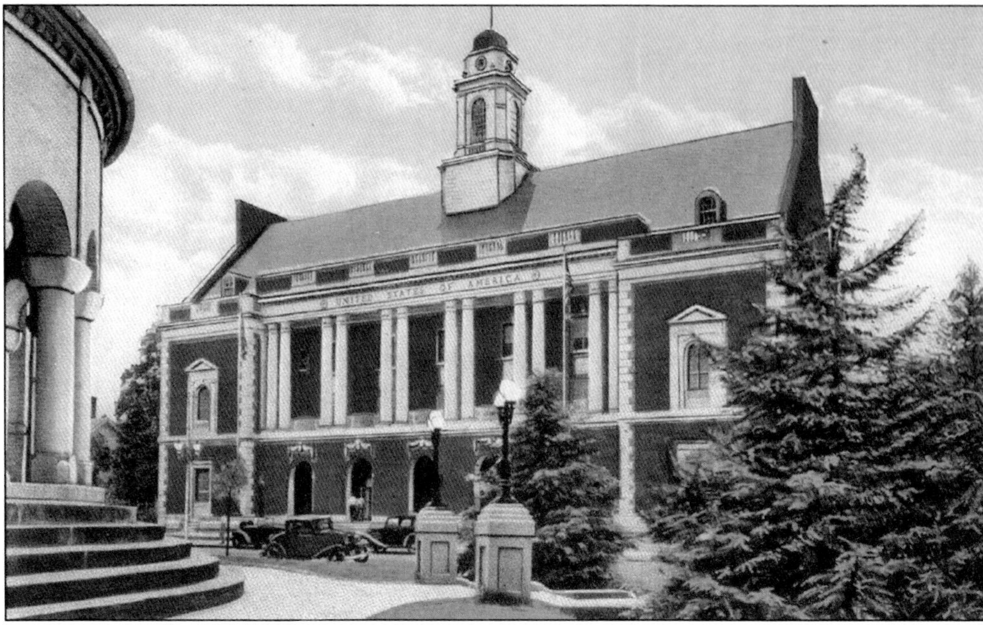

The U.S. Post Office, Courthouse, and Custom House was moved from its location at the corner of Pollock and Craven Streets to this new building at the corner of Middle and New Streets in the 1930s. Constructed from 1932–34, the building cost nearly $300,000, six times the average cost of new post office construction. Comedian Will Rogers joked that Congressman Charles L. Abernathy, who pushed the appropriation through Congress, not only brought home the bacon, but concrete as well. (Courtesy of John B. Green III Collection.)

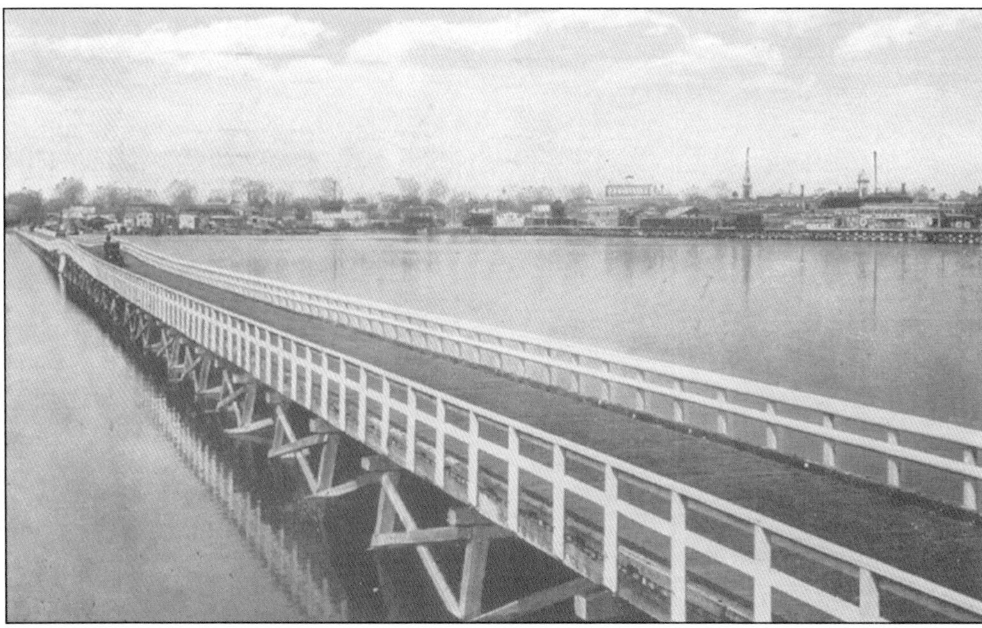

This 1930s postcard view of the Trent River Bridge showed New Bern's ever-changing, ever-beautiful waterfront area. (Courtesy of John B. Green III Collection.)

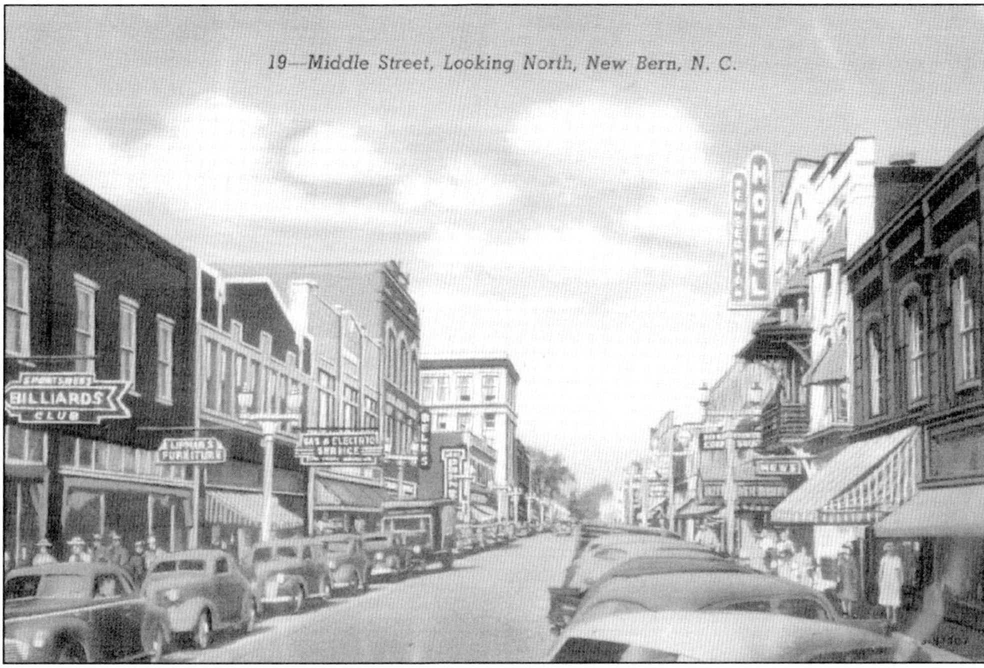

A 1930s postcard of Middle Street, looking north, shows a bustling downtown, much changed from the time of Bowden's visit in 1908. (Courtesy of John B. Green III Collection.)

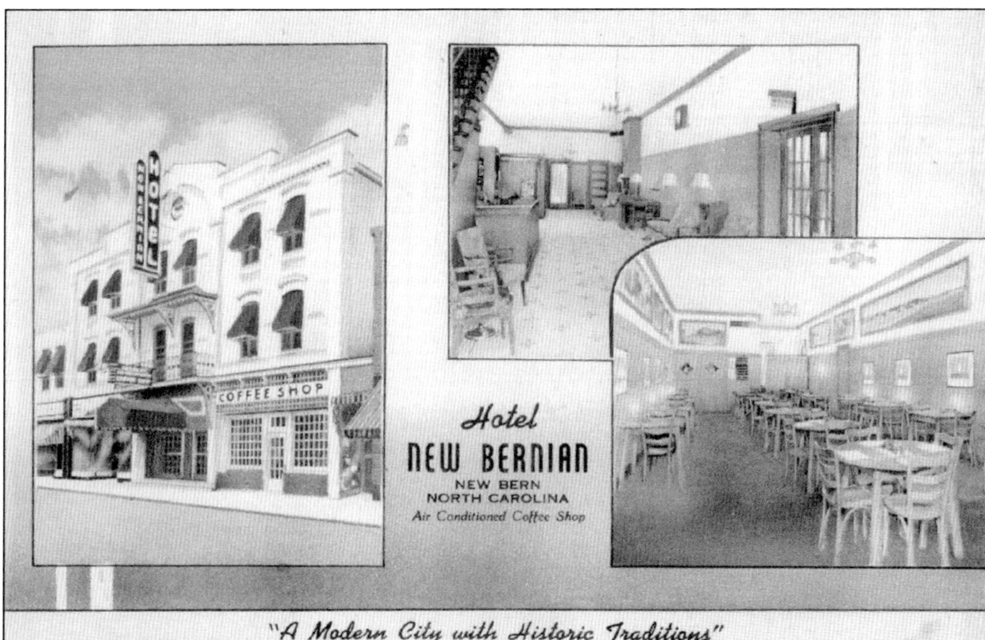

The Hotel New Bernian was another c. 1940s downtown hotel, housed in the former Hotel Albert building located in the middle of the 200 block of Middle Street. It closed in 1960. (Courtesy of John B. Green III Collection.)

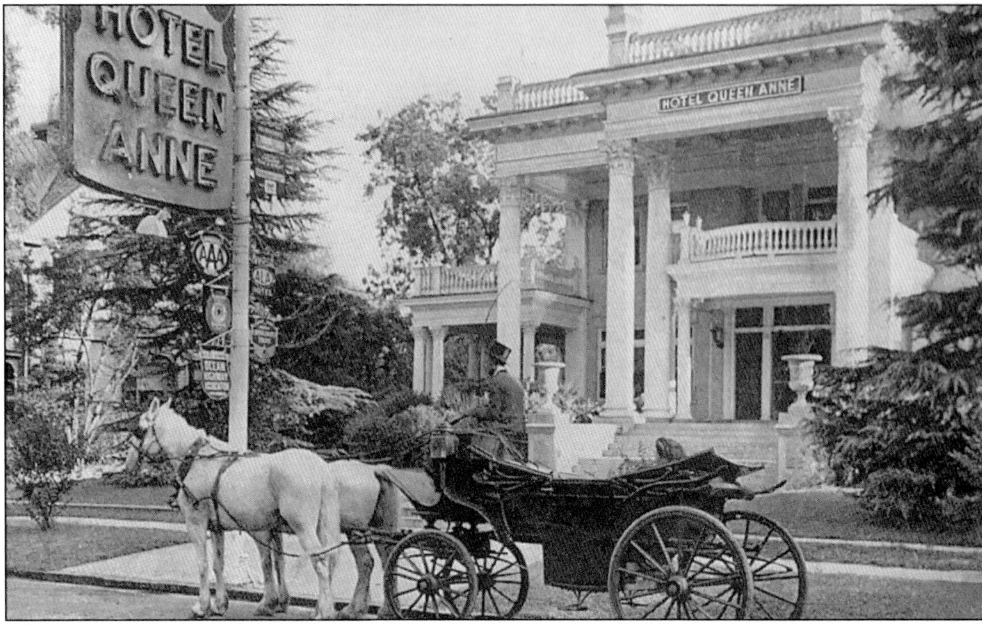

The J.B. Blades home in the 300 block of Broad Street was enlarged and converted into the Hotel Queen Anne in the late 1930s. By the early 1940s, New Bern suffered an acute housing shortage as construction workers and service personnel poured into New Bern due to the construction work at Marine Corps Air Station, Cherry Point, located in nearby Havelock. (Courtesy of New Bern Area Chamber of Commerce.)

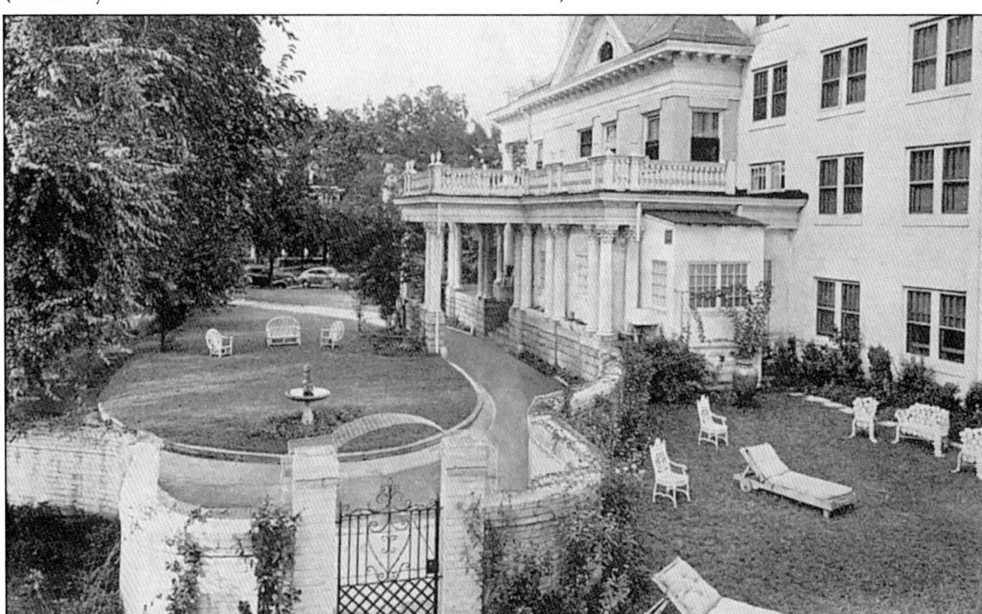

The front of the house was little changed from the day the building served as the home of J.B. Blades, as rooms for the hotel were built into a back extension. This view shows the side garden and curving driveway. Later converted into apartments, the hotel was torn down in the 1960s to make way for a new bank building. (Courtesy of New Bern Area Chamber of Commerce.)

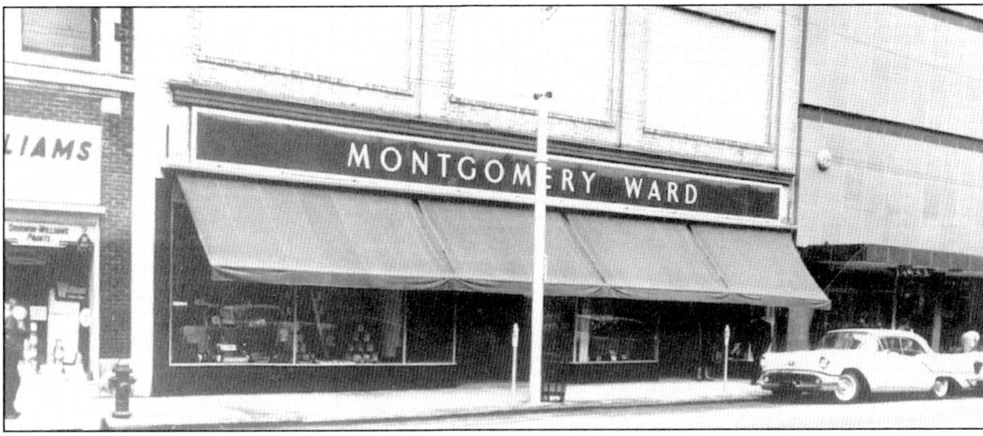

The Coplon Building was constructed in 1929 for an investment firm and occupied by Montgomery Ward until 1964. This view dates from about that time, as Belk had applied its "modernistic" metal front in early 1963. (Courtesy of Mrs. Nettie Pinnix Collection, New Bern-Craven County Public Library.)

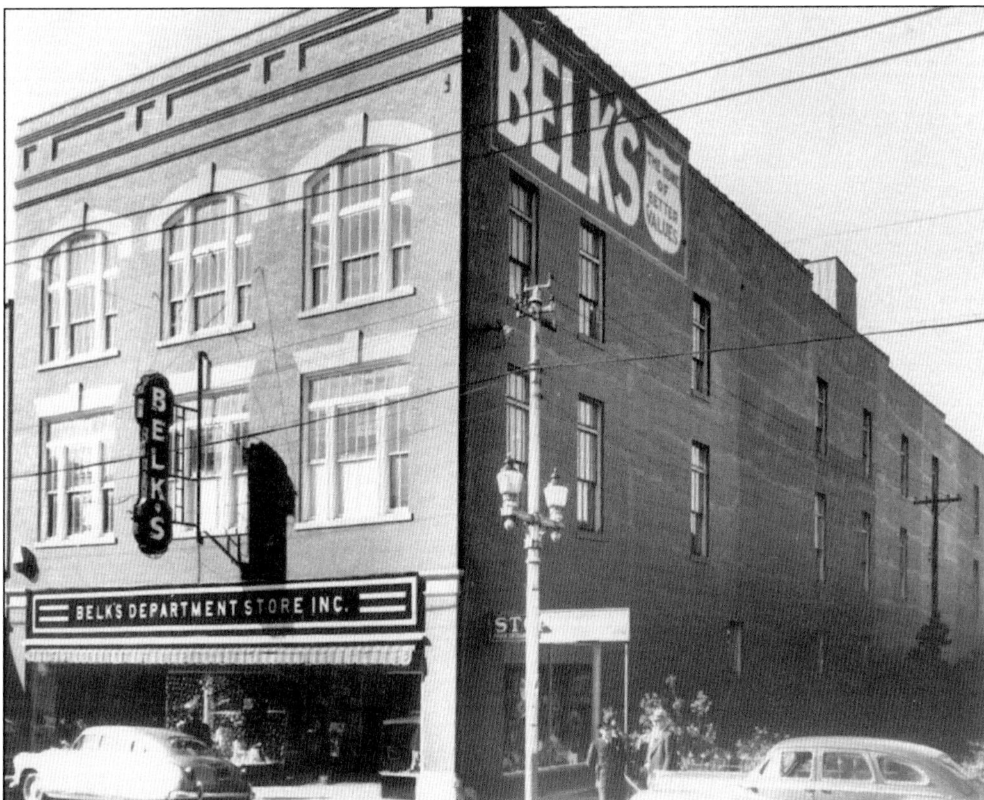

Belk's Department Store was located downtown from 1937 until its move to Twin Rivers Mall in 1979. It was located in the O. Marks Building, constructed *c.* 1915–16 for a local dry goods merchant. This 1950s view shows the building before Belk expanded in 1964 to the neighboring Coplon Building, and a false metal front was placed over both buildings to match their appearance. (Courtesy of McCotter-Rains Associates Collection, New Bern-Craven County Public Library.)

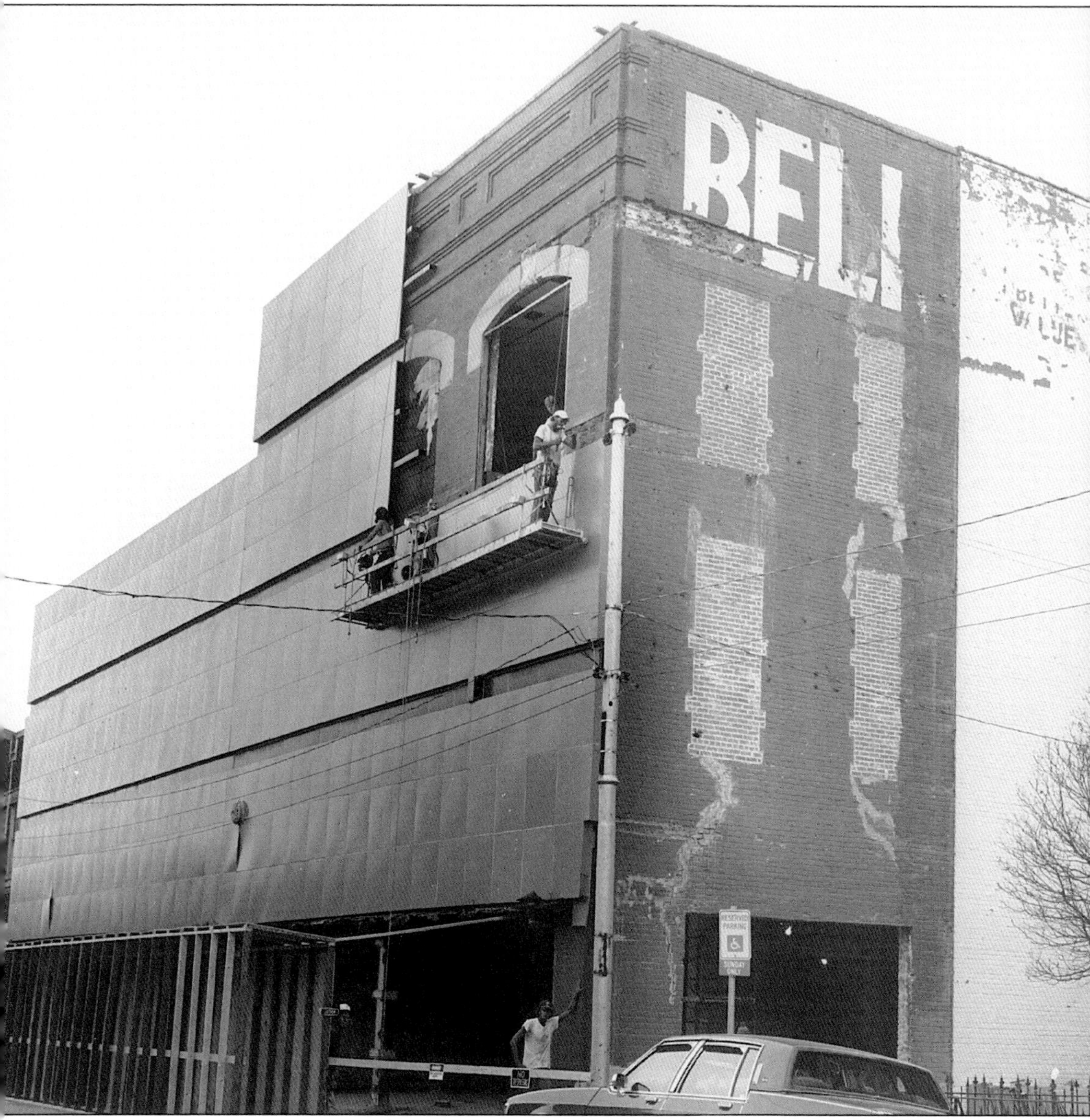

As part of outgoing rehabilitative efforts in the downtown area in the 1980s, the false metal front on the Belk building was removed, once again revealing beautiful brick work and the distinctive features on both the O. Marks and Coplon Buildings. (Courtesy of New Bern Area Chamber of Commerce.)

Six

New Bern Fire Department

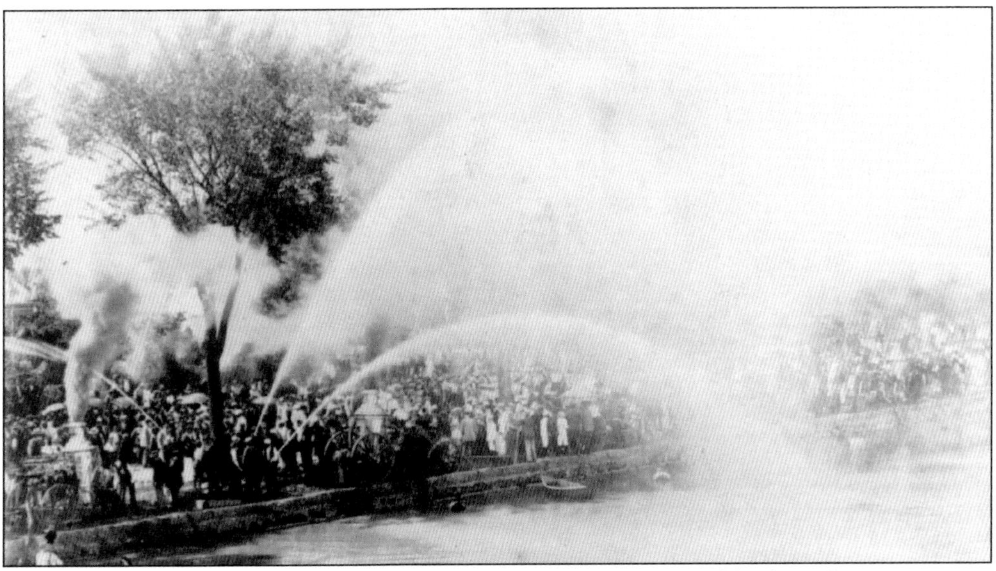

The modern-day New Bern Fire Department's origins can be traced back to the organization of the Atlantic Hook & Ladder Company on May 14, 1845. During the Civil War, when most of its members were serving in the Confederate Army and New Bern itself was occupied by Union Forces, the Atlantic Company was mostly inactive. Union soldiers, many of whom stayed on after the war was over, formed the New Bern Steam Fire Engine Company No. 1 on January 1, 1865. After the war, the two companies were fiercely competitive, even after their consolidation as the New Bern Fire Department in 1867. The department sponsored annual parades, fairs and tournaments, such as this one in August 1895. Firefighters tested the steam engines along East Front Street. (Courtesy of Mrs. G. Tull Richardson Collection, New Bern-Craven County Library.)

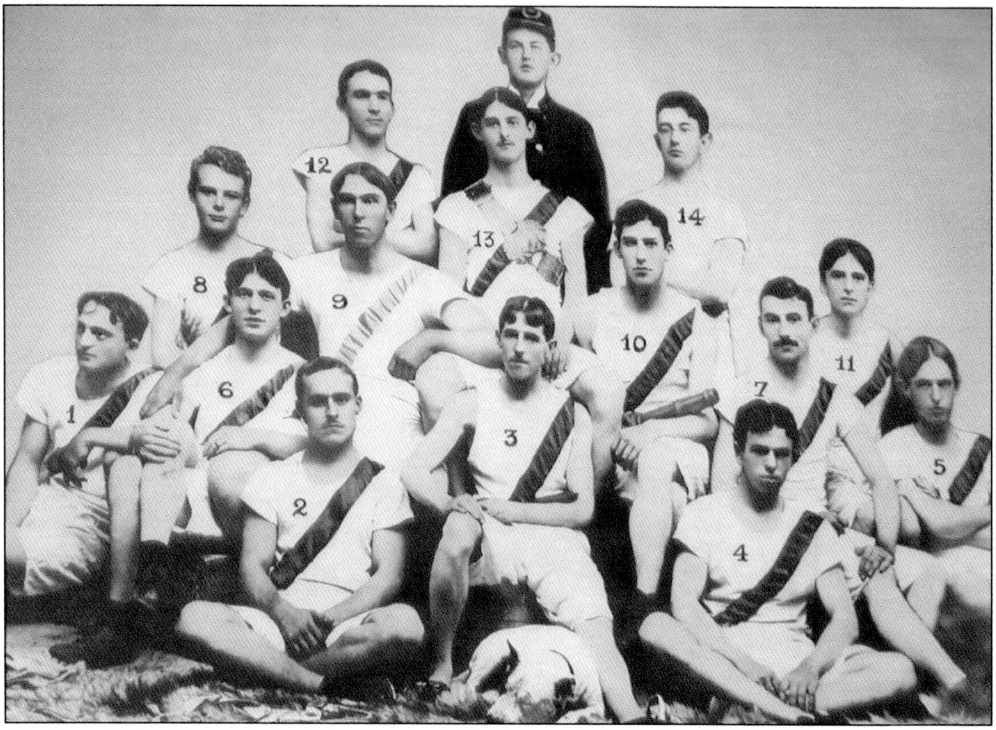

The New Bern Steam Fire Engine Company No. 1 was known throughout the community as the Button Company, after its purchase of a Button Fire Engine in 1884. Members of the fire department regularly engaged in competitions against other companies and departments. Other companies of the New Bern Fire Department included the Excelsior Bucket and Axe Company No. 4, as well as two African-American companies, the Mechanics Hooks and Ladder Company and the Reliance Company. The members of the 1900 Button Fire Company's Reel Team shown here are (1) Tom Daniels, (2) Charles Thornton, (3) Forney Justice, (4) Otis Griffith, (5) Sam Eaton, (6) Abe Cohen, (7) Leo Sultan, (8) Clarence Smith, (9) Jim Simmons, (10) Walter Brinson, (11) Johnny Gaskill, (12) Will Hay, (13) Frank Matthews, (14) Albert Bangert, and (15) Luther Taylor. (Courtesy of New Bern Firemen's Museum.)

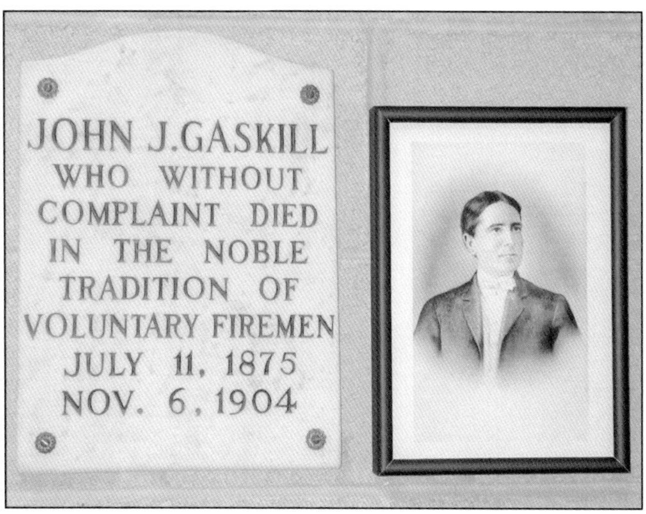

John J. Gaskill was a popular resident of New Bern who served as assistant chief of the fire department. He died November 6, 1904, two weeks after being kicked by a fire horse. His obituary in the *New Bern Daily Journal* stated that Gaskill's "brief but very distressing illness (was) from the first . . . regarded as desperate." His brother firefighters erected this tribute to him. It now hangs in the New Bern Firemen's Museum. (Courtesy of New Bern Firemen's Museum.)

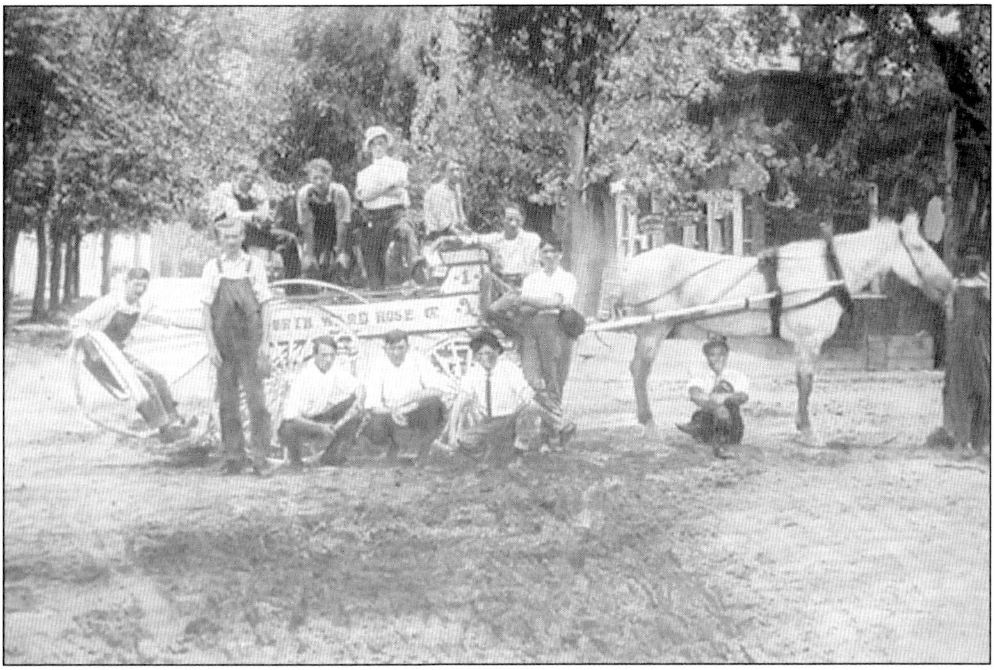

The outlying areas of New Bern were protected by their own fire companies. The Fourth Ward Fire Company (shown above) and the Riverside Fire Company (shown below) were two such companies. These pictures are dated c. 1910. (Courtesy of New Bern Firemen's Museum.)

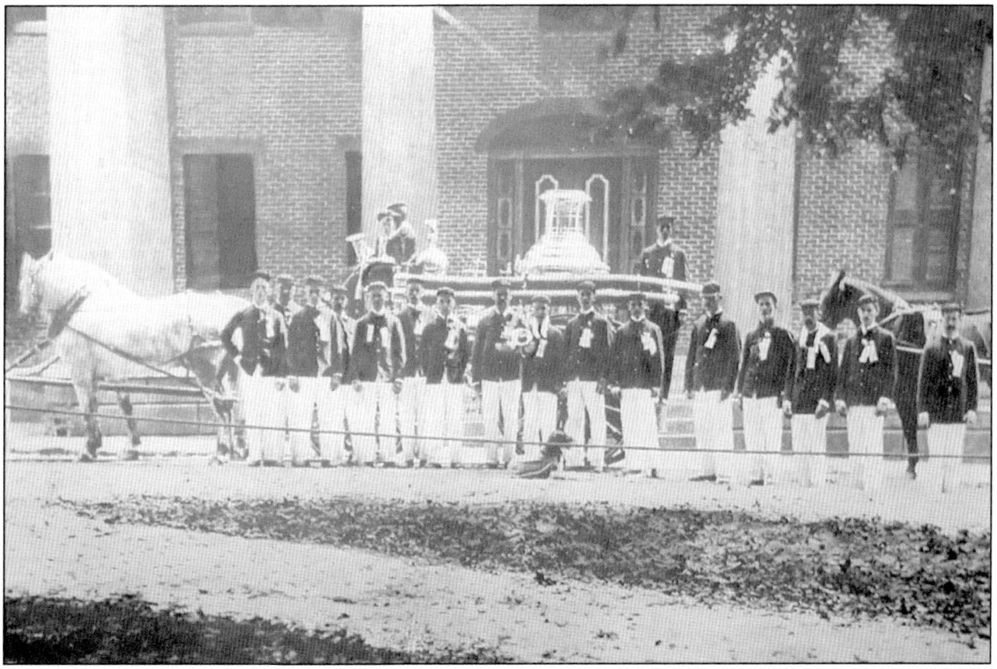

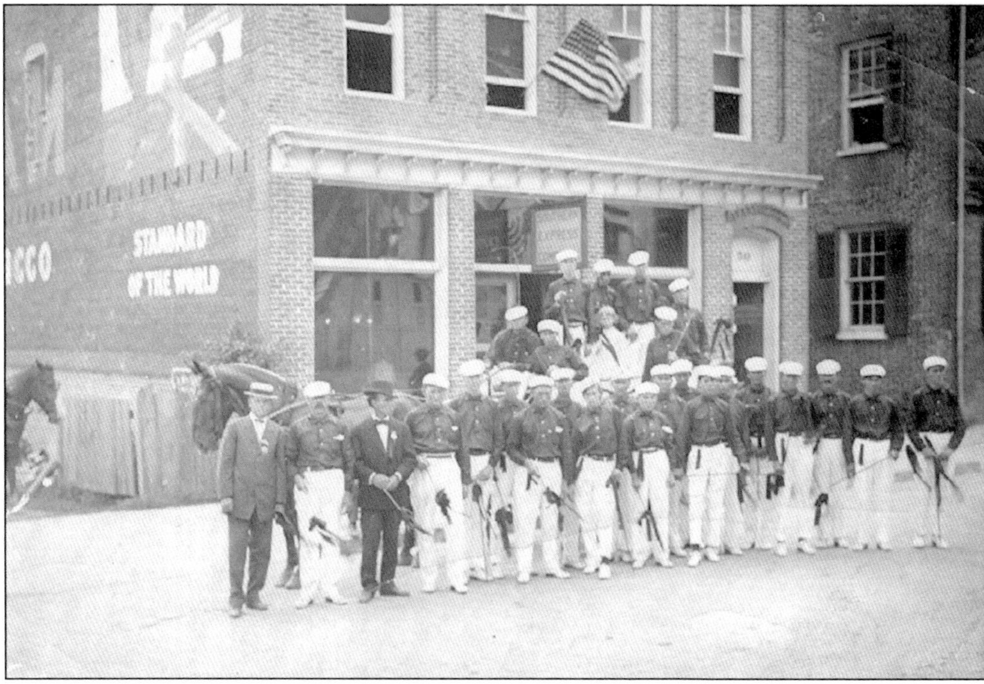

Firemen not only fought fires and protected their communities, but they also were called upon to lead parades, preside at banquets, and perform other civic duties. Each of New Bern's fire companies enjoyed their own following of fans. Members of the Button Company participated in the 1910 bicentennial celebration. (Courtesy of John B. Green III Collection.)

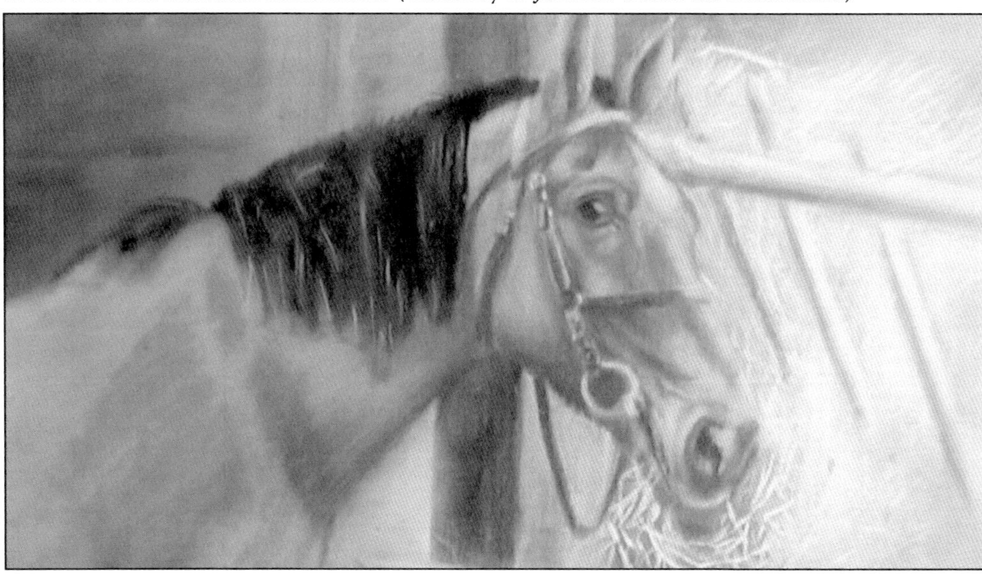

Old Jim, one of the many horses which served the New Bern Fire Department, pulled fire wagons for the fire companies from 1881 to 1909. The first fire horses were "volunteers," owned by local merchants and loaned to the fire department as emergencies dictated. The city first purchased horses to pull garbage carts. Whenever an alarm sounded, these horses were unhitched from their garbage carts and ridden to the fire department. (Courtesy of New Bern Firemen's Museum.)

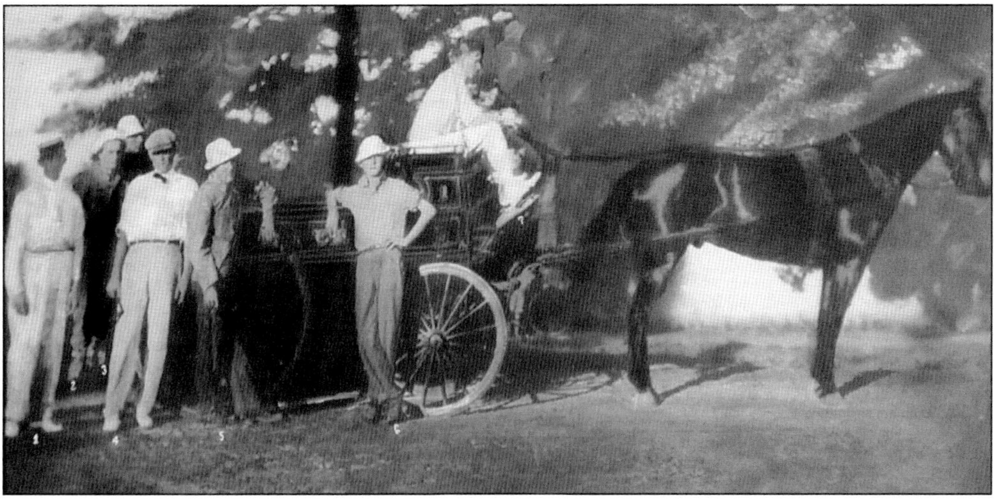

The Button Fire Company set a world record on May 19, 1911 in Charlotte, NC. While fire horse "Ben Hurst" pulled the hose wagon 200 yards, "firemen laid 228 feet of fire hose, screwed on the fire nozzle and flowed water in 26 2/5 seconds." This record has never been broken. Members of the record-setting team were, from left to right, G.Y. Herrington, Don Sparrow, L.R. Tucker, T.D. Davis, R.C. Whitley, Claud White, and E. Fleet Smallwood. (Courtesy of New Bern Firemen's Museum.)

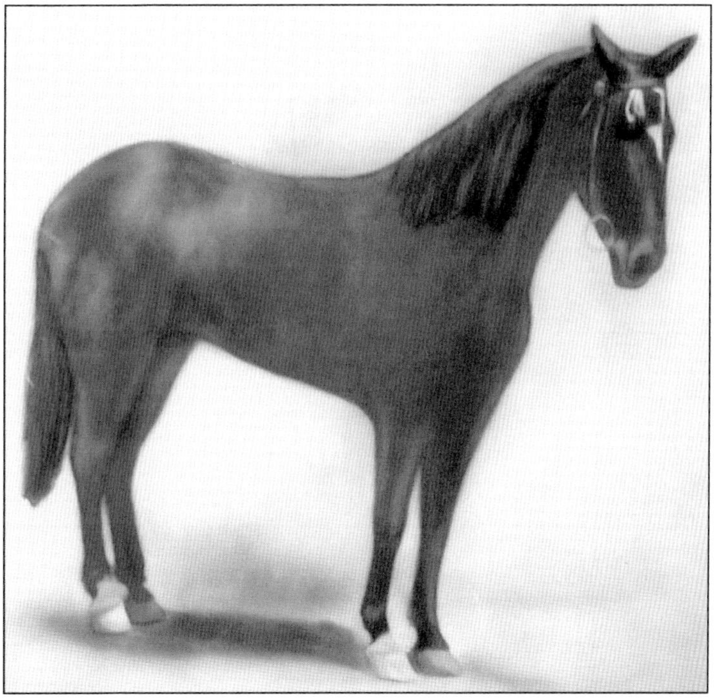

Ben Hurst pulled the hose wagon when members of the Button Fire Company set their world record in May 1911. The old Button fire engine was replaced by a motorized truck in 1945; the Atlantic company kept its horse-drawn Silsby steam fire engine until 1925. (Courtesy of New Bern Firemen's Museum.)

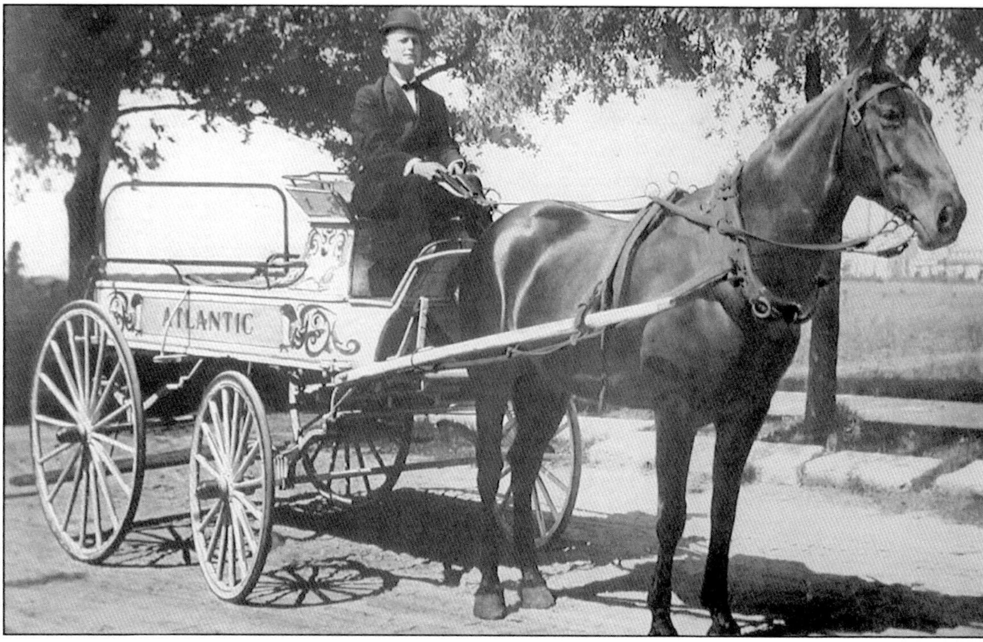

"Fire Horse Fred" is New Bern's most famous firefighting horse. Purchased for use by the Atlantic Fire Company in 1908, Fred dropped dead of a heart attack in 1925 while responding to a false alarm. Chief Sam Coward posed with Fred in this c. 1925 picture. Interestingly enough, Fred's head is on display at the New Bern Firemen's Museum. The hose wagon, built around the turn of the 20th century by G.S. Waters Buggy Works of New Bern, is also on display, along with early steam engines, fire trucks, and other historical items. (Courtesy of New Bern Firemen's Museum.)

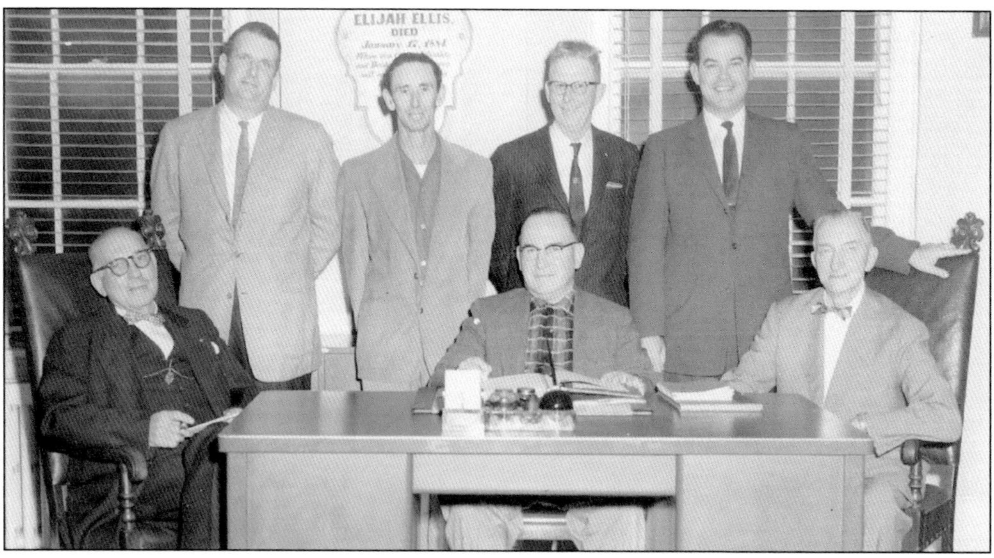

The New Bern Firemen's Museum, originally located off Broad Street, opened in June 1955; however, its official grand opening was delayed to June 24, 1957, to accommodate the schedule of Swedish ambassador Henry de Torrente. Members of the firemen's museum committee included Leroy Tucker (at left, seated) and Albert Brinson (third from left, standing). The others remain unidentified. (Courtesy of New Bern Firemen's Museum.)

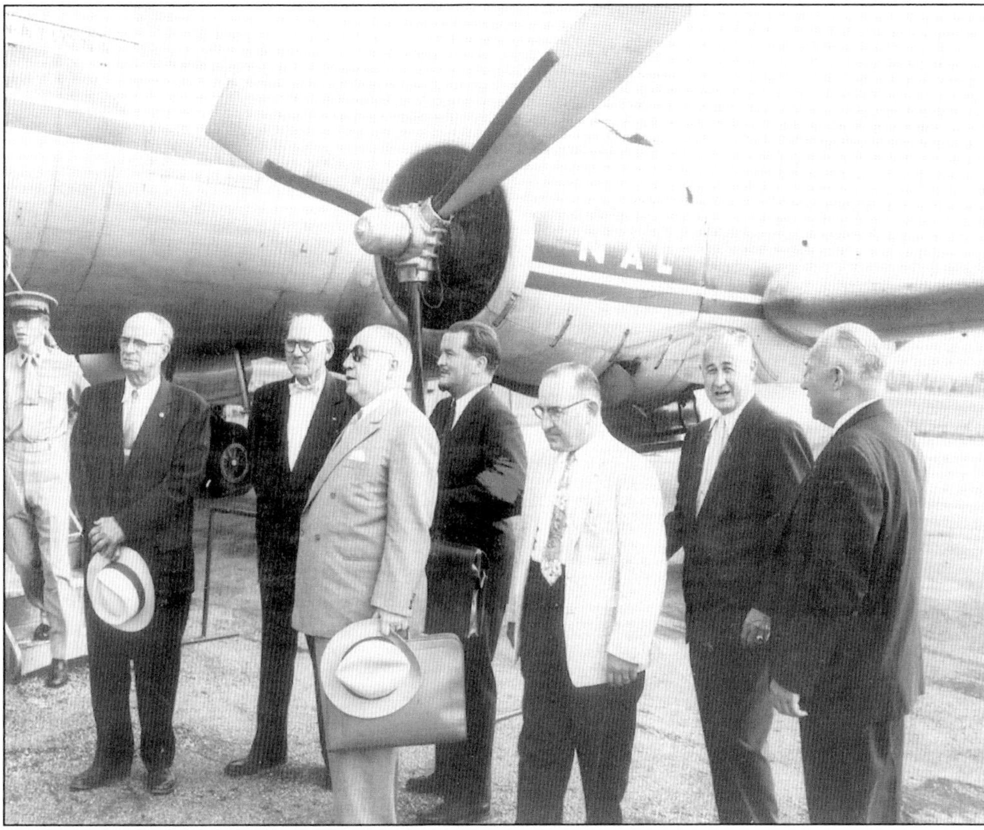

Local officials were on hand at the Simmons-Nott (Craven County) Airport to greet the arriving dignitaries. From left to right are an unidentified man, committee member Leroy Tucker, Ambassador Henry de Torrente, Von Muyden (the ambassador's attache), New Bern mayor Mack Lupton, another unidentified man, and Congressman Graham Barden of New Bern. (Courtesy of New Bern Firemen's Museum.)

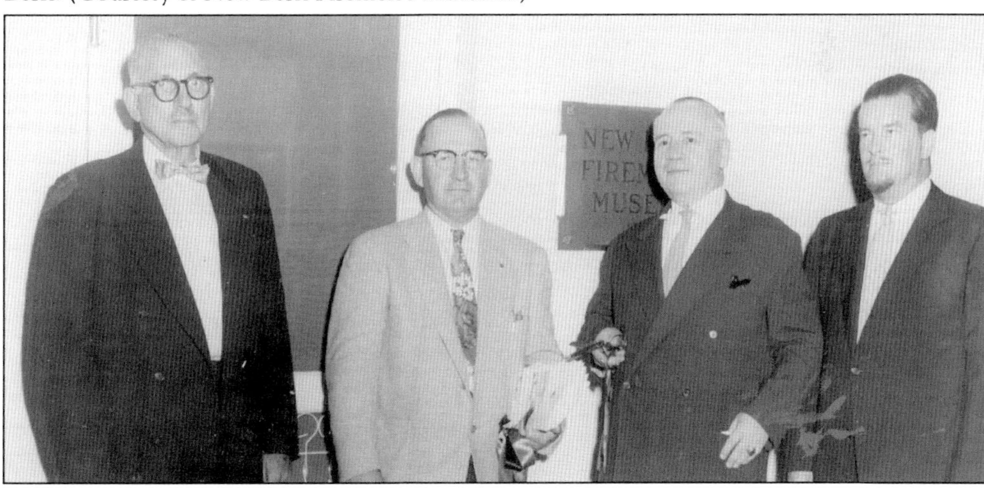

Two years after its original opening, the firemen's museum was officially dedicated and opened. Cutting the ribbon are Leroy Tucker, Mack Lupton, Henry de Torrente, and Von Muyden. (Courtesy of New Bern Firemen's Museum.)

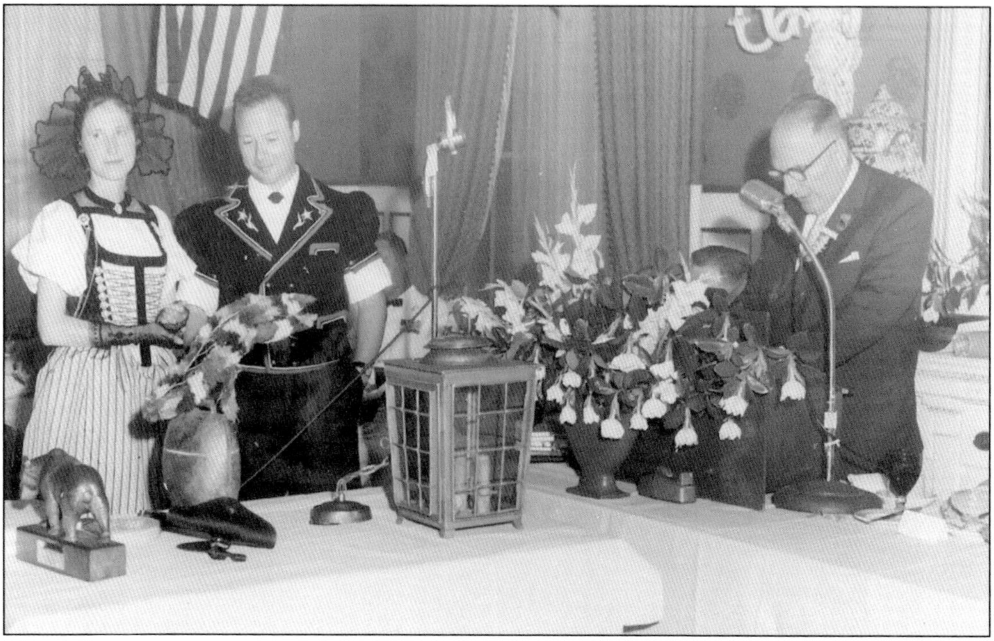

The dedication ceremony included a lavish dinner at the Hotel Governor Tryon on South Front Street. Two Swiss delegates presented a fire axe and lantern to fire museum officials as Henry de Torrente spoke. During his speech he said the museum only emphasized the bonds that existed between Berne, Switzerland, and New Bern. (Courtesy of New Bern Firemen's Museum.)

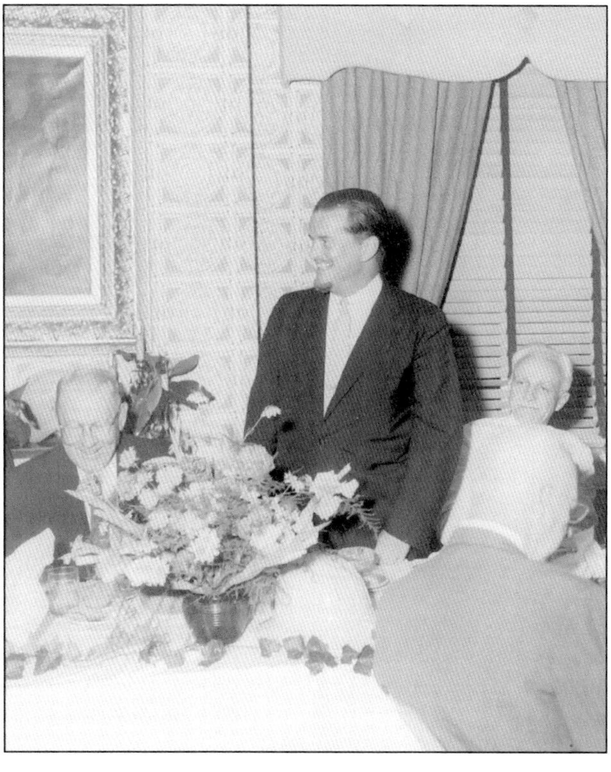

Attache Von Muyden was also recognized at the banquet marking the official dedication of the New Bern Firemen's Museum. The museum to this day contains relics and mementoes of New Bern's firefighting heritage. Also on display are many of the original fire wagons. The entrance to the museum, which was expanded in 1982, is now located at 408 Hancock Street. (Courtesy of New Bern Firemen's Museum.)

Seven

FACES OF NEW BERN

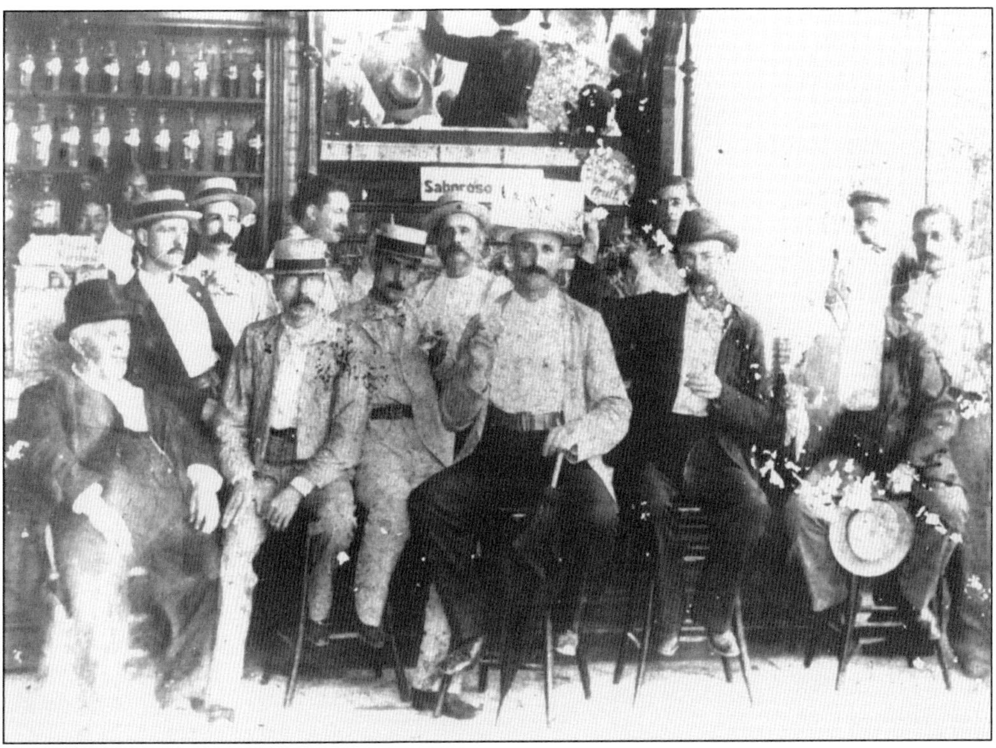

Pharmacist Caleb Bradham Davis (1867–1934) owned his first drugstore on the corner of Middle and Pollock Street. He is shown here *c.* 1900 (in profile, third from the left in the back row). Bradham, known as Brad to his friends, invented the wildly popular "Brad's Drink," later known as Pepsi-Cola, in 1898. (Courtesy of New Bern Historical Society Collection, New Bern-Craven County Public Library.)

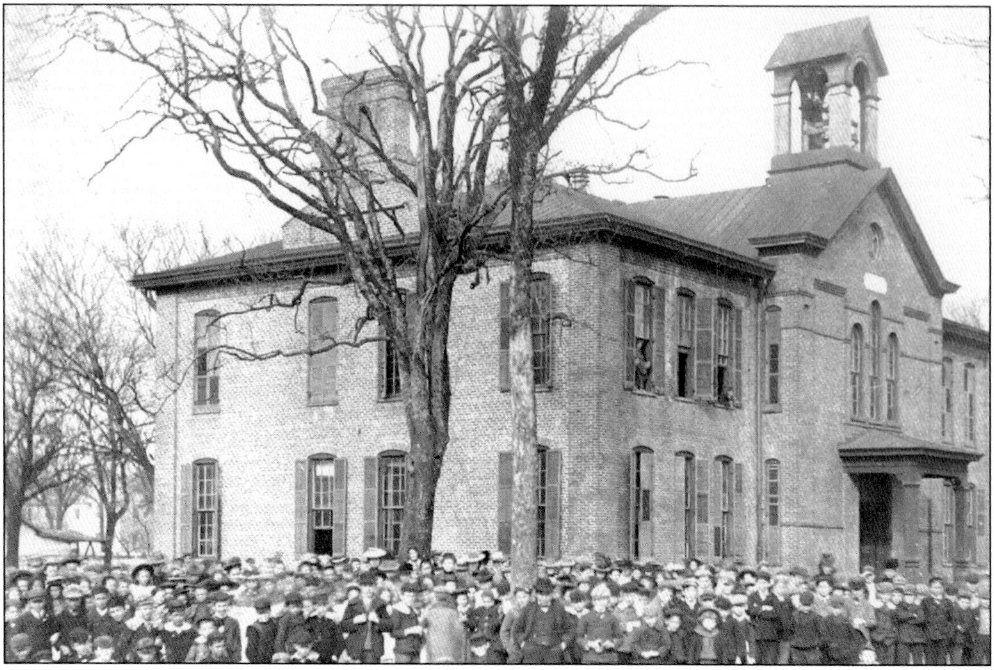

Students at New Bern Graded School, 517 Hancock Street, paused outside for this school portrait. This building, nicknamed the Bell Building because of the school bell, was opened in 1885; along with New Bern Academy, it was used as a school until 1972. It stood empty for a number of years before its eight classrooms were converted into four apartments during the 1980s. (Courtesy of Sadie Whitehurst Collection, New Bern-Craven County Public Library.)

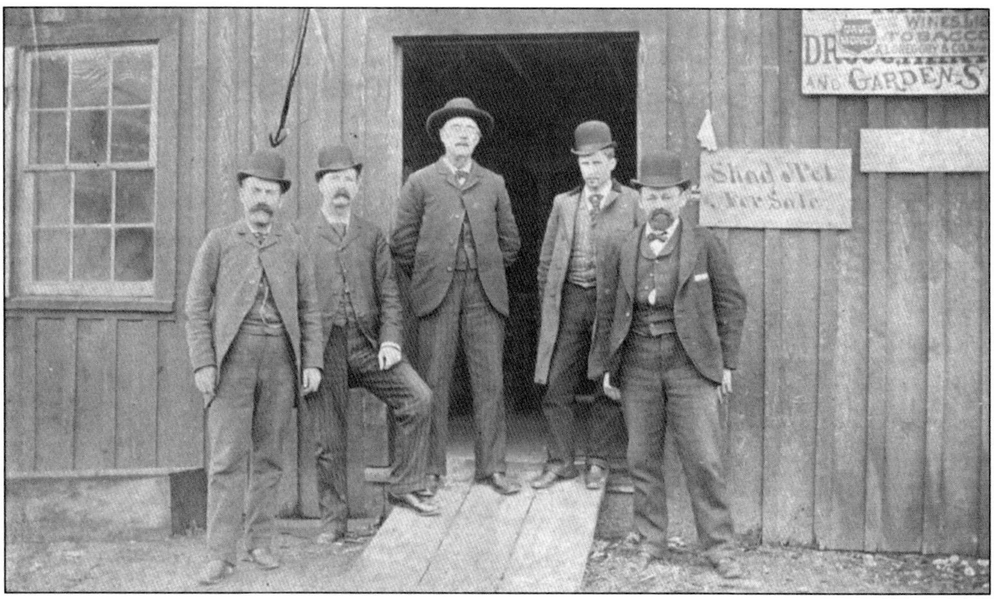

A group of local businessmen paused *c.* 1910 outside Tom Watson's Fish House, located at the foot of Middle Street on the Trent River waterfront. (Courtesy of Mrs. Nettie Pinnix Collection, New Bern-Craven County Public Library.)

G.S. Waters built his first "Buggymobile," powered by a gasoline engine, in 1899, but he was unable to find the financial backing to go into production. Still, he drove his modified 1903 Buggymobile, complete with buggy whip, around New Bern for 35 years. This photograph was taken on Broad Street around 1925. (Courtesy of Mrs. Elizabeth Crowley Collection, New Bern-Craven County Public Library.)

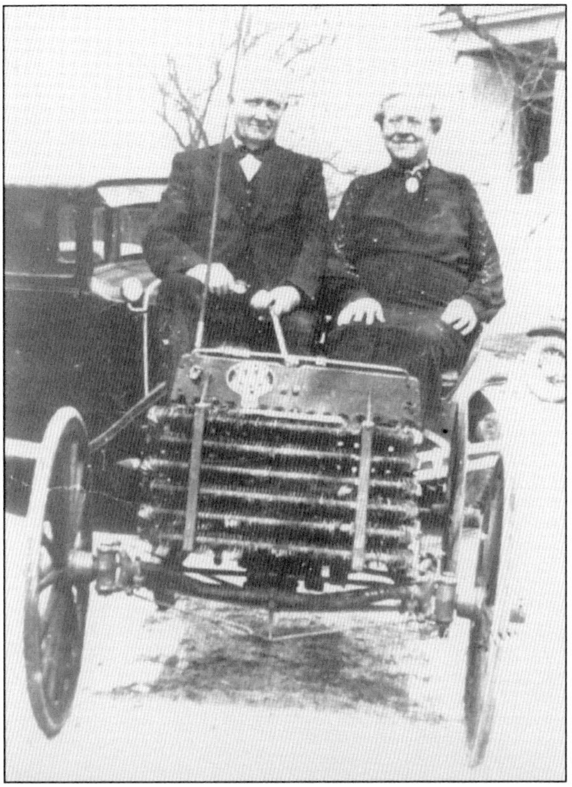

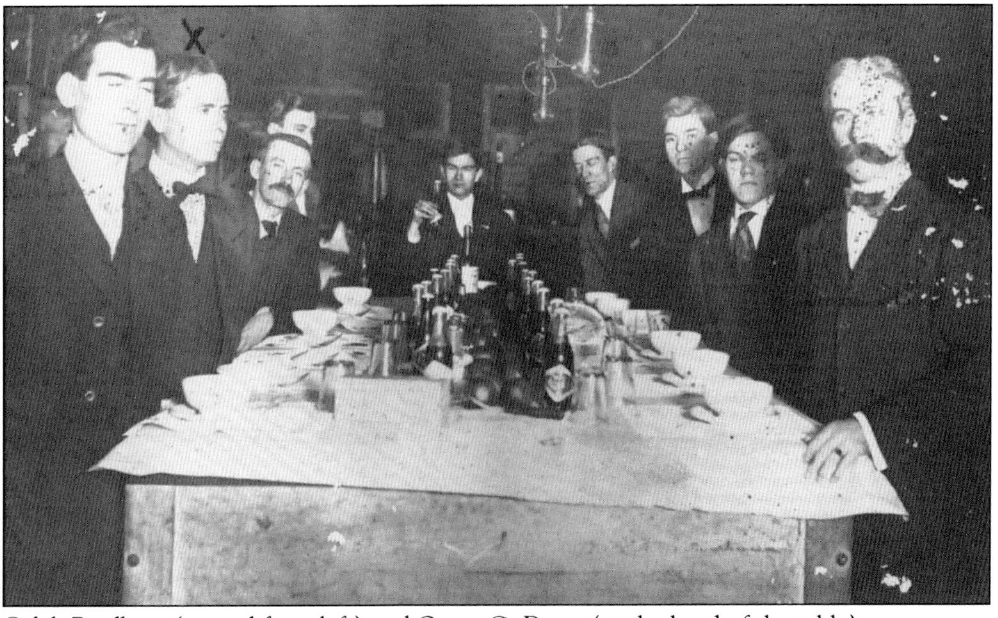

Caleb Bradham (second from left) and Owen G. Dunn (at the head of the table) were among the businessmen seated at this banquet table, c. 1910. Dunn operated a prolific printing business and later founded the *New Bern Sun*, where he served as editor, manager, and printer until its merger in 1914 with the *New Bern Journal*. (Courtesy of Pepsi-Cola Bottling Company Collection, New Bern-Craven County Public Library.)

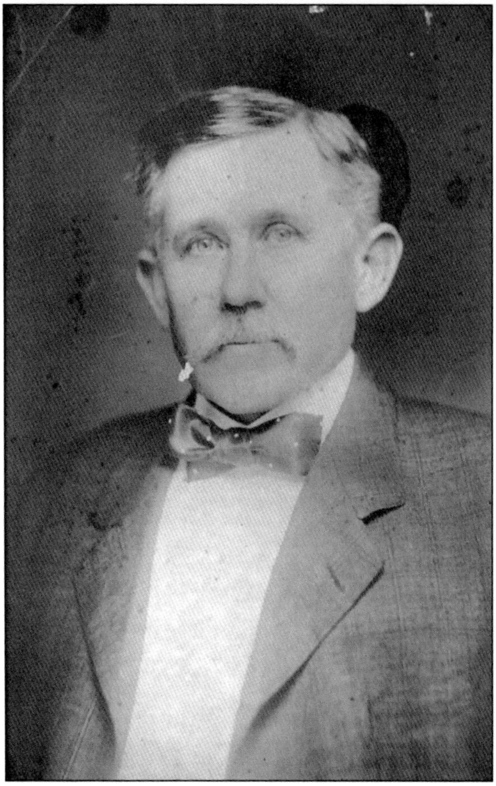

John W. Stewart was a local businessman whose first business venture included a livery stable with T.J. Mitchell. Later, he sold the livery business and enjoyed successful real estate and farming ventures. He owned a grand Victorian mansion at the corner of Craven and Pollock Streets, where he died in 1919 at age 66. (Courtesy of Tom Faulkenberry Collection.)

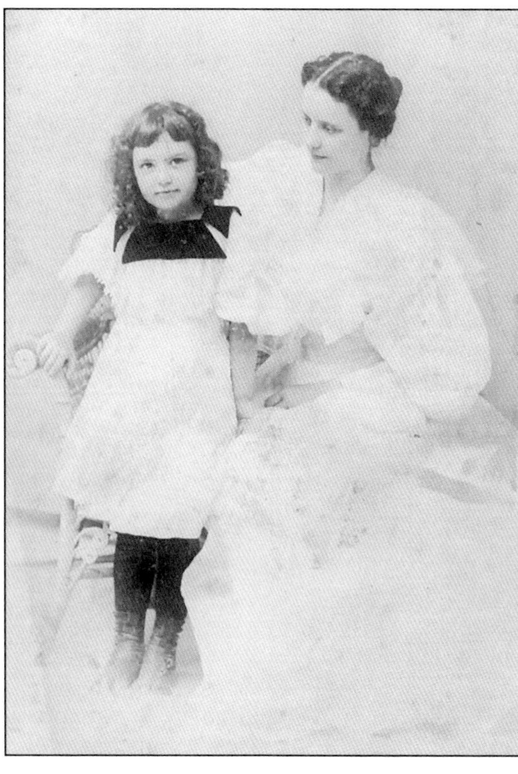

Sarah Louise Stewart (1890–1961), the daughter of New Bern businessman John Stewart, posed with Mrs. Annie Calhone, possibly her nurse or governess, in this c. 1896 photograph. (Courtesy of Tom Faulkenberry Collection.)

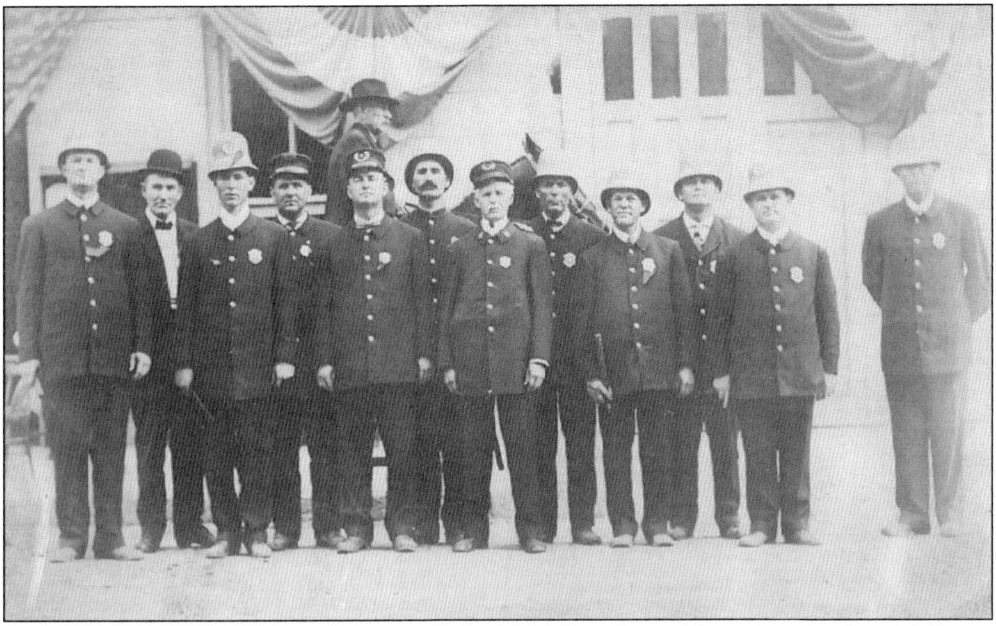

Members of the New Bern Police Department posed in front of city hall on Craven Street for this c. 1910 photograph. Policemen in New Bern were expected to be "circumspect in deportment, erect in carriage, discreet in languages and actions, and firm but courtesy in exercising authority." (Courtesy of John B. Green III Collection.)

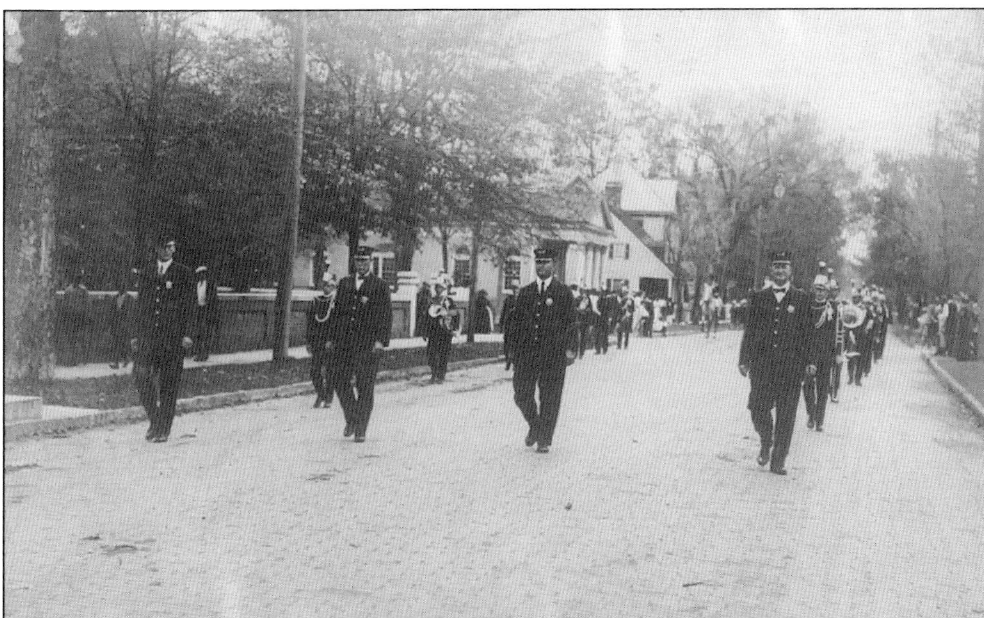

A staple of any parade, along with firefighters, these policemen proudly marched in a c. 1910 parade. (Courtesy of John B. Green III Collection.)

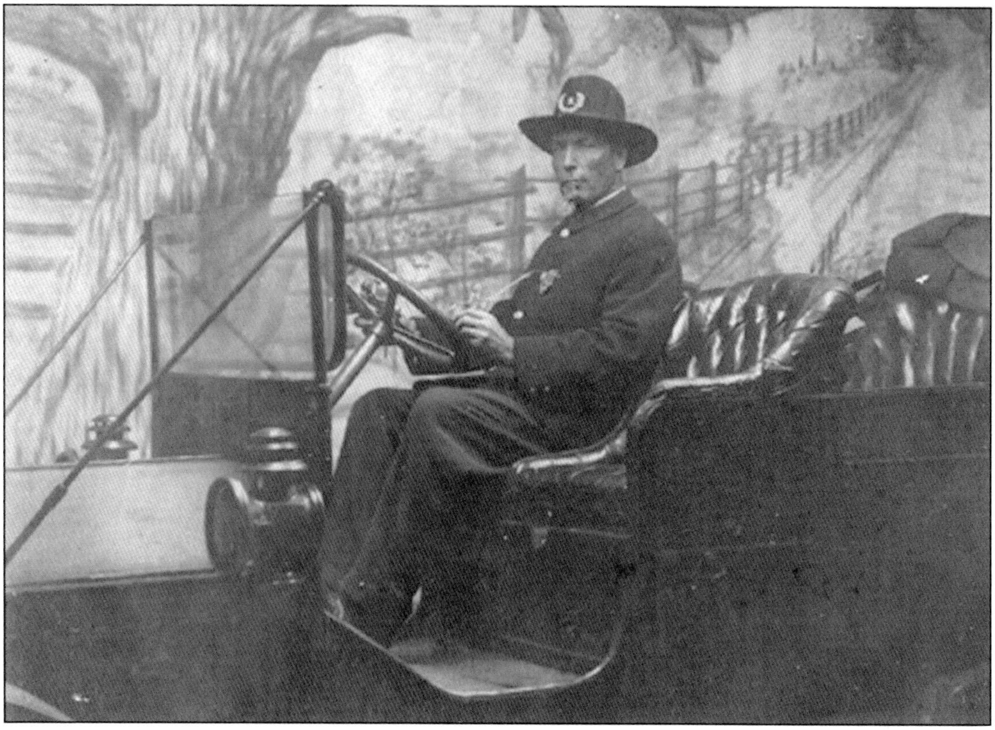

Another of New Bern's finest posed in a car against a false backdrop for this c. 1910 postcard. (Courtesy of John B. Green III Collection.)

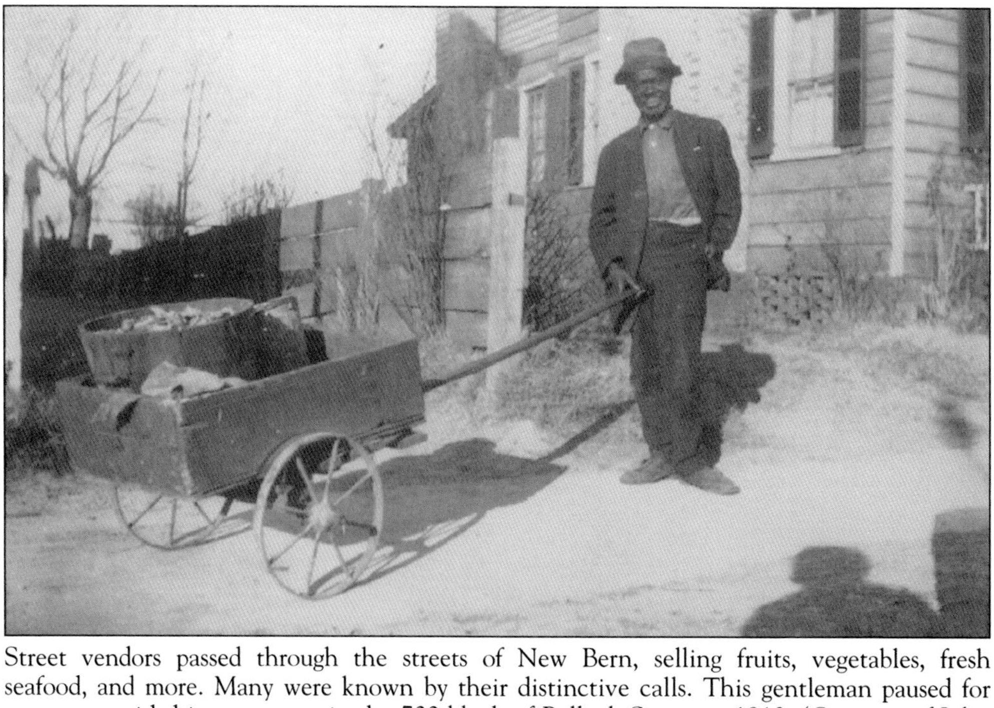

Street vendors passed through the streets of New Bern, selling fruits, vegetables, fresh seafood, and more. Many were known by their distinctive calls. This gentleman paused for a moment with his oyster cart in the 700 block of Pollock Street, c. 1910. (Courtesy of John B. Green III Collection.)

This unidentified woman was photographed *c.* 1910 in the 400 block of Metcalf Street. (Courtesy of John B. Green III Collection.)

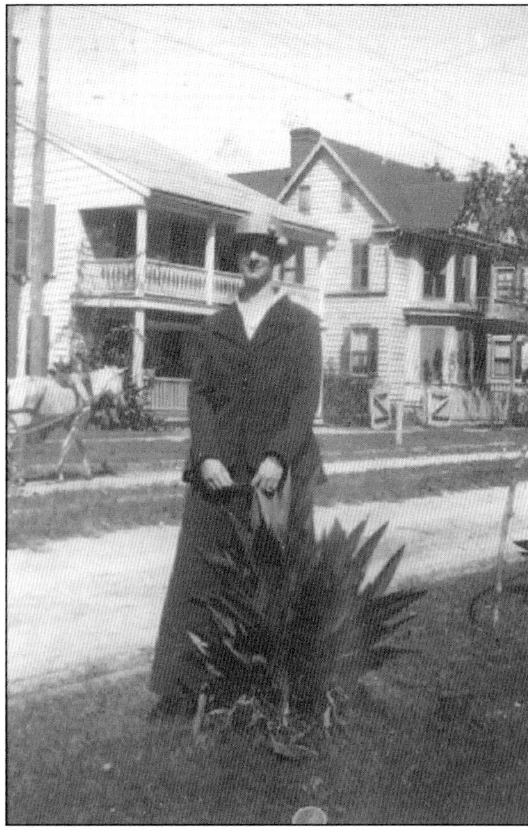

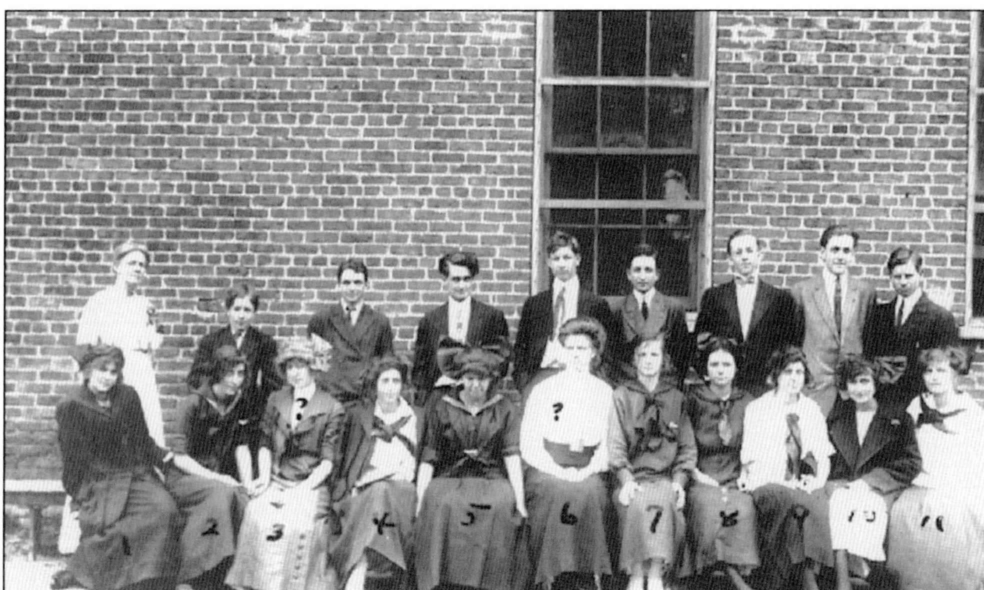

The New Bern High School Class of 1913 posed for this class portrait. (Courtesy of Mrs. G. Tull Richardson Collection, New Bern-Craven County Public Library.)

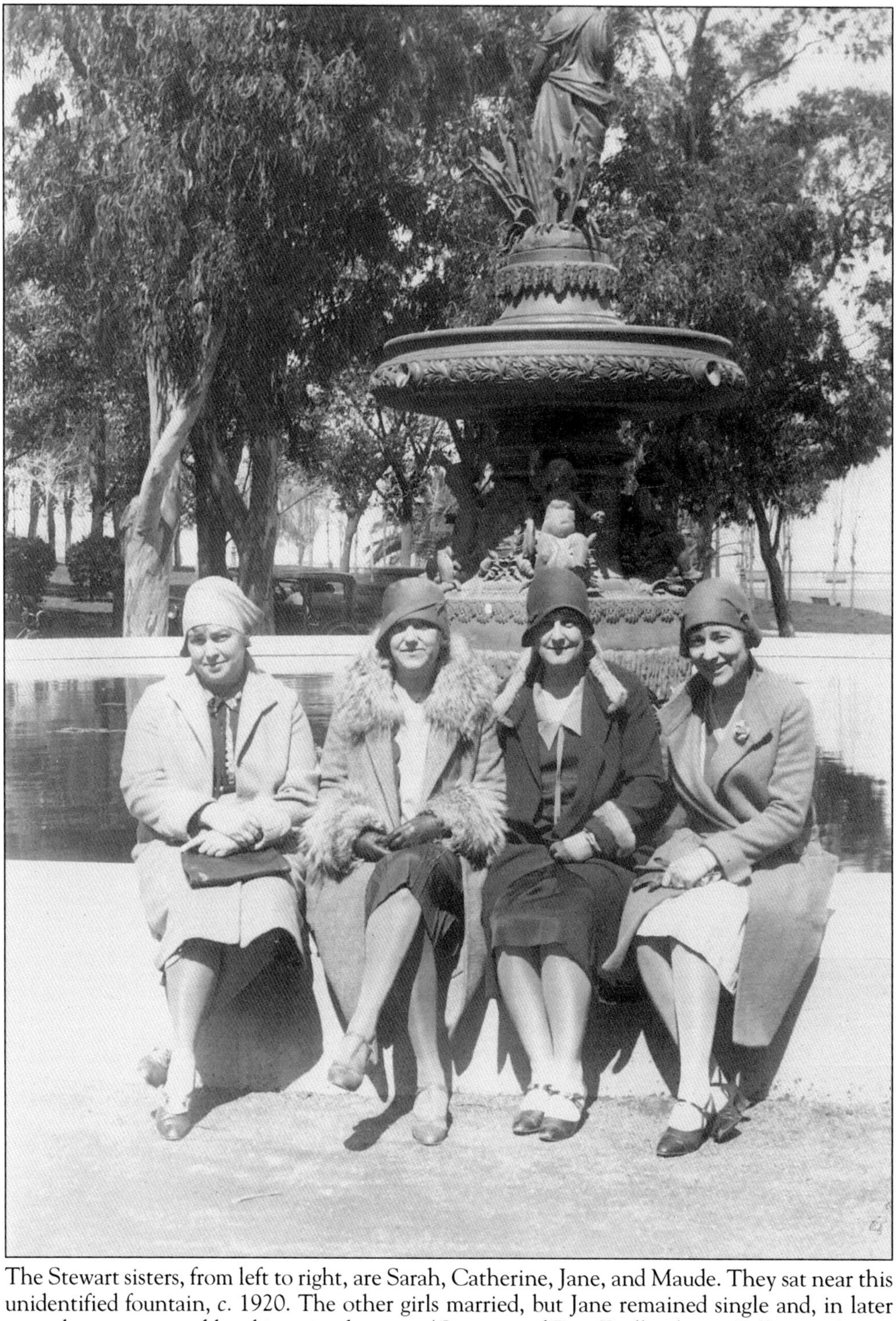

The Stewart sisters, from left to right, are Sarah, Catherine, Jane, and Maude. They sat near this unidentified fountain, *c.* 1920. The other girls married, but Jane remained single and, in later years, became a noted local interior designer. (Courtesy of Tom Faulkenberry Collection.)

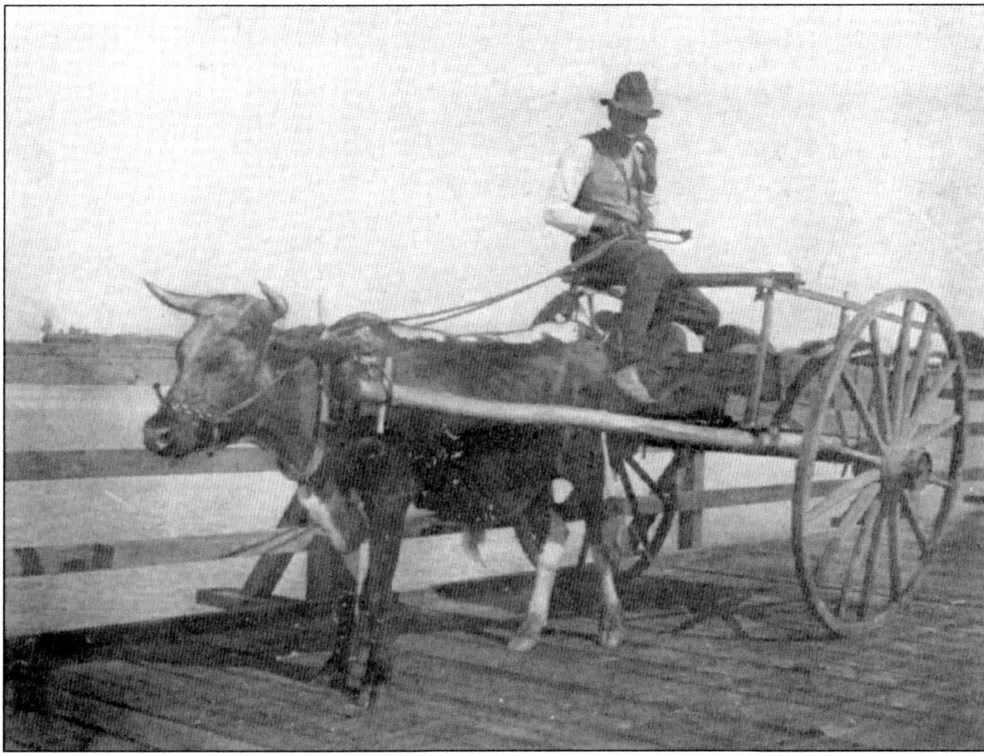

The ox cart was one way of getting around town, as shown on this c. 1910 postcard taken on the Neuse River bridge. (Courtesy of John B. Green III Collection.)

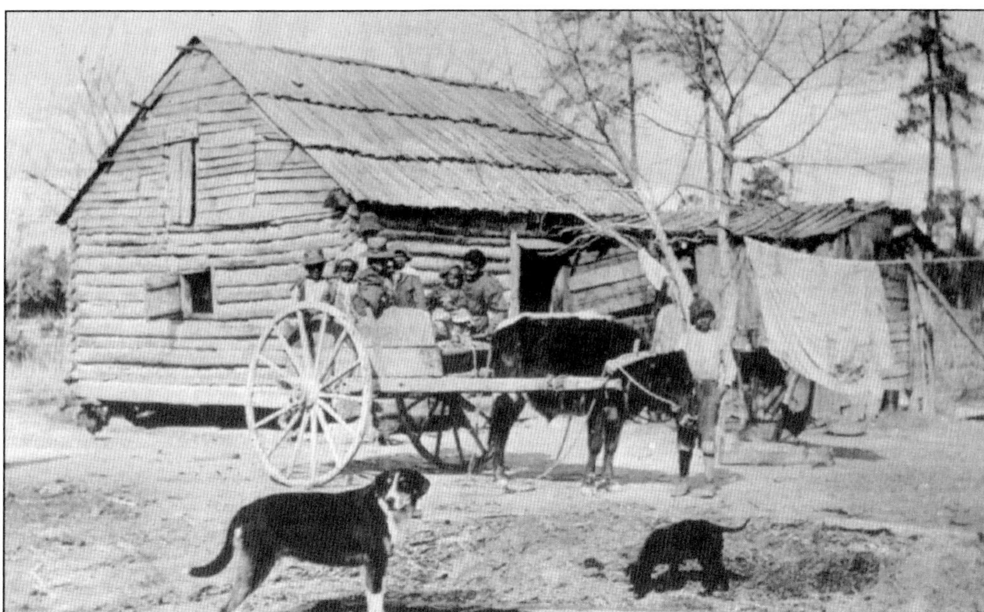

The poverty of many New Bern African-American residents is demonstrated on this c. 1916 postcard, rather insensitively titled "Off For a Joy Ride." (Courtesy of John B. Green III Collection.)

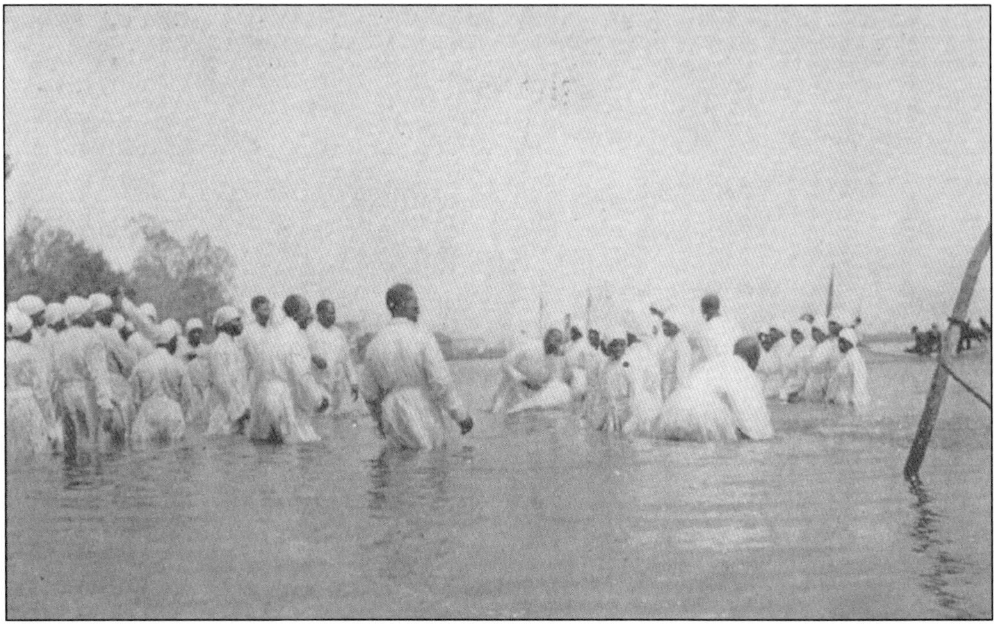

African-American baptisms, such as this one in the Neuse River c. 1900, were popular events not only for participants but also for spectators. (Courtesy of John B. Green III Collection.)

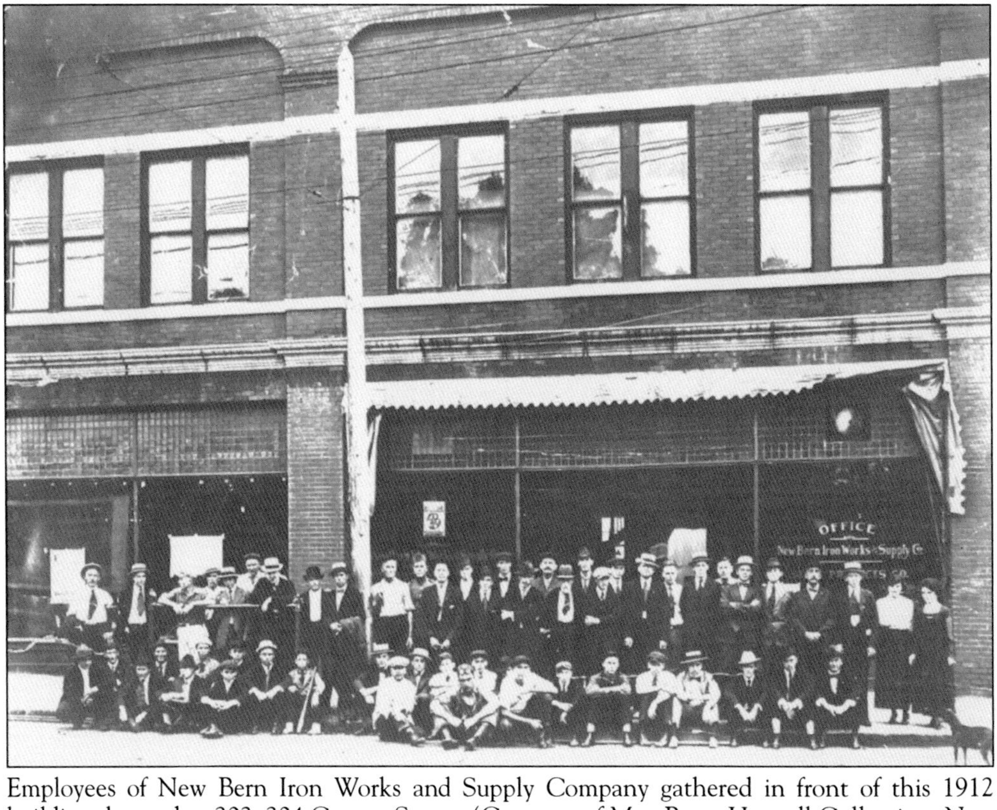

Employees of New Bern Iron Works and Supply Company gathered in front of this 1912 building, located at 202–204 Craven Street. (Courtesy of Mrs. Betty Hartsell Collection, New Bern-Craven County Public Library.)

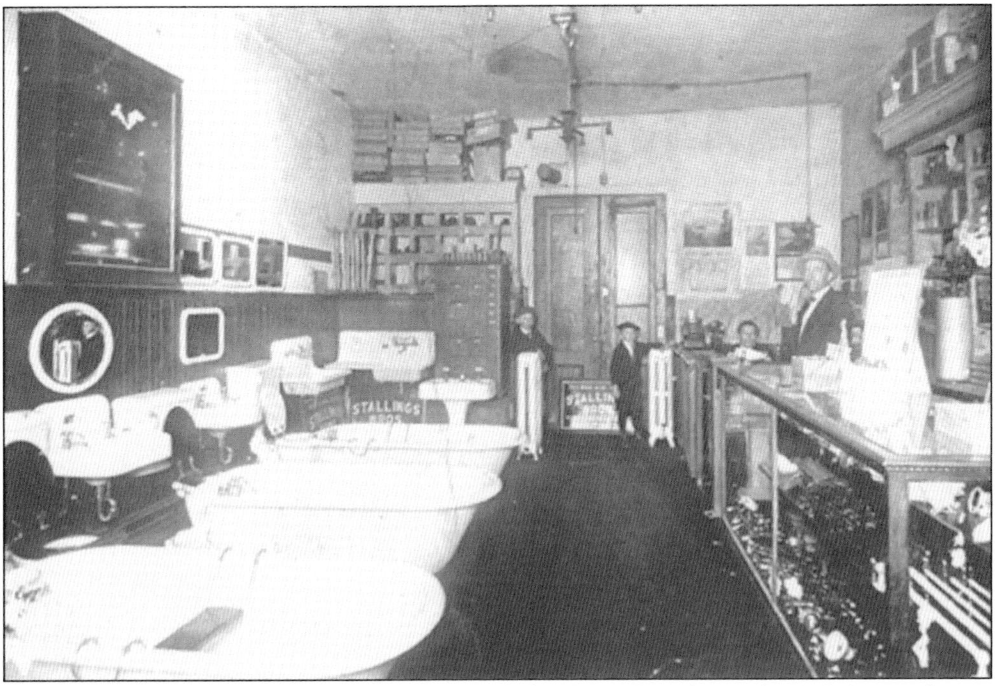

The proprietors of Stalling Brothers Heating and Plumbing Shop, located at 243 Craven Street, proudly displayed their wares in March 1925. Established in 1905, the business was owned by R.L. Stallings, who was described as "a gentleman of remarkable skill in all kinds of heating and plumbing trade and [who] executes perfect work." (Courtesy of New Bern-Craven County Public Library Collection.)

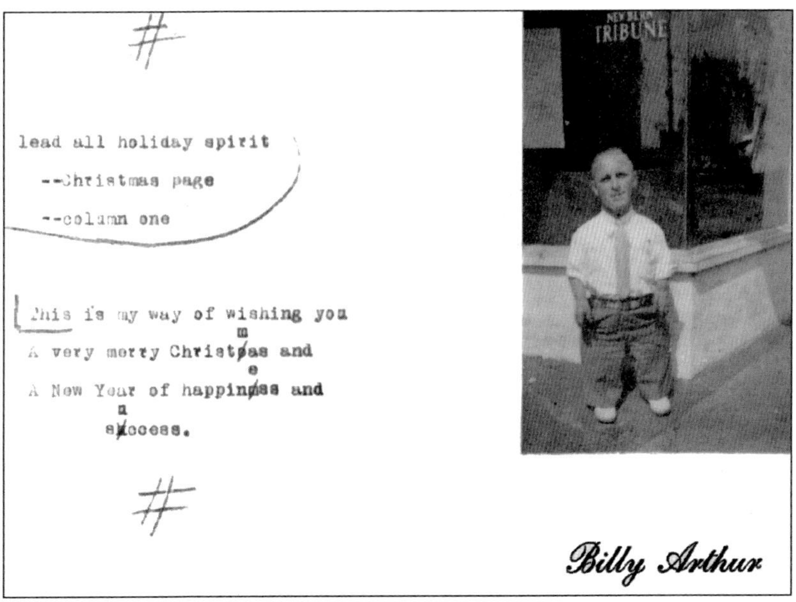

Billy Arthur was a local newspaperman who had quite a sense of humor, as evidenced by this c. 1930 Christmas postcard. He wrote for the *New Bern Tribune* before moving on to Chapel Hill. (Courtesy of John B. Green III Collection.)

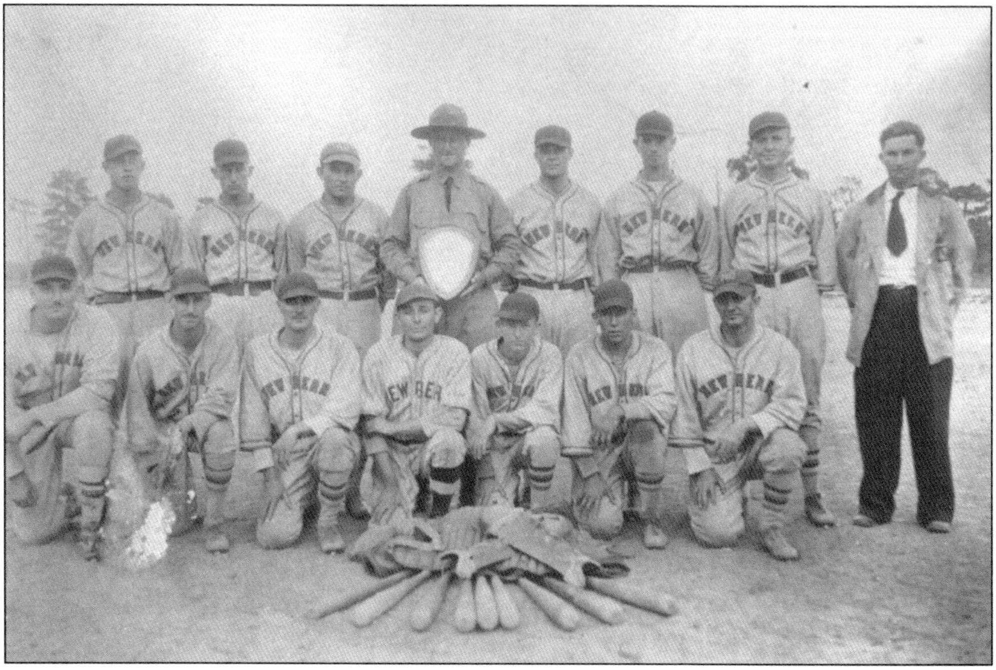

The New Bern Bears, shown here *c.* 1935, were a local baseball team who played in Kafer Park on George Street during the 1930s. War and money woes in the early 1940s spelled the end of the team for awhile, but in 1946, the New Bern Bears reappeared as a Coastal Plain League team. They played against teams from other eastern North Carolina towns for over 20 years. (Courtesy of New Bern-Craven County Public Library Collection.)

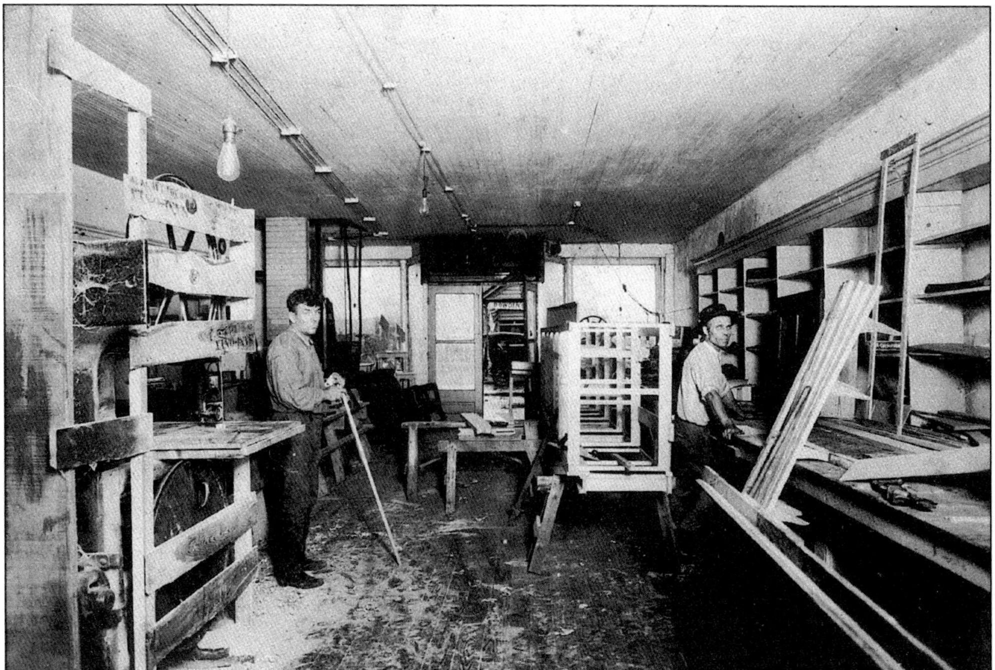

This undated photograph shows Mr. Dewey's cabinet shop, located on lower Middle Street.

Eight

TRYON RESTORATION

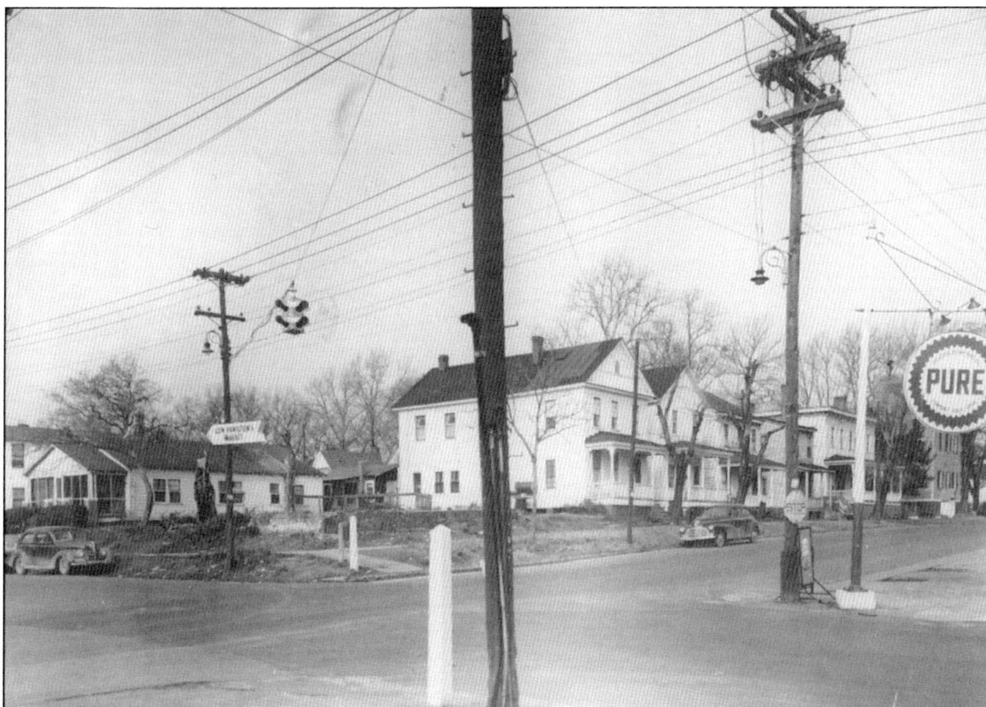

By the 1920s, many local people shared a dream that Tryon Palace, which burned to the ground in February 1798, could be reconstructed where it had originally stood when it was built for Royal Governor William Tryon in the 1770s. The Tryon Palace Commission was appointed by North Carolina governor Gregg Cherry in 1945, and by 1953, the commission had been authorized by the state legislature to proceed with the work. Homes and businesses, including those depicted in this *c.* 1950 photograph taken from the corner of South Front and George Streets looking northeast, were purchased and either moved or torn down. (Courtesy of Tryon Palace Historic Sites and Gardens.)

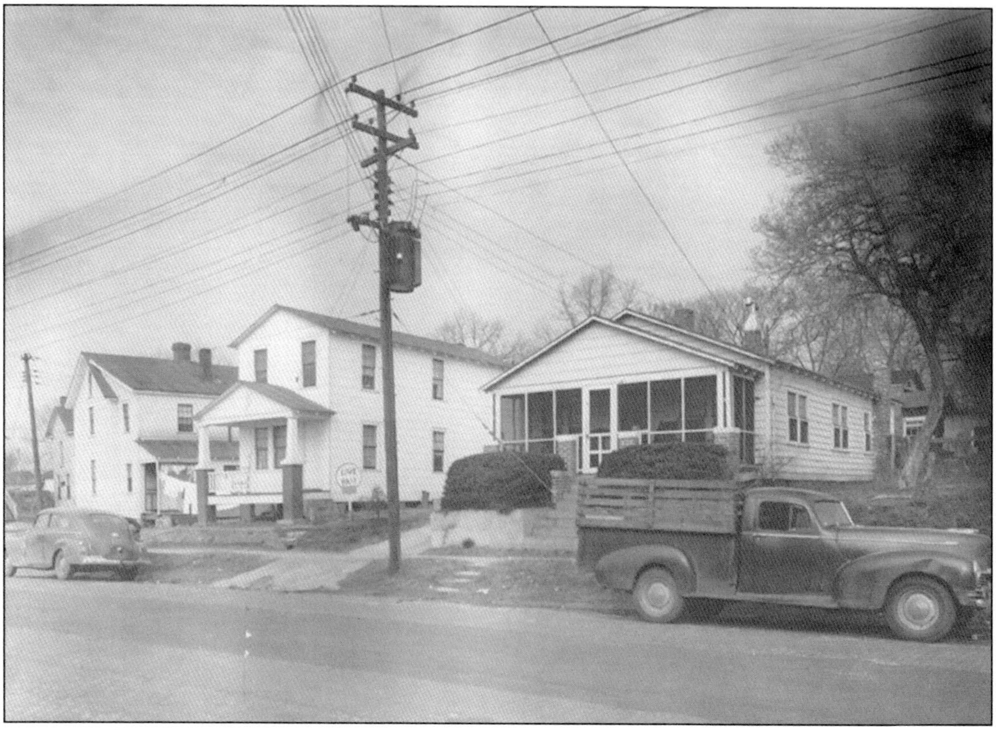

Many residents and property owners in the affected area did not want to give up their homes and mounted a legal challenge with the help of attorneys L.A. Stith, John Beaman, and Jesse Jones. Ultimately, they were unsuccessful, and around 54 homes and businesses, such as these along South Front Street, were removed. The picture is dated *c.* 1950. (Courtesy of Tryon Palace Historic Sites and Gardens.)

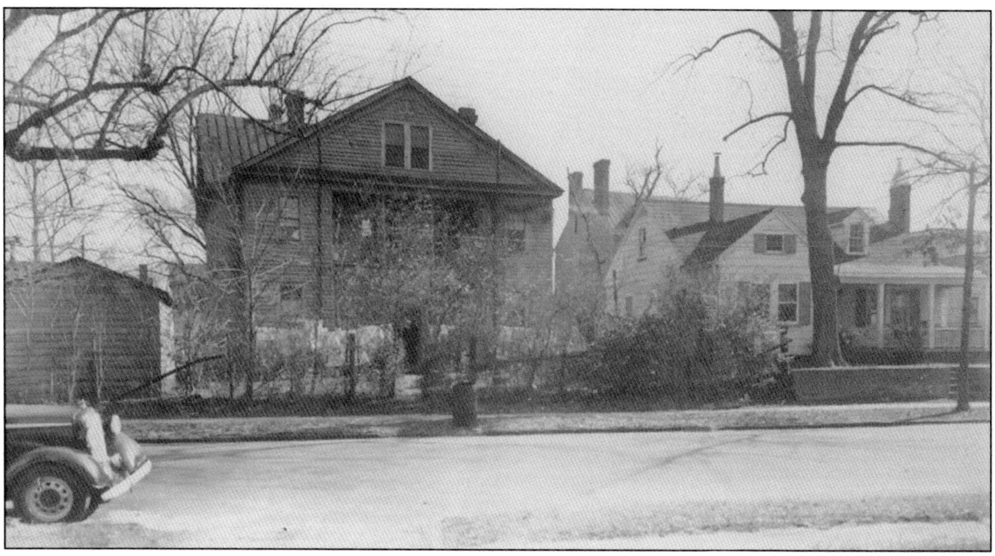

The house at the left in this *c.* 1950 photograph was the only original building remaining of the Tryon Palace complex. Formerly the West Wing Stable, by the 1950s it had been renovated into a stucco-covered apartment building. Its restoration as a stable was completed in November 1953. (Courtesy of Tryon Palace Historic Sites and Gardens.)

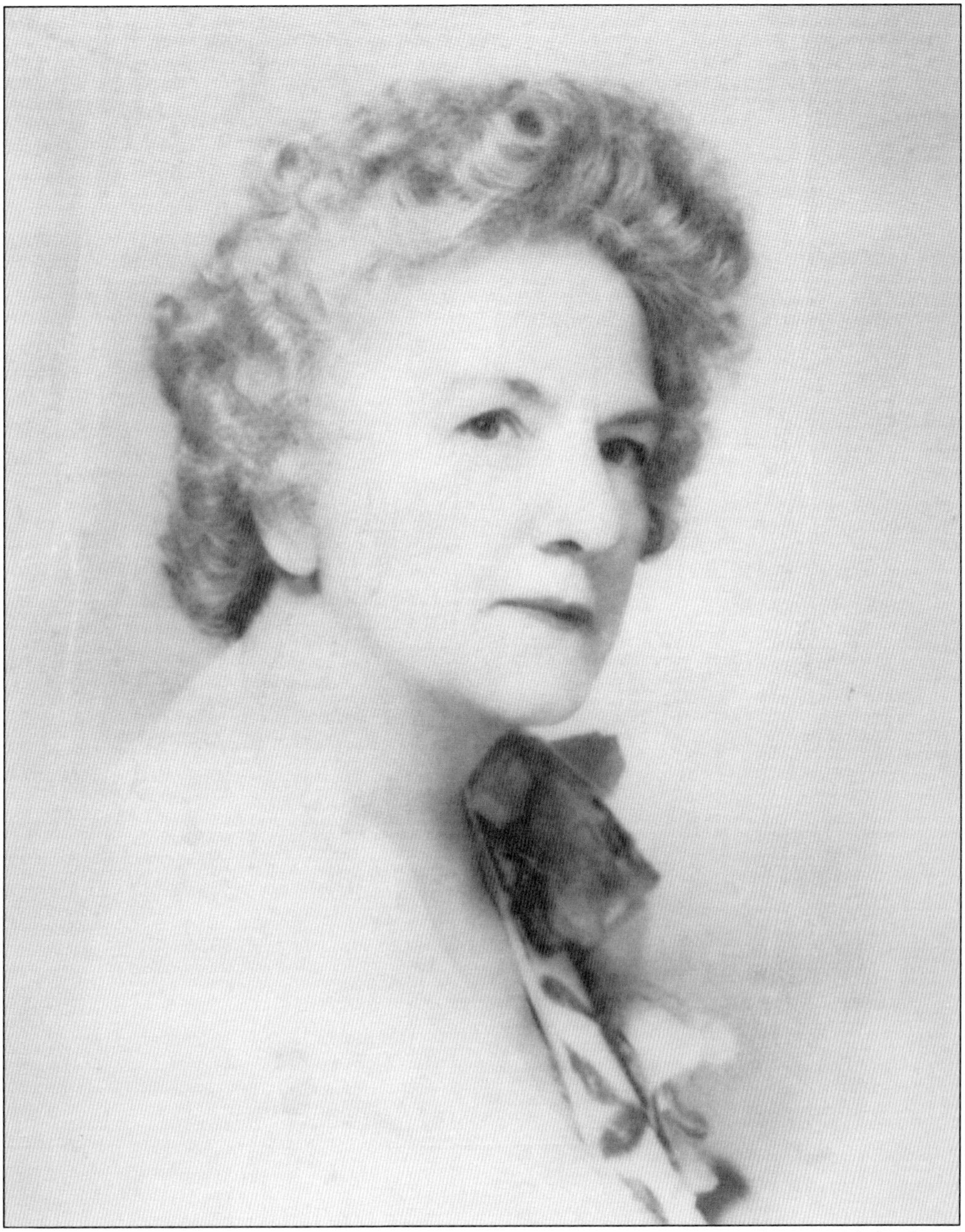

Maude Moore Latham, a New Bern native who lived in Greensboro, at first established two trusts totaling $250,000 for the restoration effort. Upon her death, and with the blessing of her daughter, May Gordon Kellenberger, Mrs. Latham gave over $1 million to the Tryon Palace Commission, on which she served as chairman. Her daughter took over these duties when Mrs. Latham died in 1951. (Courtesy of Tryon Palace Historic Sites and Gardens.)

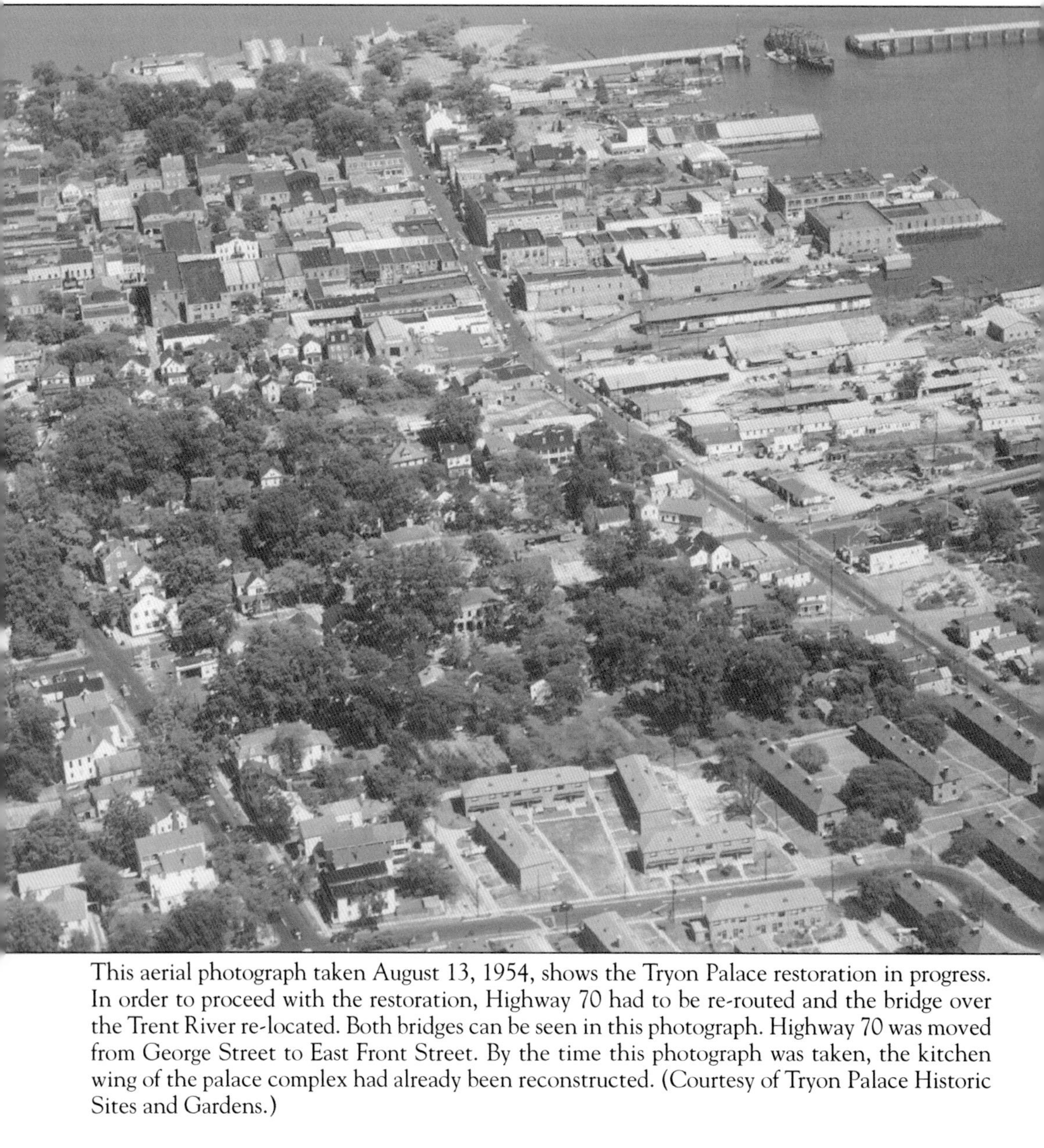

This aerial photograph taken August 13, 1954, shows the Tryon Palace restoration in progress. In order to proceed with the restoration, Highway 70 had to be re-routed and the bridge over the Trent River re-located. Both bridges can be seen in this photograph. Highway 70 was moved from George Street to East Front Street. By the time this photograph was taken, the kitchen wing of the palace complex had already been reconstructed. (Courtesy of Tryon Palace Historic Sites and Gardens.)

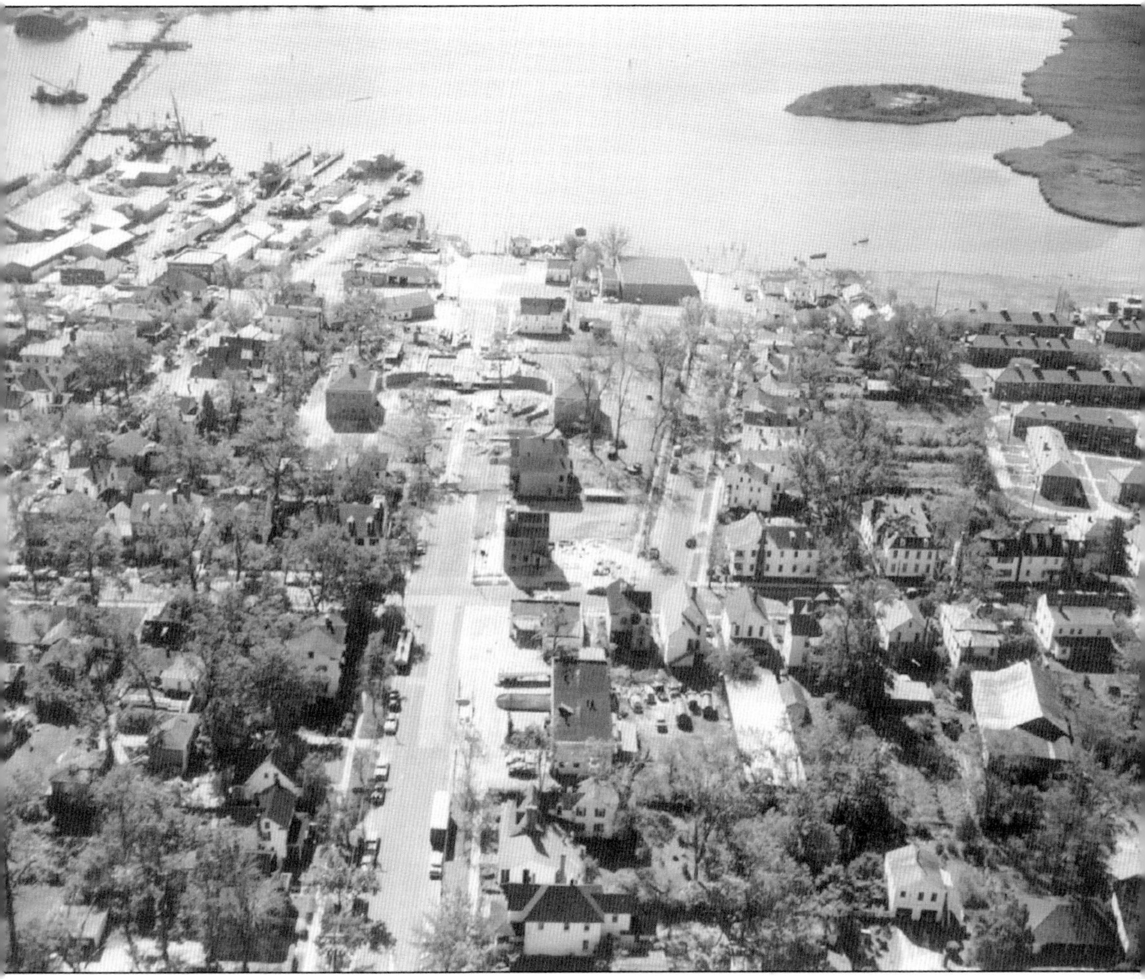

This photograph, taken October 16, 1955, depicts work on the palace already underway. Archaeological work at the site had already uncovered the east and west walls of the palace's original basement still standing at a depth of about 5 feet. Other artifacts found included pieces of plaster mouldings, marble and brass fragments, and lead from the roof. Houses continued to be removed from the neighborhood. (Courtesy of Tryon Palace Historic Sites and Gardens.)

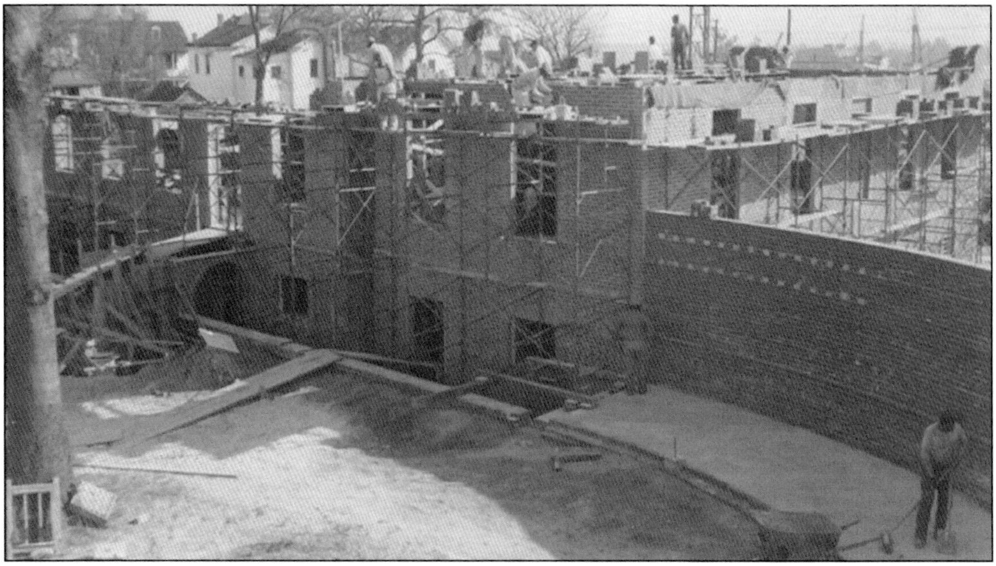

As other buildings in the neighborhood were removed, the palace, shown here on November 15, 1955, was indeed rising "like the regenerated phoenix from the fury of the flame." Meanwhile, commission members, aided by an inventory of Tryon's property filed after a fire destroyed his New York residence in 1773, were busy acquiring antiques and furnishings for the palace's interior. Mrs. Latham, who died in 1951, had not only left her money to the Tryon Palace Commission, but also her valuable collection of English antiques. (Courtesy of Tryon Palace Historic Sites and Gardens.)

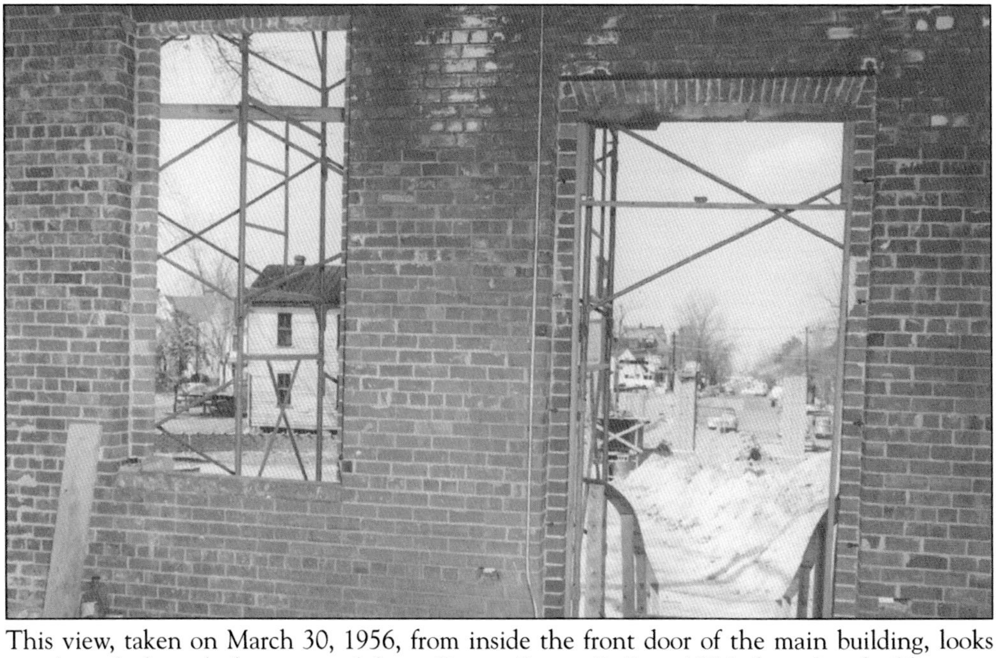

This view, taken on March 30, 1956, from inside the front door of the main building, looks out through through the gates and down George Street. By June 1956, the palace building was nearly complete. That same month, Gertrude Carraway, who had served on the Tryon Palace Commission since 1945, resigned her commission to become the first Tryon Palace director. (Courtesy of Tryon Palace Historic Sites and Gardens.)

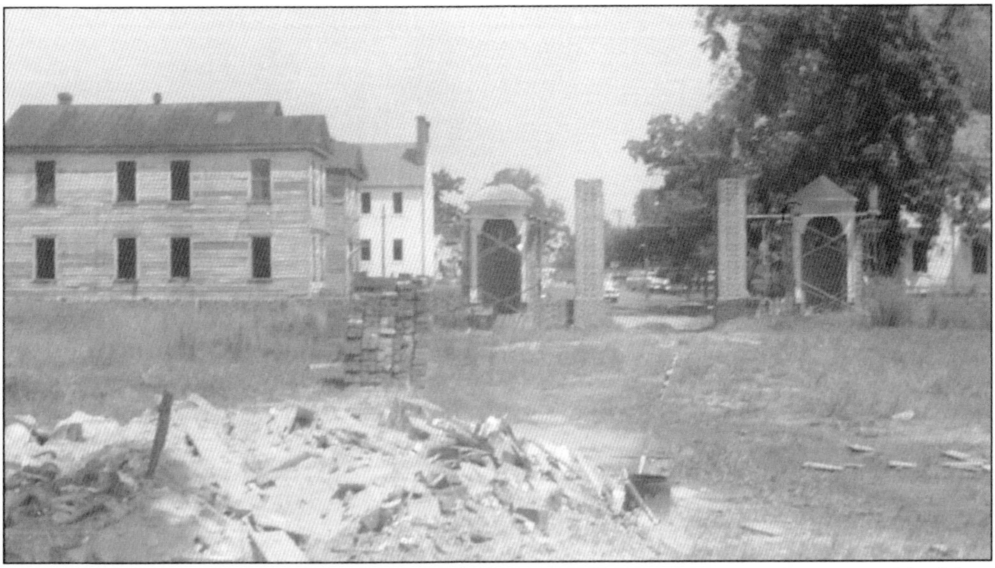

As the walls of the palace went up, so did the gates. Construction on the original building took place in 1767–71, under the supervision of architect John Hawks. Governor Tryon moved into the building in mid-1770 and held an assembly meeting in the palace's council room that December. The governor left North Carolina in 1771 for a similar post in New York, and his successor only lived there for four years before New Bern lost its status as the state capital. (Courtesy of Tryon Palace Historic Sites and Gardens.)

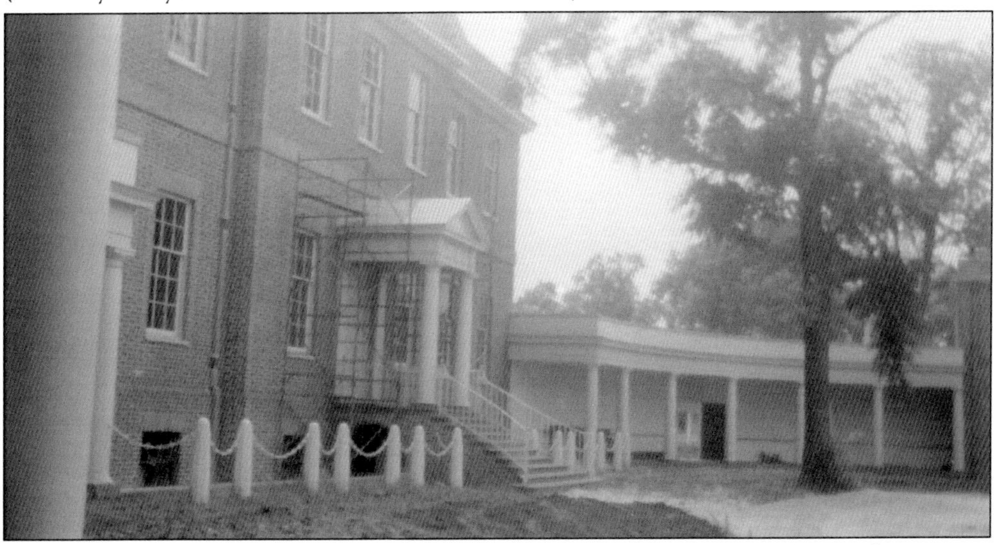

Carraway said in May 1957 that work on the palace was "99 percent complete." This exterior shot of July 1957 shows the final touches being added to the palace's entryway. One of the final touches of the restoration work would include the raising of King George III's Royal Coat-of-Arms to the exterior pediment on the north side of the palace. Features on the coat-of-arms included the shield of the House of Hanover, topped with a jeweled crown and flanked by a gold lion and silver unicorn. Added touches include the white and red rose of England, purple thistle of Scotland, green shamrock of Ireland, and fleur-de-lis of France. The mottoes on Royal Coat-of-Arms are *Honi Soit qui mal y pense* ("Shame be to him who evil thinks") and *Dieu et mon driot* ("God and my right"). (Courtesy of Tryon Palace Historic Sites and Gardens.)

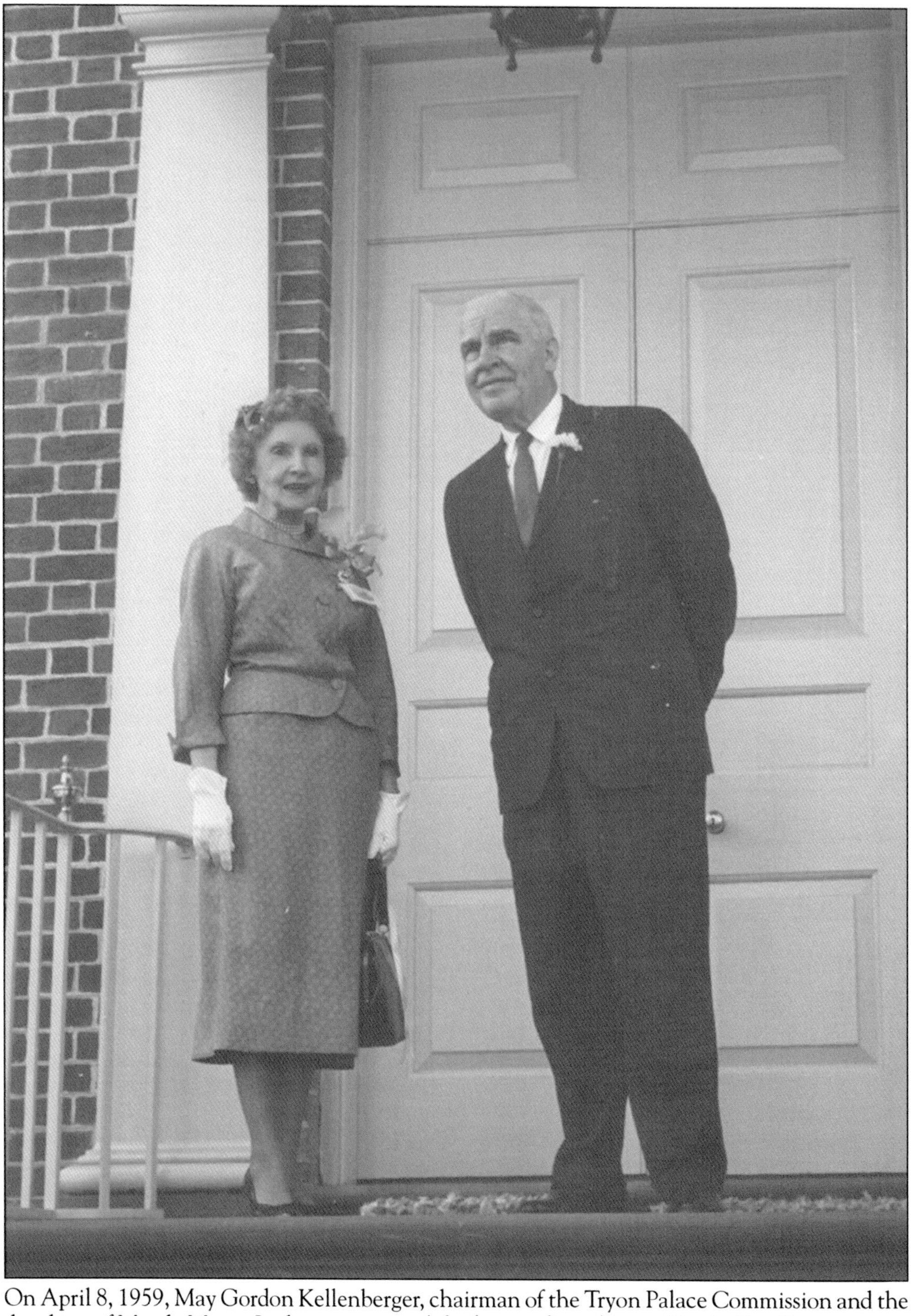

On April 8, 1959, May Gordon Kellenberger, chairman of the Tryon Palace Commission and the daughter of Maude Moore Latham, presented the key to the palace to North Carolina governor Luther Hodges, who then cut the ribbon and officially opened the palace to the public. It was the eighth anniversary of Maude Moore Latham's death. (Courtesy of Tryon Palace Historic Sites and Gardens.)

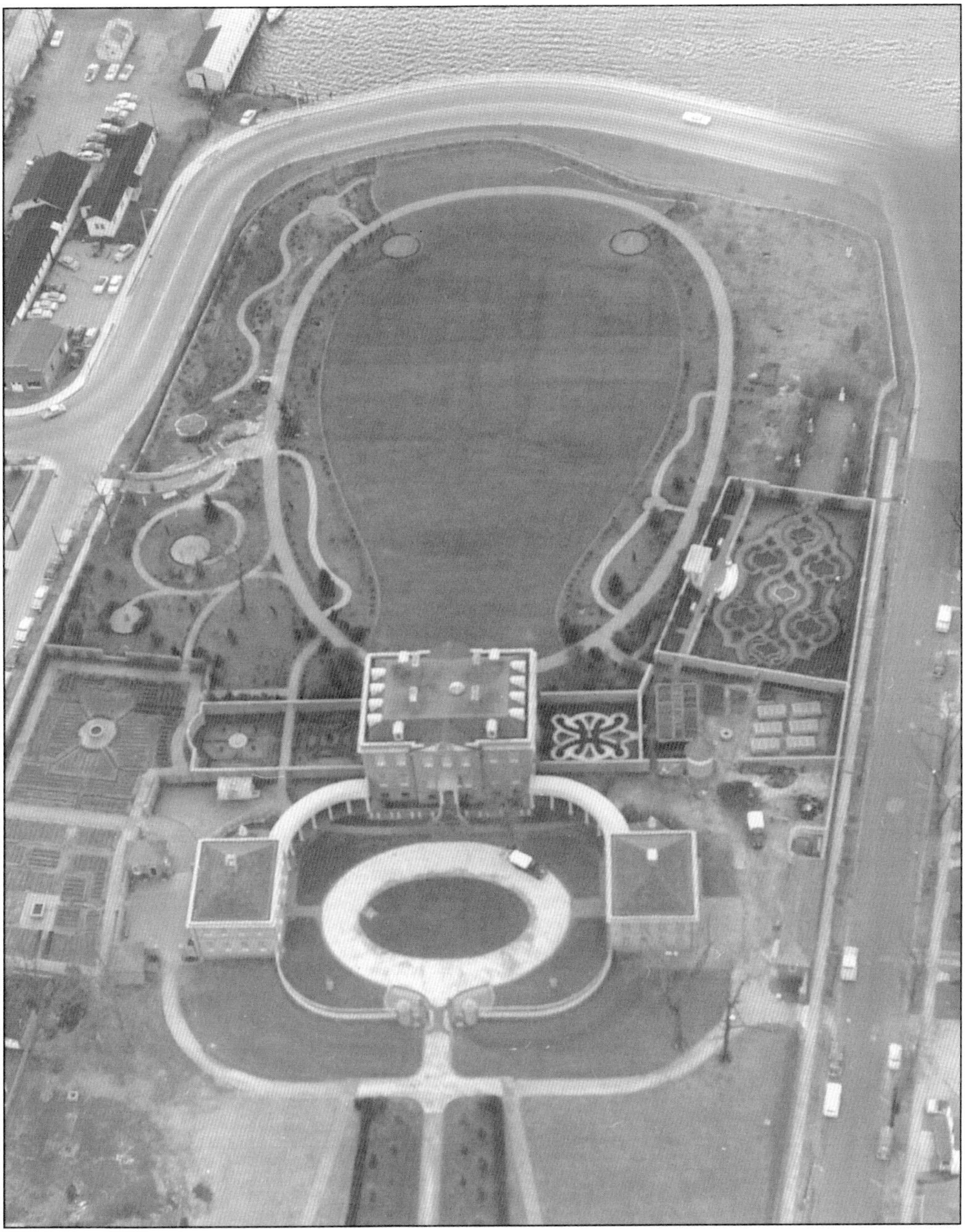

The original garden plans of John Hawks were not recovered until 1992. Noted landscape architect Morley Jeffers Williams created the gardens, seen here in an early 1960s aerial view, including two gardens that honor the women who worked so hard to make New Bern's palace dreams a reality. Immediately to the left of the palace is the Kellenberger Garden while the larger garden immediately adjacent is the Maude Moore Latham Memorial Garden. (Courtesy of Tryon Palace Historic Sites and Gardens.)

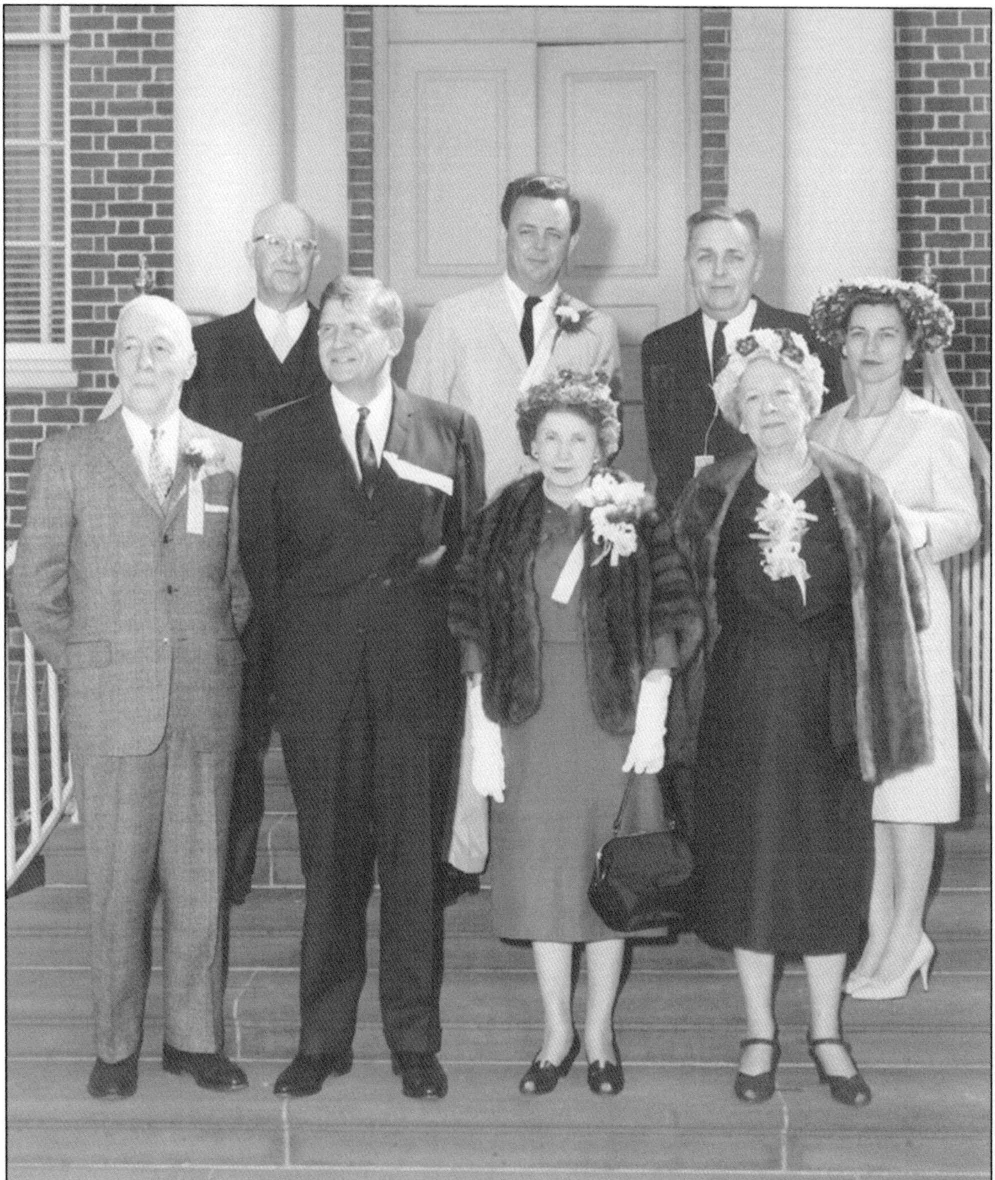

The Maude Moore Latham Memorial Garden was dedicated on April 8, 1961. Dignitaries present for the garden's dedication included the following, from left to right: (front row) John Kellenberger, North Carolina Governor Terry Sandford, May Kellenberger, and Gertrude Carraway, (back row), two unidentified men, and New Bern Mayor and Mrs. Robert L. Stallings. (Courtesy of Tryon Palace Historic Sites and Gardens.)

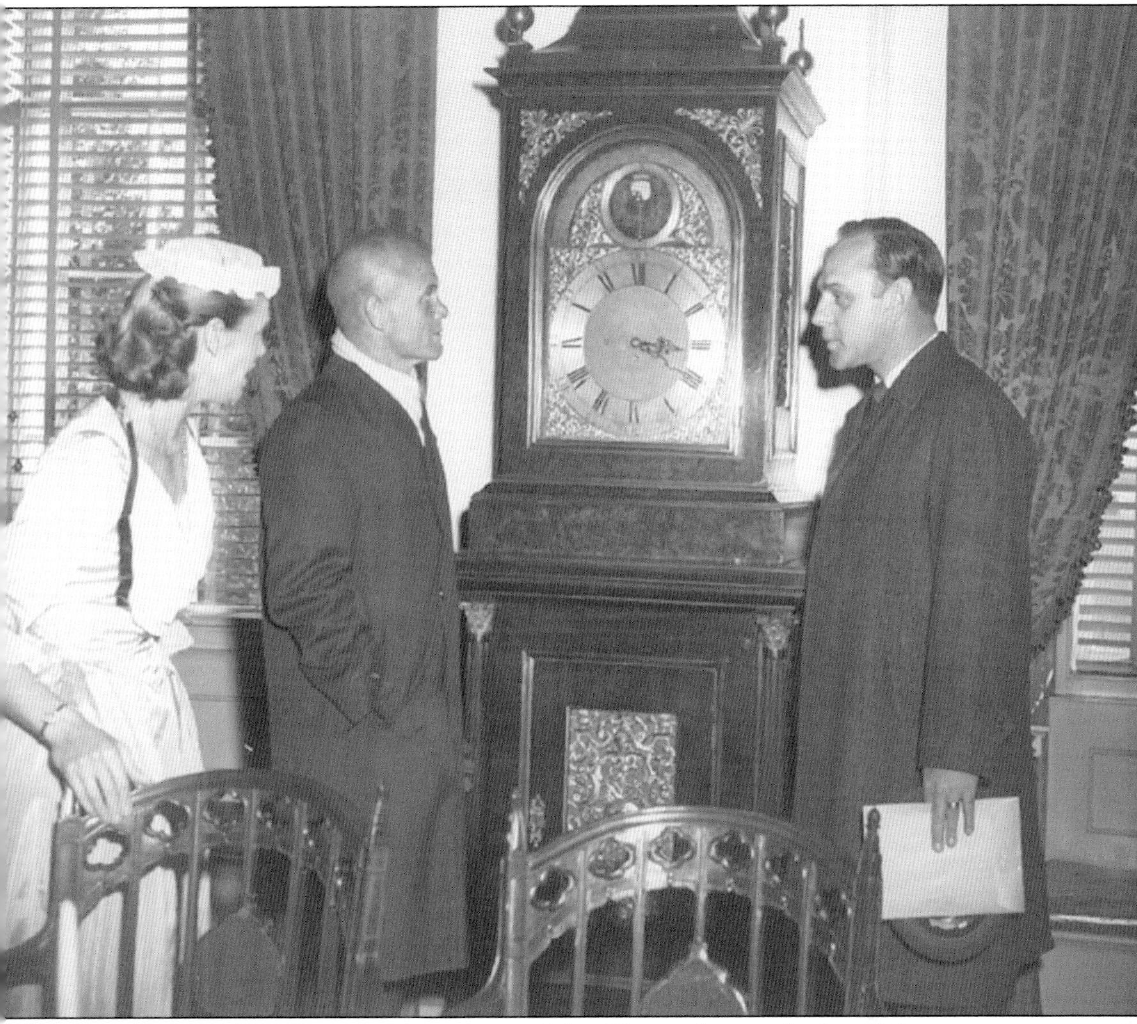

Among Tryon Palace's more famous visitors is John Glenn, who was the first U.S. astronaut to orbit the earth as part of Project Mercury in 1962. Glenn came to the North Carolina coast for the 60th anniversary of the Wright Brothers flight on December 17, 1903. He also visited the U.S. Corps Air Station, Cherry Point, near Havelock, where he had been formerly stationed, and he was honored in New Bern with a luncheon and a key to the city. In the council chamber, Glenn examined the palace's 18th-century musical clock as Congressman David Henderson and Mrs. Ray C. Ipock, Tryon Palace hostess, looked on. (Courtesy of Tryon Palace Historic Sites and Gardens.)

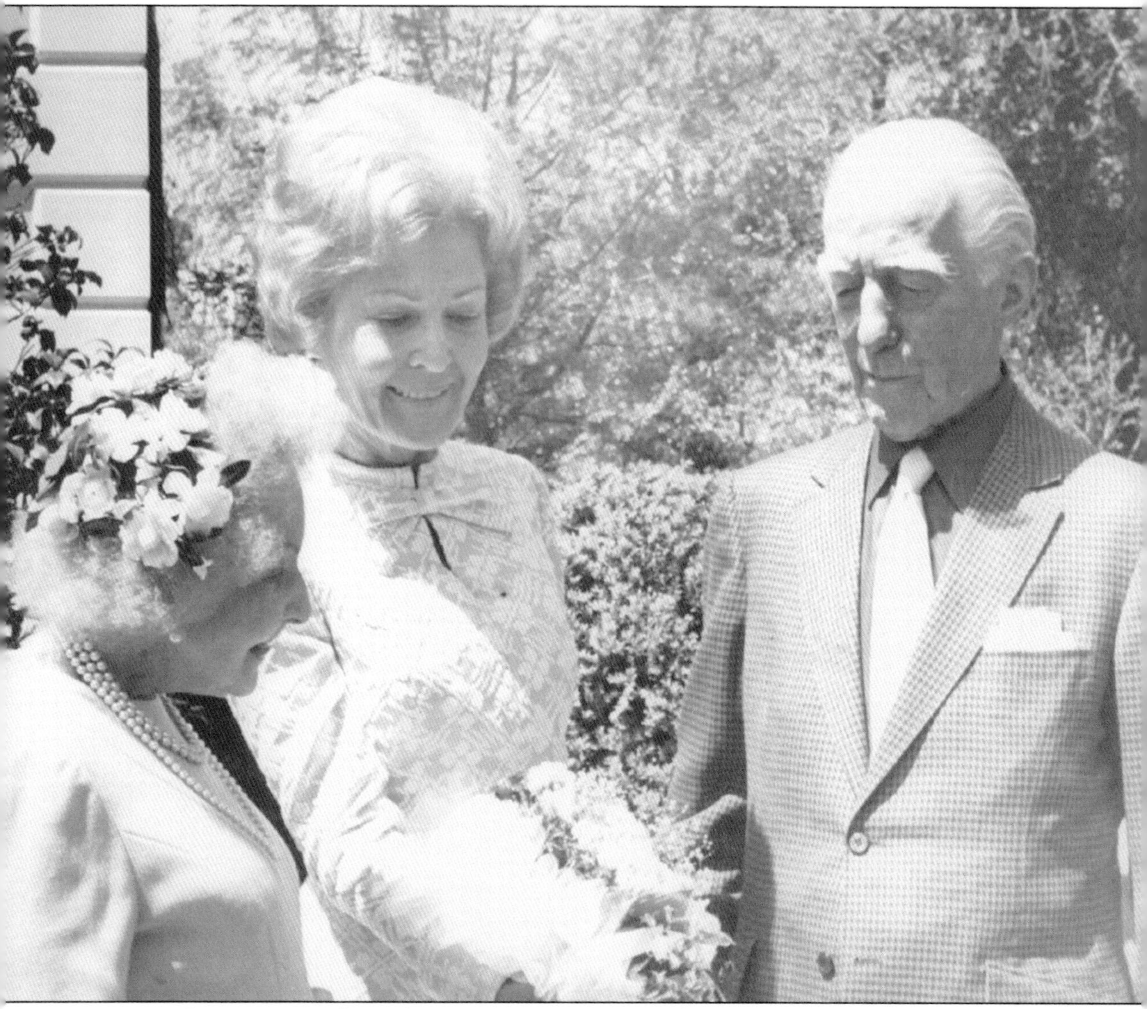

First Lady Pat Nixon, shown here with Mr. and Mrs. Kellenberger, came to New Bern in 1971 for the grand re-opening of the John Wright Stanly House. The house, which was originally constructed in late 1700s, had been moved once before, from its location on the corner of Middle and New Streets to a lot just around the corner on New Street, in order to make way for the post office in the 1930s. From 1935 to 1965, the Stanly House was the home of New Bern's public library. When the new library was constructed in the late 1960s, the library board gave the Stanly House to the Tryon Palace Commission. The Stanly House was moved in 1966 to its present location on George Street, renovated, and reopened as part of the Tryon Palace complex. (Courtesy of Tryon Palace Historic Sites and Gardens.)

Nine

LANDMARKS

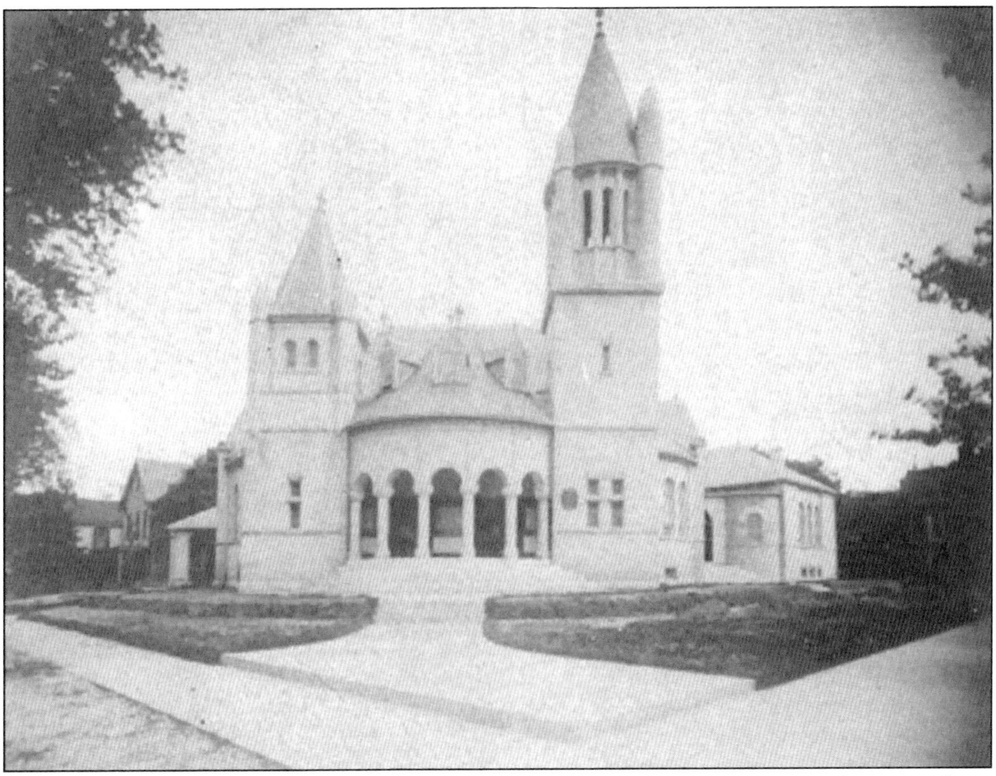

New Bern prides itself on its impressive range of architecture. However, some places stand out more than others. This short chapter includes a few of the author's very favorite places in New Bern. Centenary Methodist Church, on the southeast corner of Middle and New Streets, was built in 1904 and dedicated on October 22, 1905. This photograph was taken *c.* 1910. New Bern has several interesting old churches, but Centenary's unusual architecture makes it one of the most visually appealing. (Courtesy of John B. Green III Collection.)

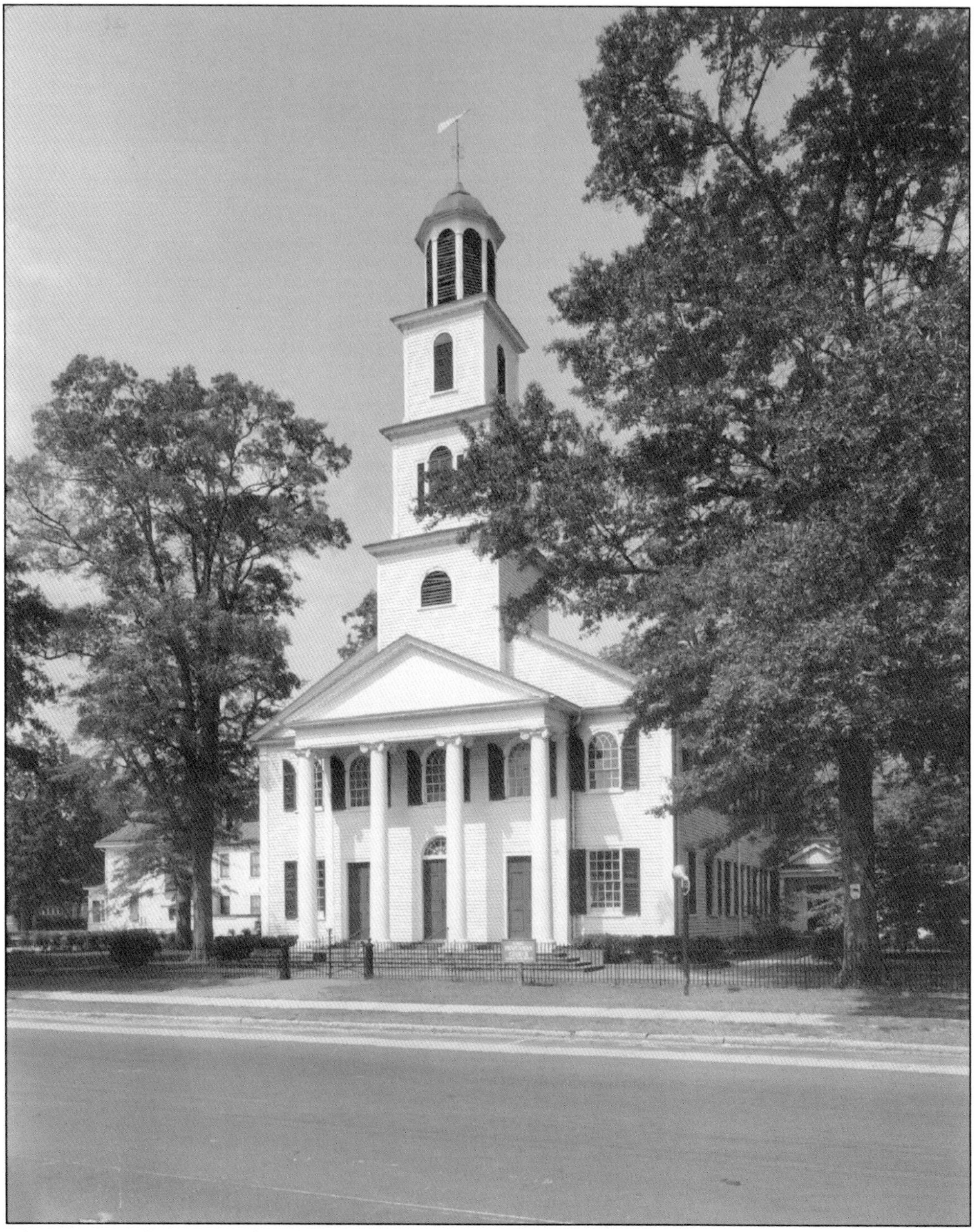

The First Presbyterian Church at 412 New Street was dedicated in 1822. The church itself was organized in 1817, and its cornerstone was set in place in 1819. The iron fence surrounding the church dates from 1905. It is the oldest church building still in use in New Bern. (Courtesy of Tryon Palace Historic Sites and Gardens.)

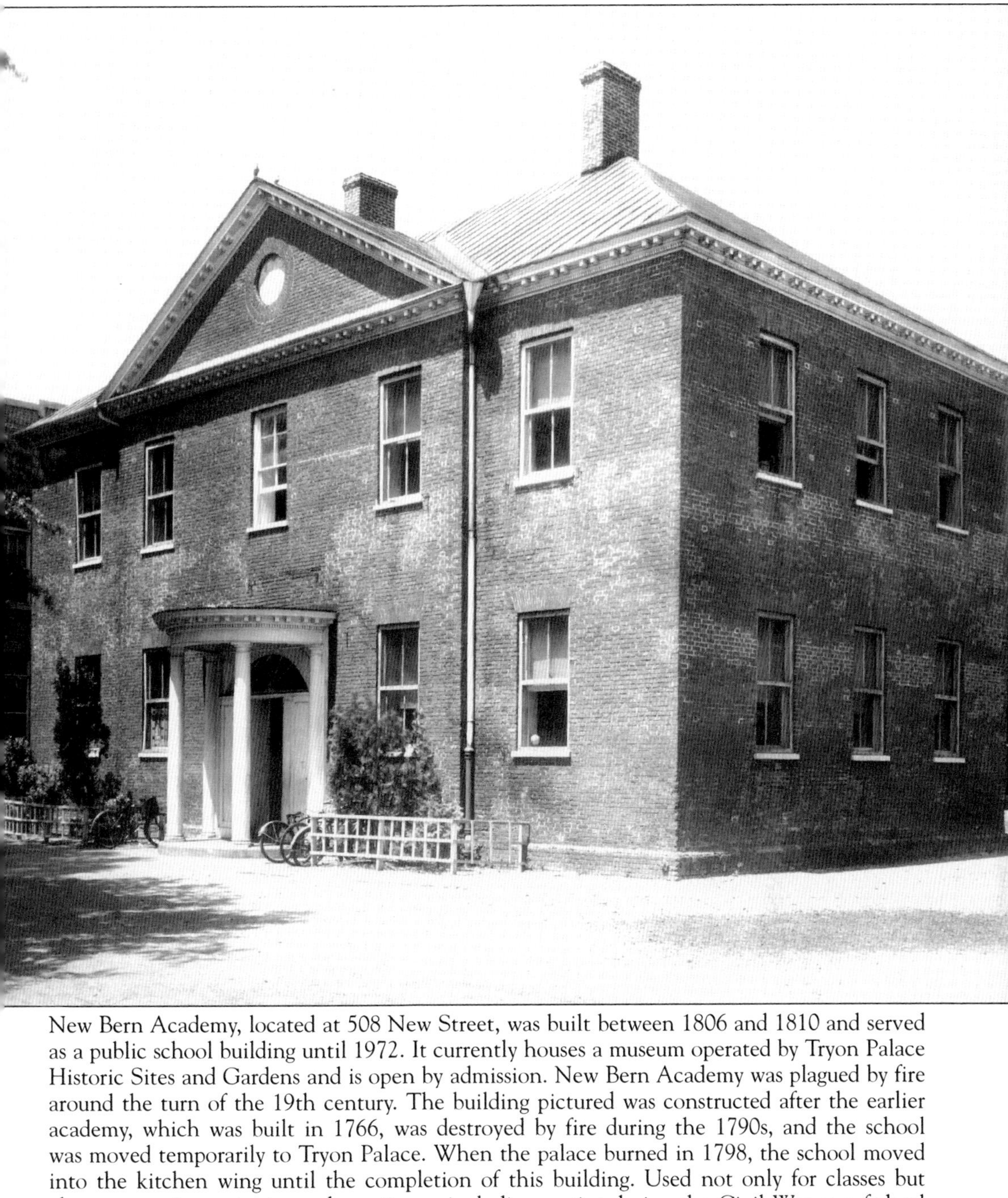

New Bern Academy, located at 508 New Street, was built between 1806 and 1810 and served as a public school building until 1972. It currently houses a museum operated by Tryon Palace Historic Sites and Gardens and is open by admission. New Bern Academy was plagued by fire around the turn of the 19th century. The building pictured was constructed after the earlier academy, which was built in 1766, was destroyed by fire during the 1790s, and the school was moved temporarily to Tryon Palace. When the palace burned in 1798, the school moved into the kitchen wing until the completion of this building. Used not only for classes but also community activities and meetings—including a stint during the Civil War as a federal hospital—the building was closed in 1972. After a damaging fire in 1977, the building was fully restored by 1982 and reopened as a museum. (Courtesy of Library of Congress.)

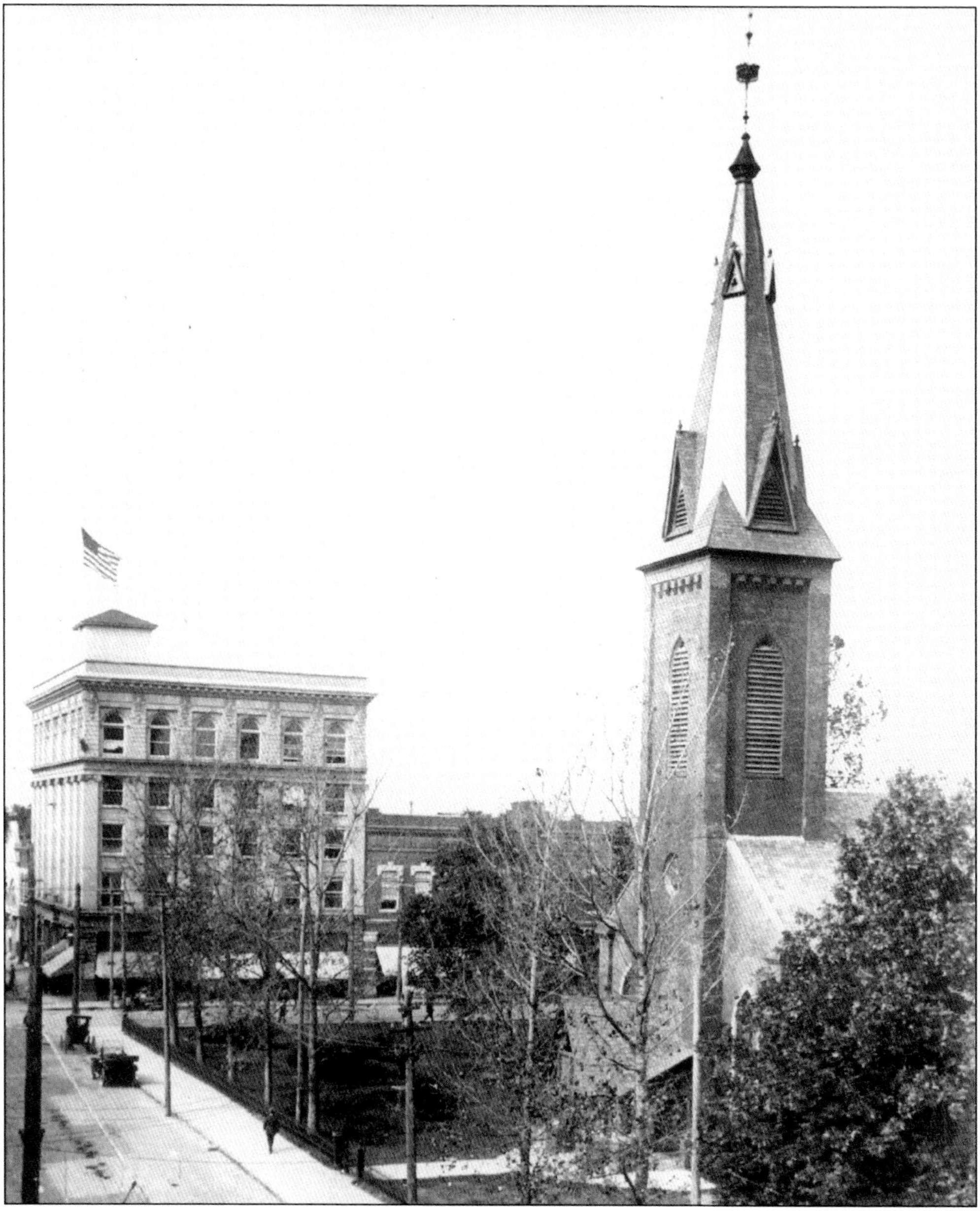

This *c.* 1910 view shows two impressive structures located in downtown New Bern—Christ Episcopal Church, located in the 300 block of Pollock Street, and the Elks Temple, located on the corner of Pollock and Middle Streets. Established in 1715, Christ Episcopal Church remains an oasis of calm in the midst of a busy downtown. The current church building was remodeled in the 1870s following a fire that gutted the original church constructed in the 1820s. The grounds of Christ Episcopal Church contains New Bern's oldest grave markers, while the churchyard itself is surrounded by a cast-iron fence erected *c.* 1900. The Elks Temple was constructed in 1908 as part of an optimistic commercial building boom around that time—it contains commercial and professional office space. The Elks Temple is one of downtown's tallest commercial structures. (Courtesy of New Bern Historical Society Collection, New Bern-Craven County Public Library.)

Ten

A New Look

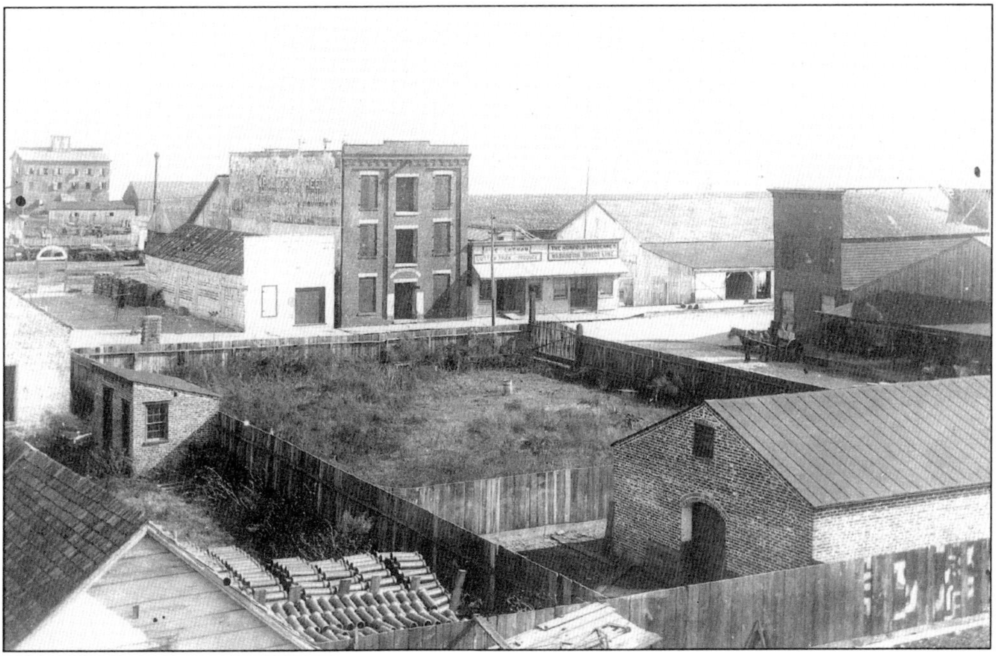

New Bern's waterfront at the turn of the 20th century, as shown here in this view of the foot of Craven Street, consisted of shipping offices and fish markets. This area would change dramatically over the next 100 years. (Courtesy of North Carolina Division of Archives and History).

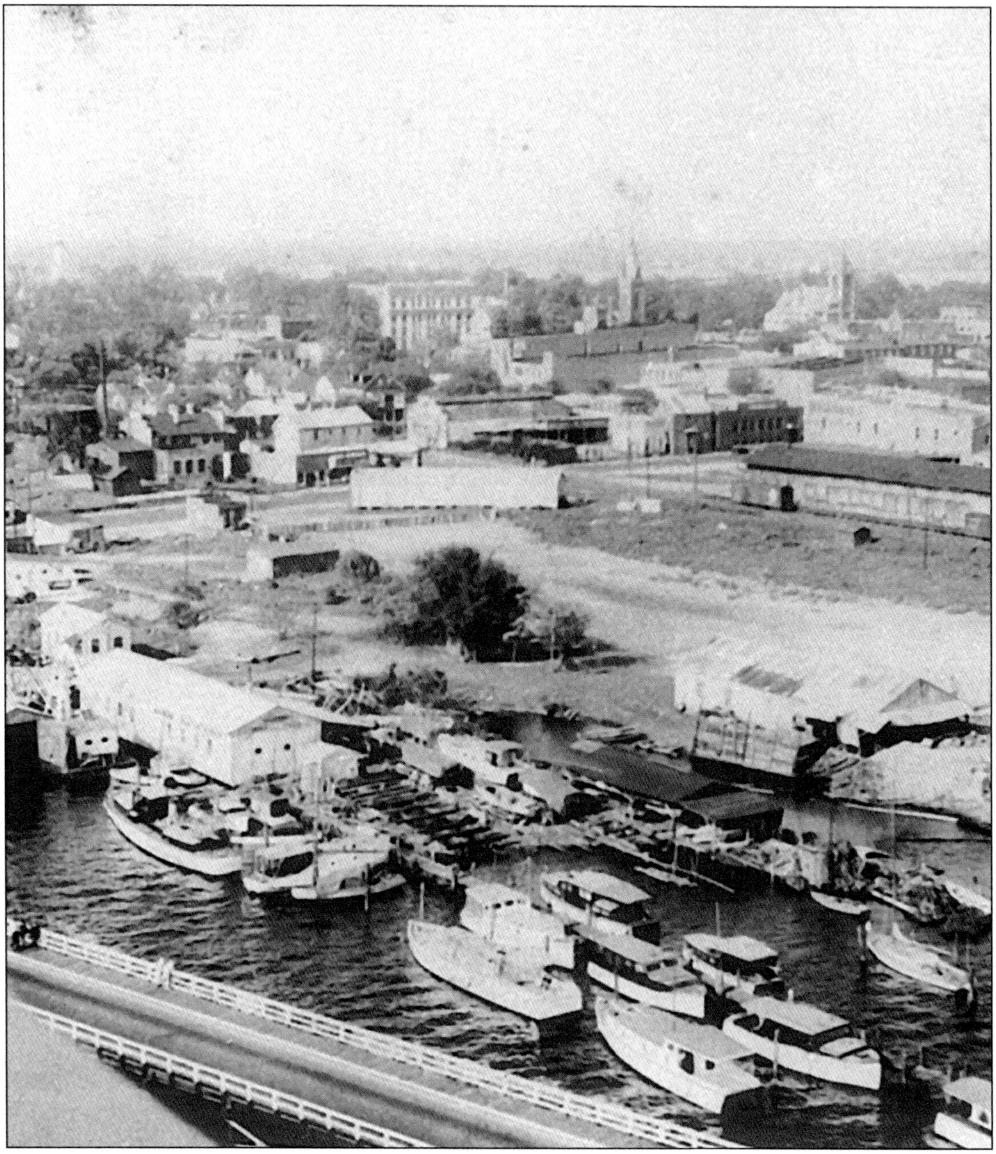

Barbour Boat Works was located on the Trent River waterfront from 1932 until 1997. Known for its small wooden boats, outboards, runabouts, sea skiffs, and other boats, Barbour Boats Works expanded during the 1940s to enter military production, constructing mine sweepers and salvage ships. After the war, in addition to fishing vessels, Barbour Boat Works produced ferries, tugboats, and barges, among other vessels. This picture dates before the removal of the Trent River bridge in the early 1950s. The site today is under reconstruction and renovation as an education and living history center for Tryon Palace. (Courtesy of Ida Harrison Collection, New Bern-Craven County Public Library.)

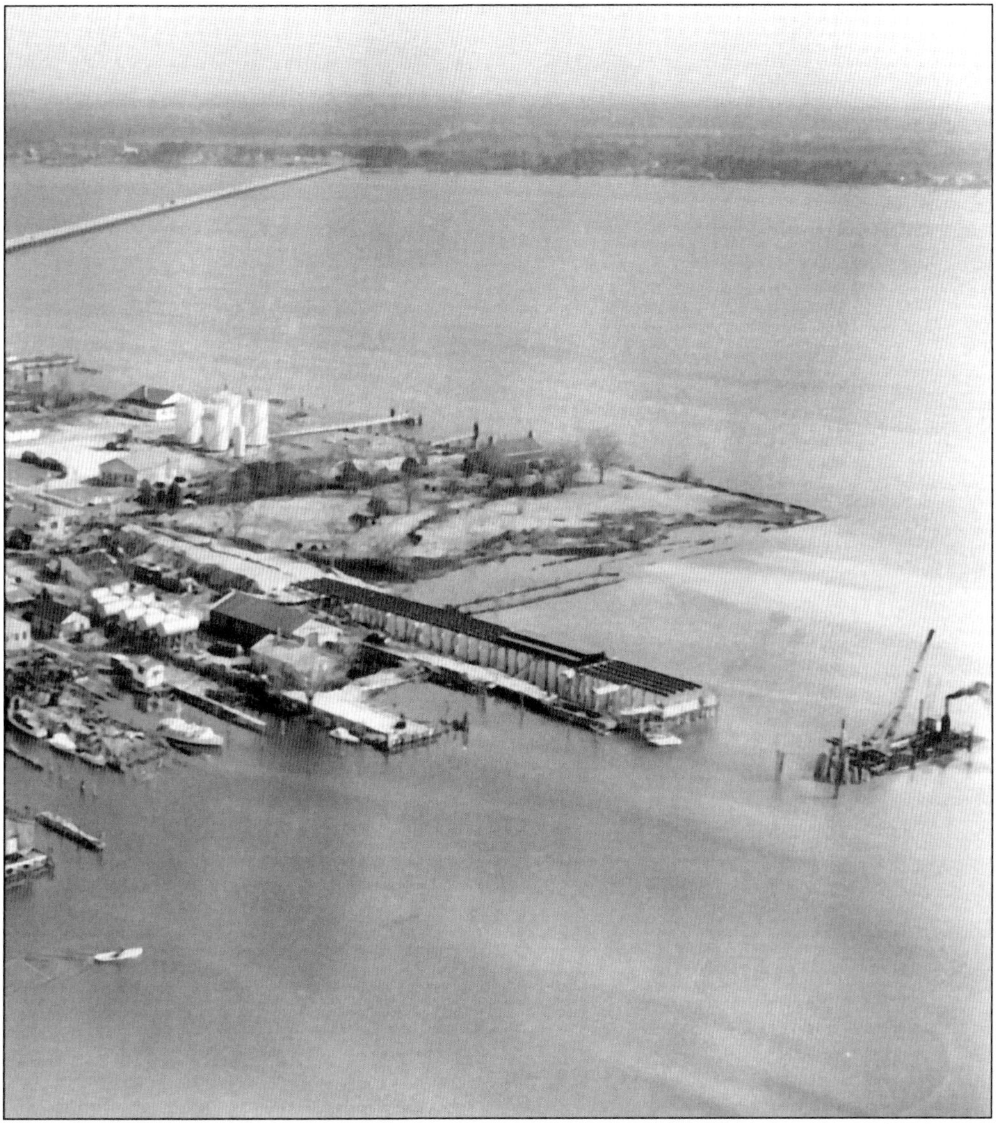

The bridge over the Trent River was moved from the foot of George Street to the foot of East Front Street in the early 1950s to make way for the reconstruction of Tryon Palace. The reconstruction of the palace called not only for the removal of the bridge but also the removal of houses in the area bordered by Pollock, Eden, South Front, and Metcalf Streets. The Tryon Palace complex today remains one of New Bern's and eastern North Carolina's top tourist attractions. (Courtesy of New Bern Area Chamber of Commerce Collection, New Bern-Craven County Public Library.)

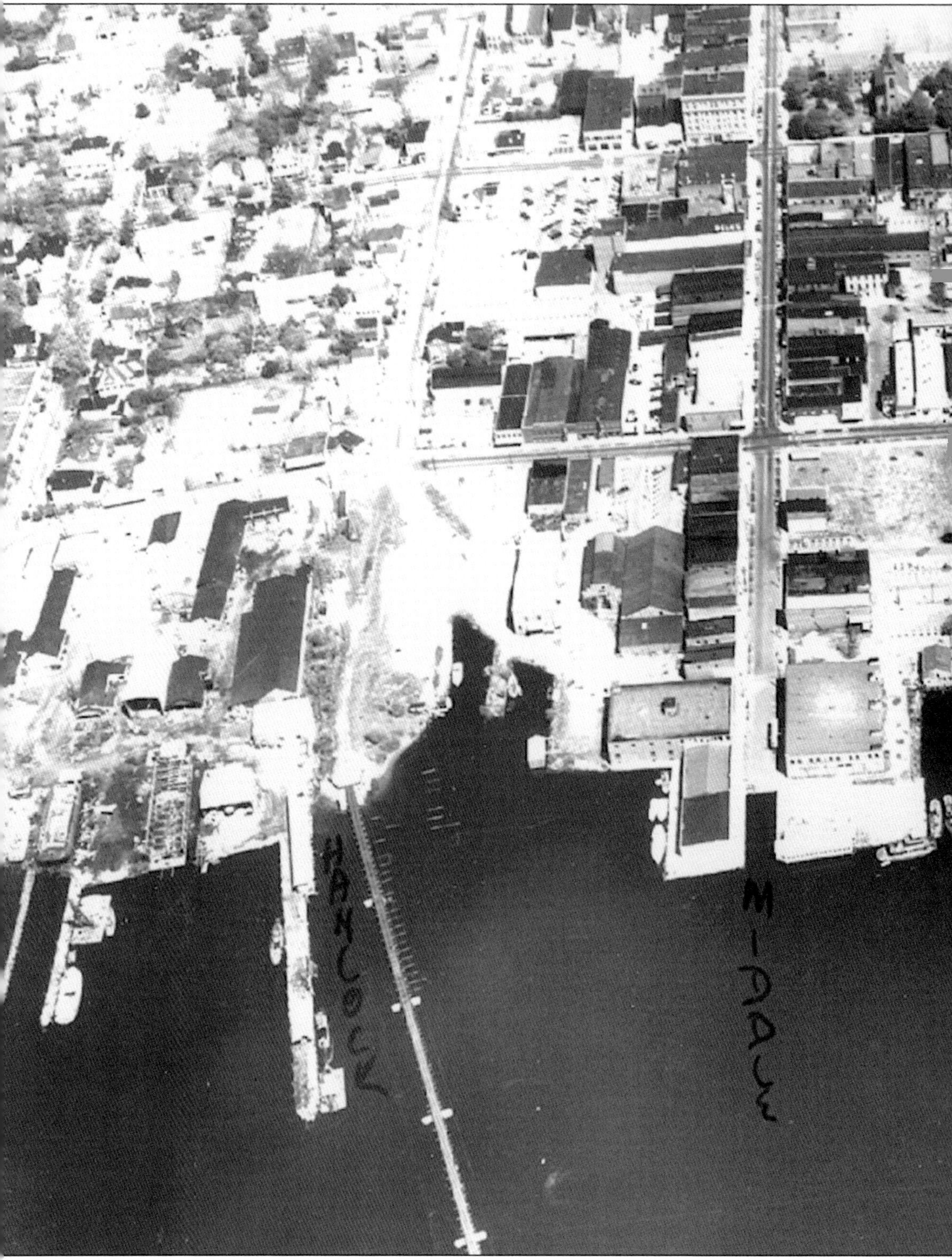

This aerial view of New Bern, dating from 1965–70, shows many of the changes the town

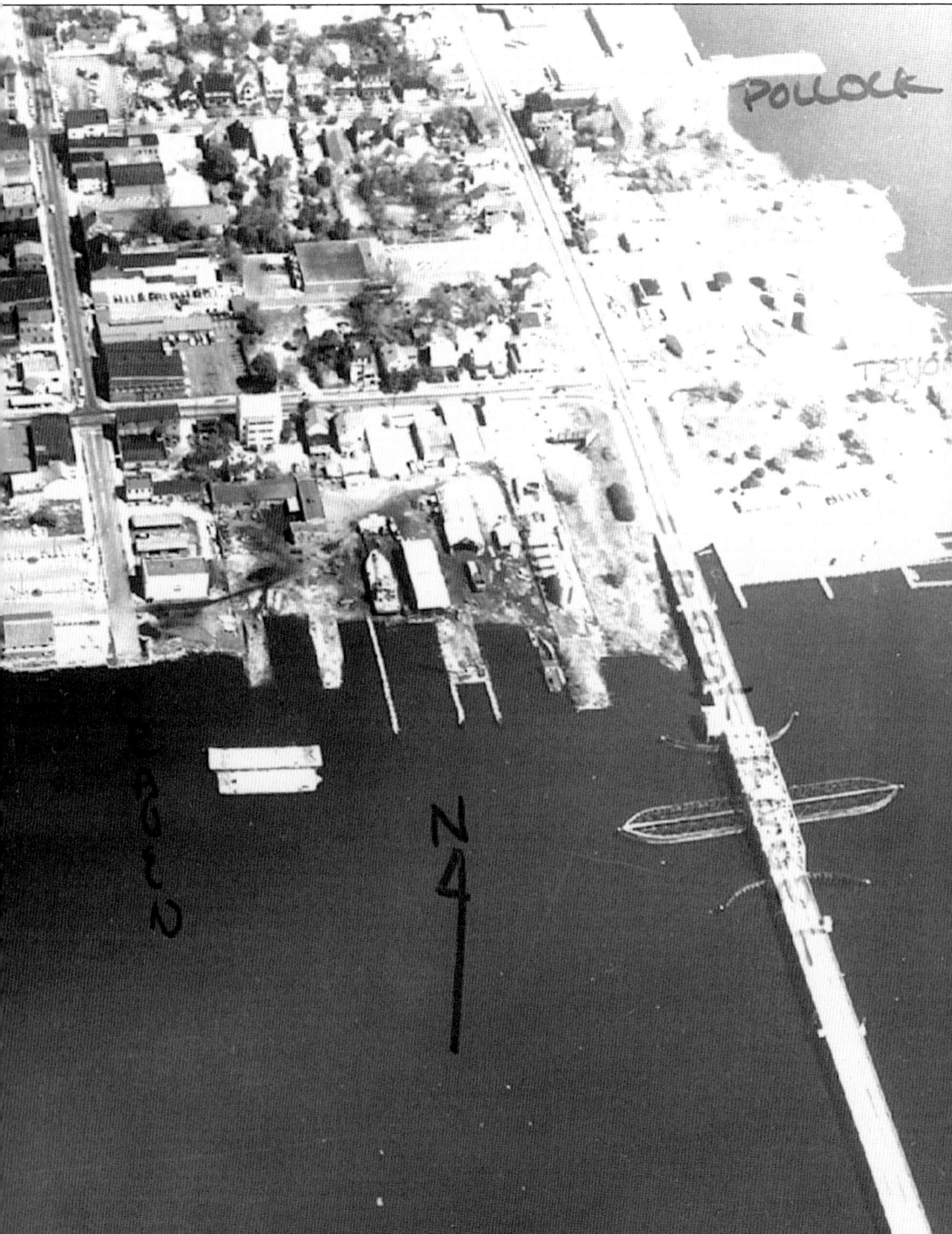

experienced around that time. (Courtesy of North Carolina Division of Archives and History.)

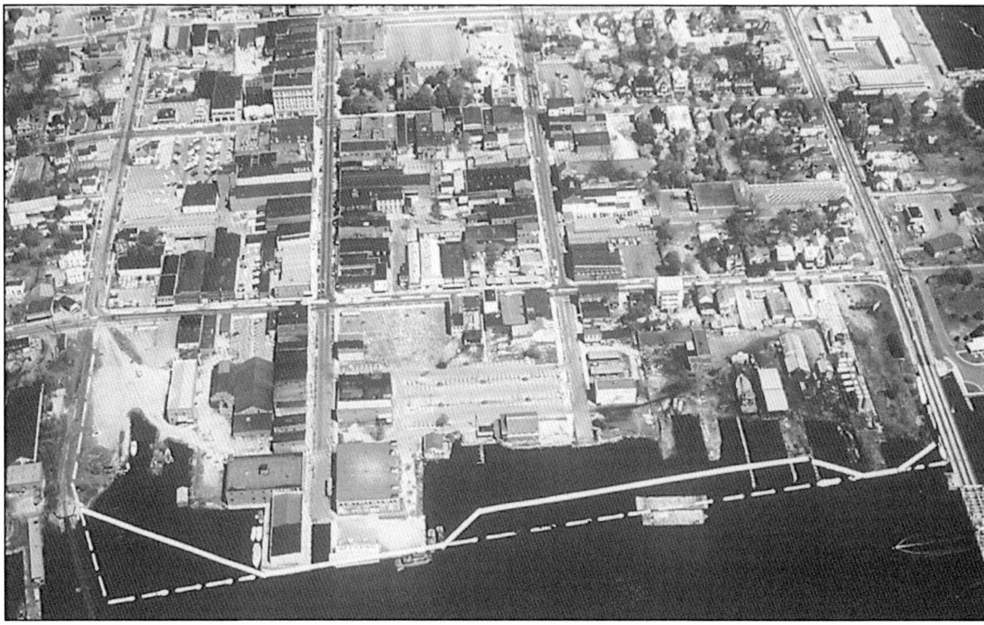

The dotted lines in this c. 1965 aerial view of New Bern represent the area that was later filled in and is currently the site of the Sheraton Grand Hotel. As growth accelerated on the outskirts of town, New Bern's downtown area took on a neglected air. Although urban renewal funds in the early 1970s led to the demolition of many waterfront buildings, local leaders with vision developed a revitalization plan and formed an organization to see that plan implemented. Thus, Swiss Bear was born in 1979. (Courtesy of Swiss Bear.)

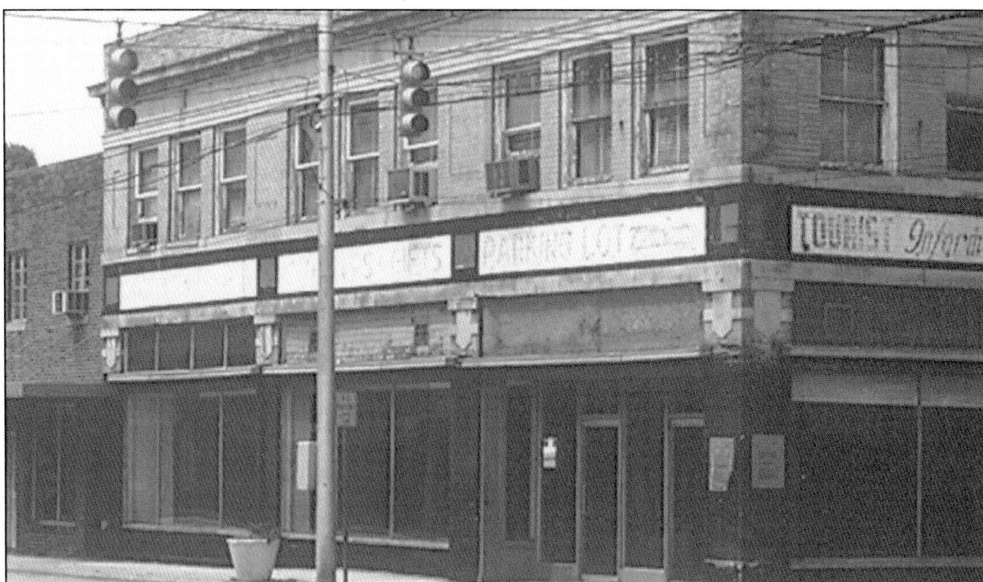

Boarded up storefronts and neglected buildings were a common sight in the late 1970s, as this view along the 400 block of Broad Street shows. The turn-around of the downtown area started in the late 1970s with the development of a central business district plan that called for bringing a new market to the downtown area and expanding the tourism industry. (Courtesy of Swiss Bear.)

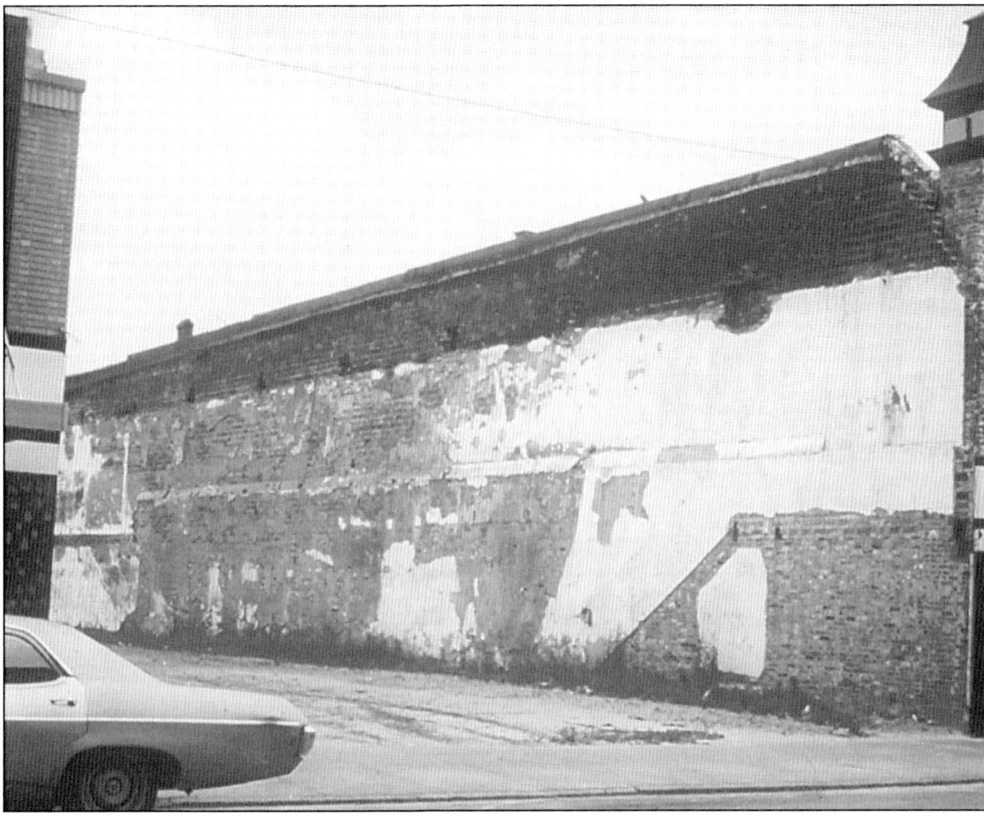

One of Swiss Bear's first projects was to take this unattractive site of a burned-out department store on Middle Street and transform it into a park, now known as Bear Plaza. Swiss Bear also acquired other properties around town for improvement, including the site of a Texaco gas station on East Front Street, which was rehabilitated for use as part of Union Point Park. (Courtesy of Swiss Bear.)

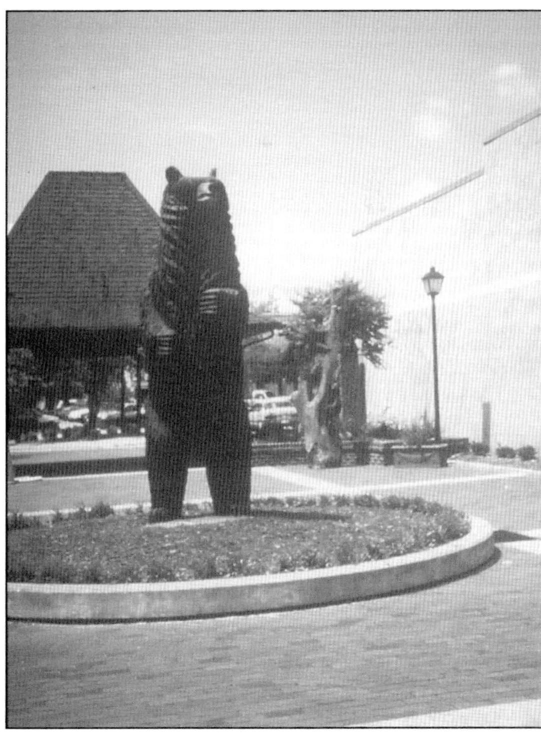

A fund-raising drive in the mid-1990s led to the purchase of the Bear Plaza bears, adding a touch of whimsey to an already beautified area. The park includes a shaded bench area perfect for a rest or an outdoor lunch. In 1999, the original bears were replaced by new bear sculptures due to deterioration caused by weather and termites. (Courtesy of Swiss Bear.)

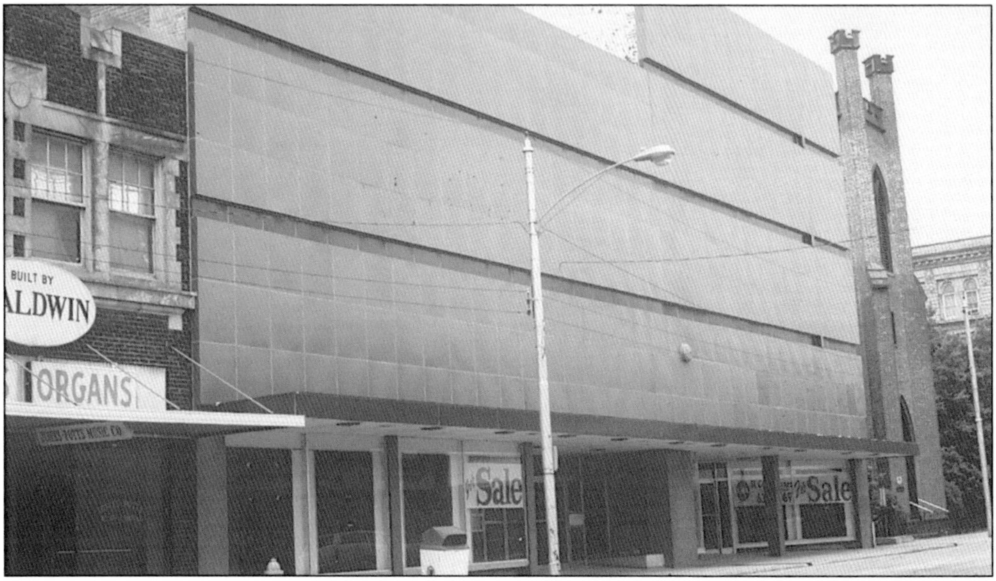

Fears that the empty Belk building would be adapted for an unsuitable use led to Swiss Bear's purchase of the 57,000-square-foot building. Swiss Bear's dream to totally recreate the downtown area, with New Bern's historic heritage in mind, was slowly coming true, one project at a time. (Courtesy of Swiss Bear.)

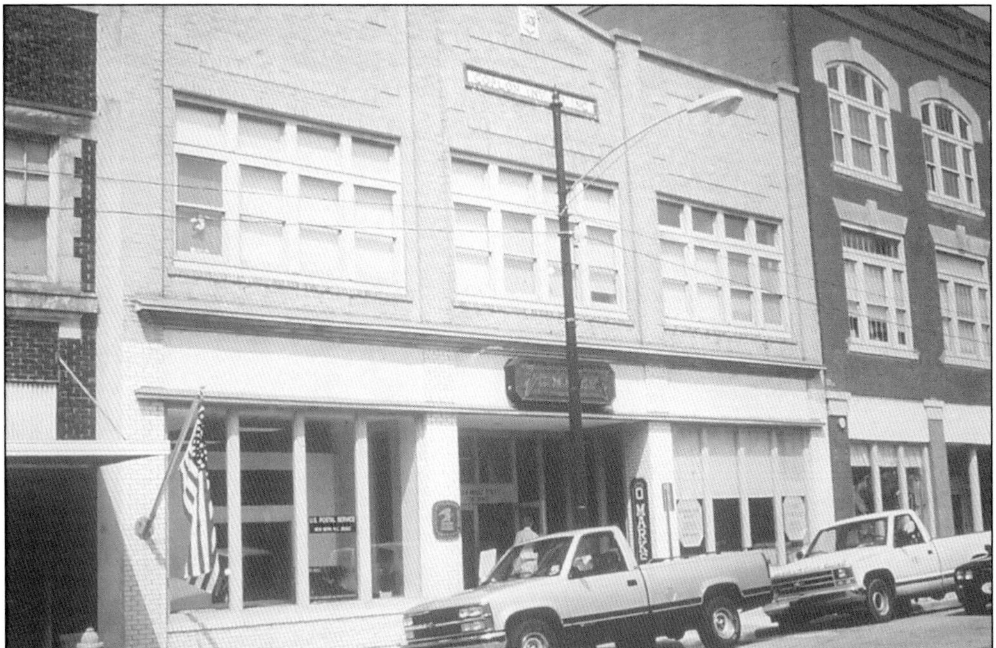

Swiss Bear sold the Belk building to a local partnership, which rehabilitated the structure into a mixed-use multi-level office complex. Today, it houses offices, a sandwich shop, and a branch of the New Bern Post Office. Business buildings and residences in the area have been restored and renovated to bring out the best of their historical features and heritage. Over the past 20 years, property values in downtown New Bern have increased 336 percent, and tourism generated $67 million in 1998. (Courtesy of Swiss Bear.)

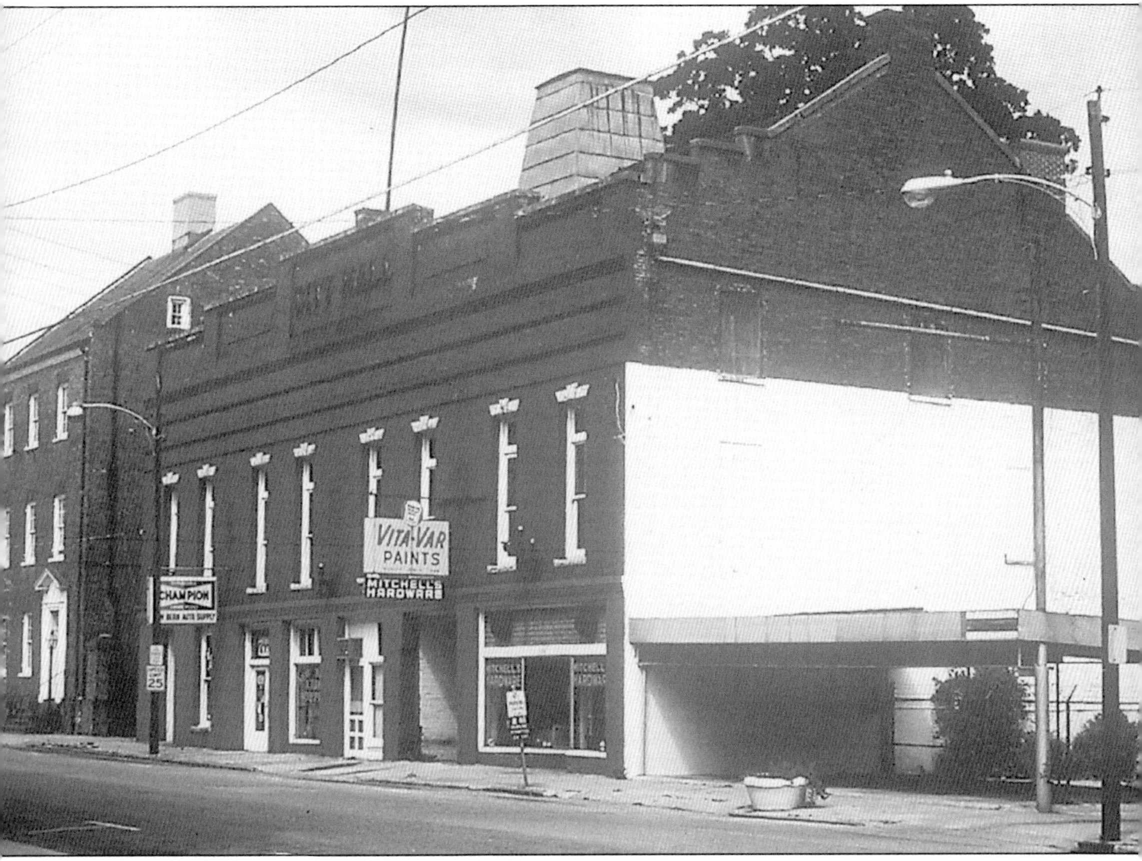

New Bern moved its city hall to the old federal building at the corner of Craven and Pollock Streets in 1935. The old city hall at 220–226 Craven Street was originally built in 1817. Known as Stephens' Brick Block, it housed four storefronts. The city had purchased the separate storefronts by 1888 and subsequently remodeled the building for use as city hall. By the 1970s, the building, once again in private hands, housed a variety of businesses. (Courtesy of Swiss Bear.)

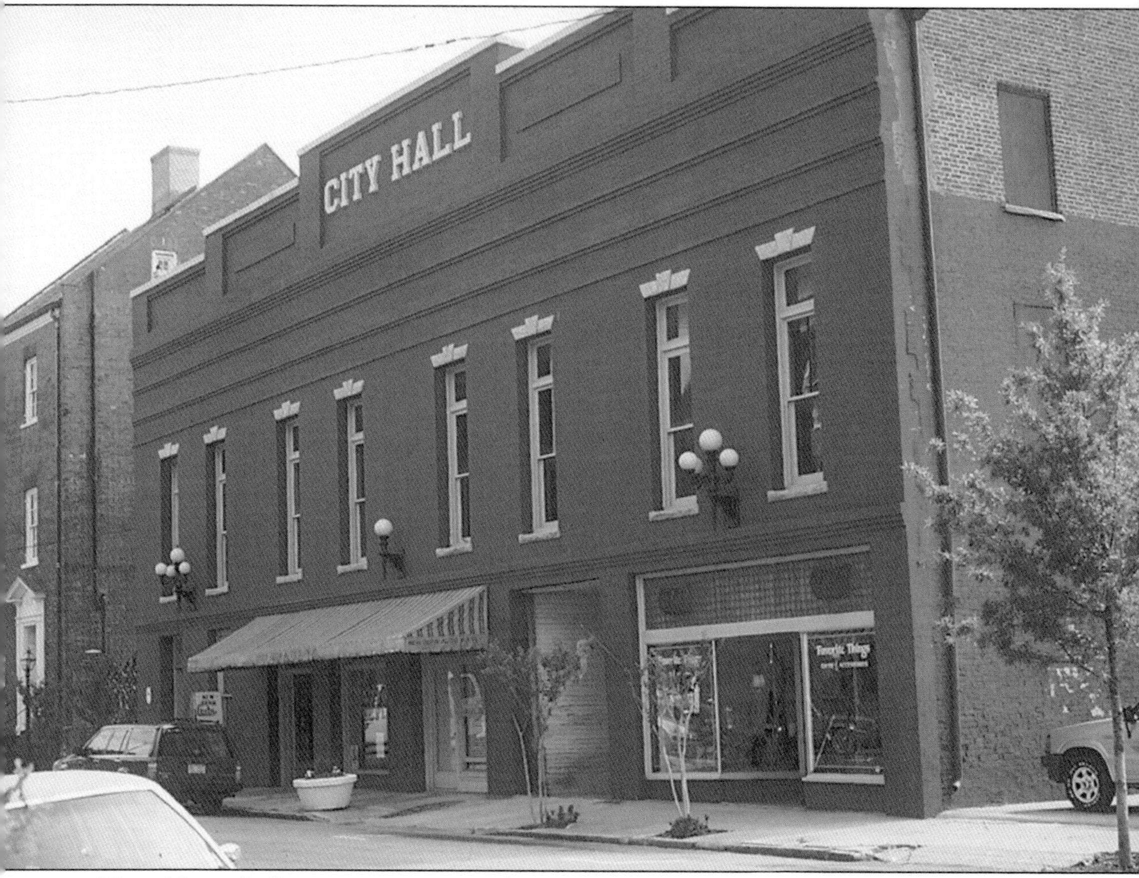

The old city hall, as it appears now, features three restored c. 1915 cast-iron trochere-style electric light fixtures. Although the upper floors are not in use, the building at present houses an eclectic mix of art shops. (Courtesy of Swiss Bear.)

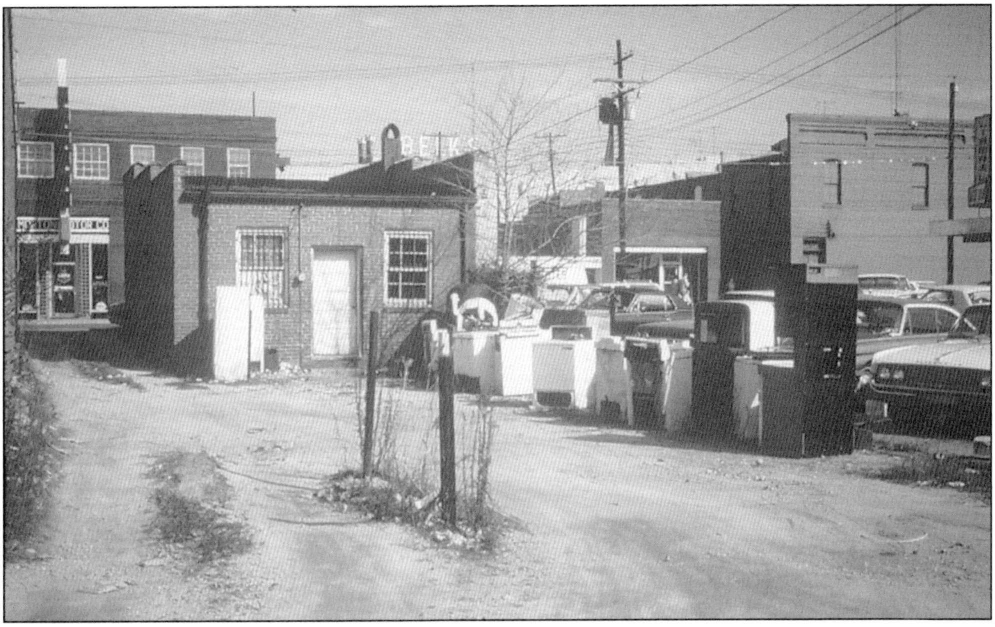

Parking was, and remains, a major source of concern in the city of New Bern. Each year, the city draws more and more visitors to its lovely downtown, making parking hard to come by during the busy tourism season. One solution was to take areas such as this, clean up the debris, and develop a new municipal parking lot. (Courtesy of Swiss Bear.)

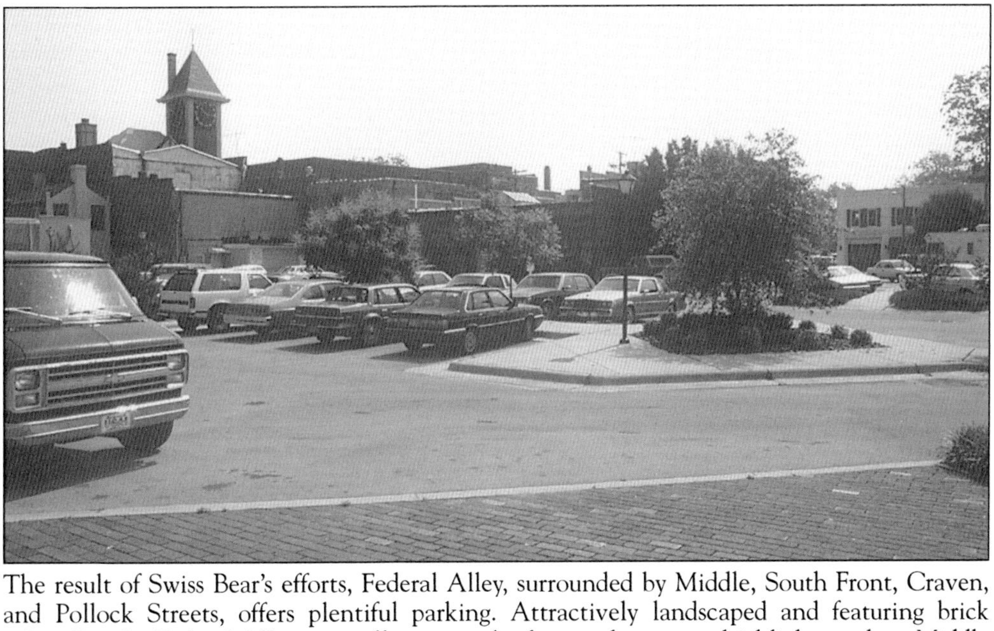

The result of Swiss Bear's efforts, Federal Alley, surrounded by Middle, South Front, Craven, and Pollock Streets, offers plentiful parking. Attractively landscaped and featuring brick sidewalks, the Federal Alley area offers access by foot to downtown highlights such as Middle Street through the lovely Bear Plaza and Pollock Street through James Reed Lane. (Courtesy of Swiss Bear.)

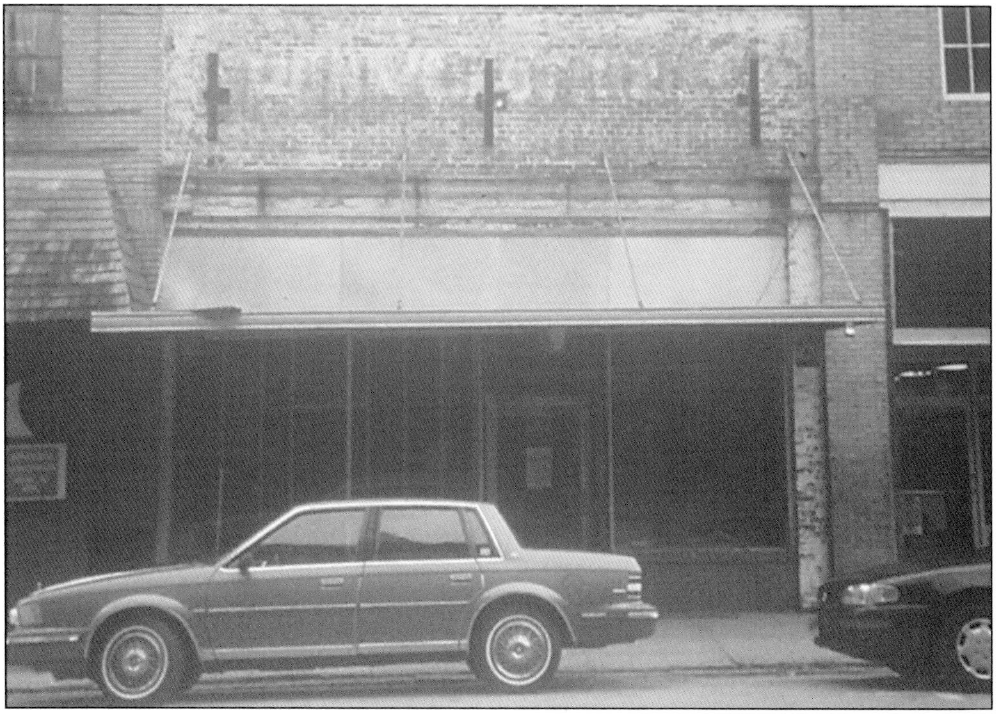

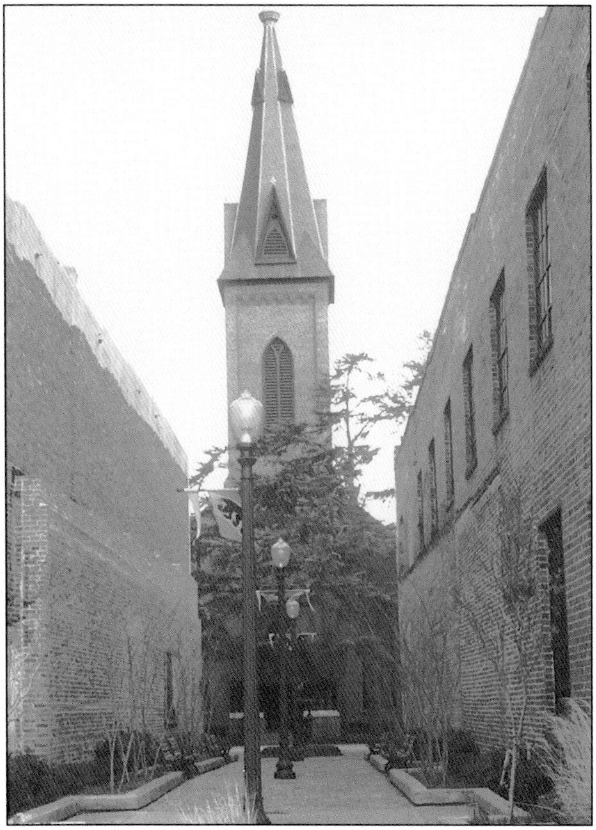

This building in the 300 block of Pollock Street, located directly across the street from the Christ Episcopal Church building, was torn down, and the resulting alleyway was transformed into one of New Bern's loveliest hidden treasures. (Courtesy of Swiss Bear.)

Now known as James Reed Lane, the alleyway honors James Reed, who was the first rector of Christ Episcopal Church (shown here) and the man who led the establishment of colonial New Bern's first public school. The park, featuring a bricked walkway, benches, and beautiful landscaping, offers a quiet respite from New Bern's busy streets. James Reed Lane also contains a memorial fountain to former school superintendent H.J. MacDonald and his wife, Kathryn. (Courtesy of Swiss Bear.)

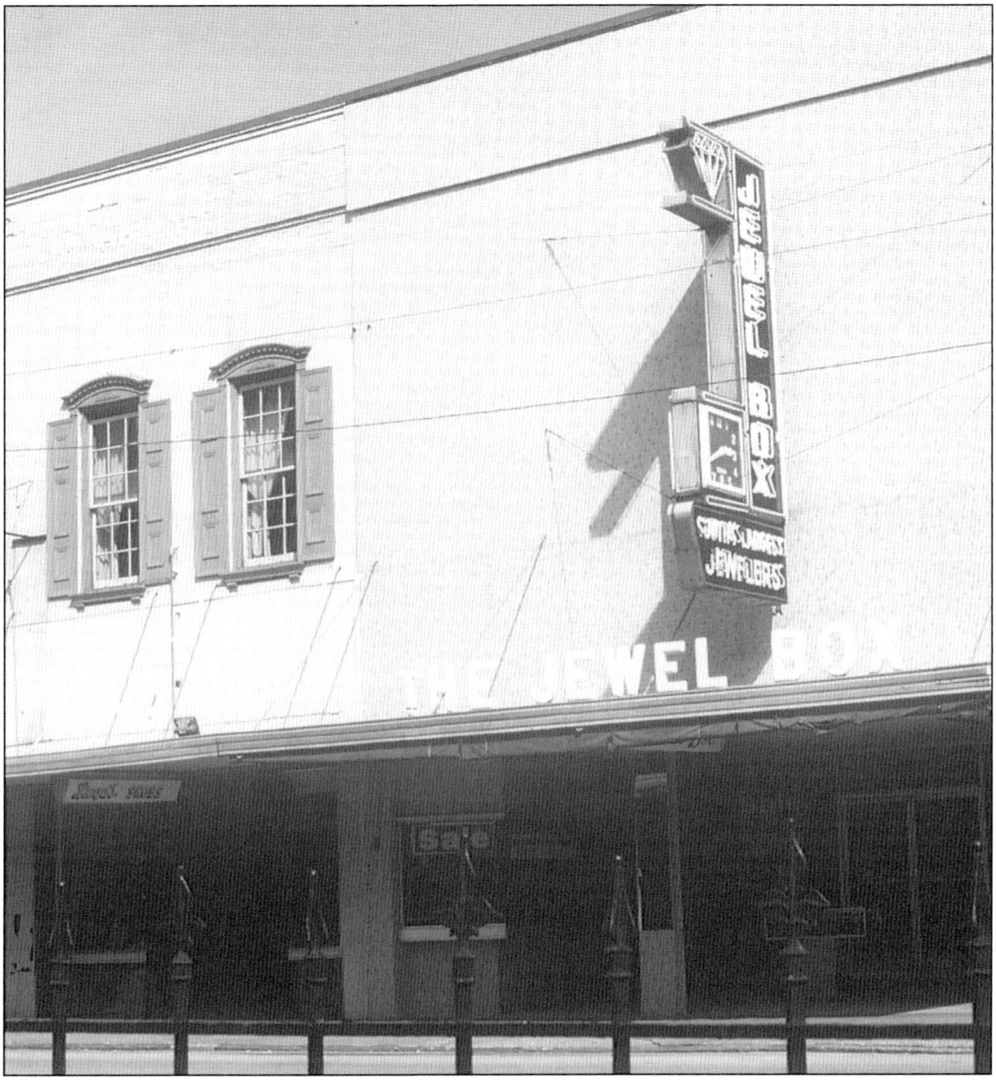

The facades of many old buildings were covered up with tile or sheet metal in order to give them an "updated" look. The results sometimes could look dated after only a short period of time. One goal of the business plan was to improve the look of the city by making major streetscape improvements, including new streetlights and outdoor benches. (Courtesy of Swiss Bear.)

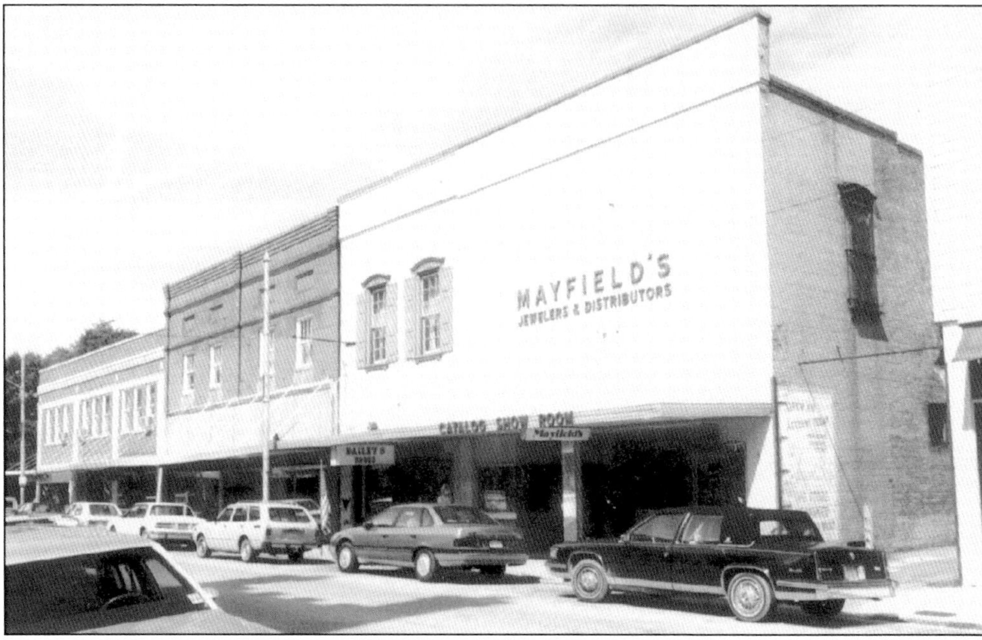

This view of 244–246 Middle Street from 1988 displays a typical storefront of that time. What looks like two storefronts was actually one building—the Patterson Building. Built *c.* 1873–76 by Moses Patterson, it has been and remains a valuable commercial property, over the years housing such operations as a jewelry shop, clothing store, furniture display showroom, stationer, and bookseller, among others. The Patterson Building is one of the oldest surviving commercial structures on Middle Street. (Courtesy of Tom Faulkenberry Collection.)

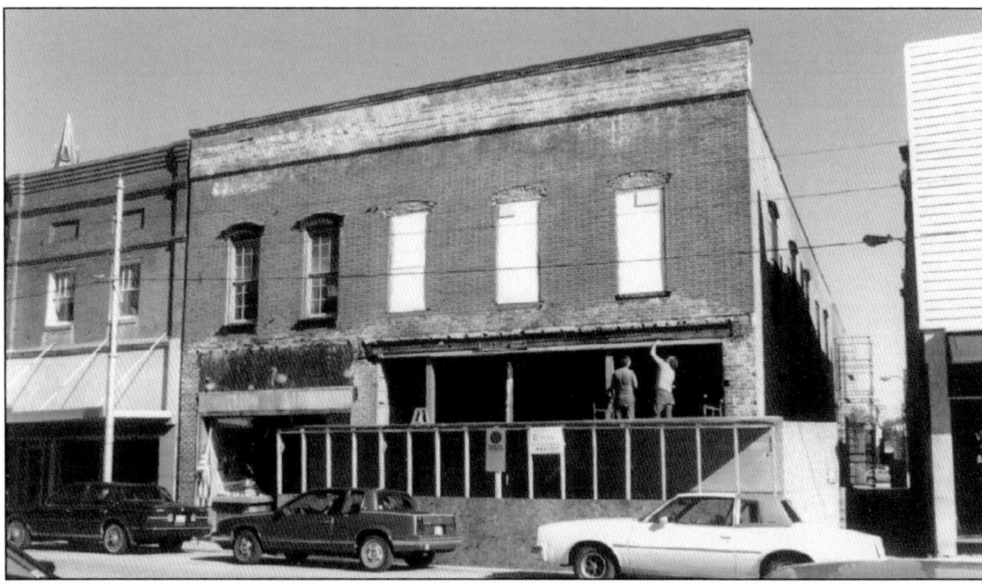

During 1988–89, antique dealer Tom Faulkenberry renovated the Patterson Building to its original appearance. Through his renovation efforts, Faulkenberry has retained one of the building's most unique features—ornamental cast-iron hoods and sills on several of the windows. Today, the building houses Tom's Coins and Antiques, where antique hunters and browsers alike can find many New Bern treasures. (Courtesy of Tom Faulkenberry Collection.)

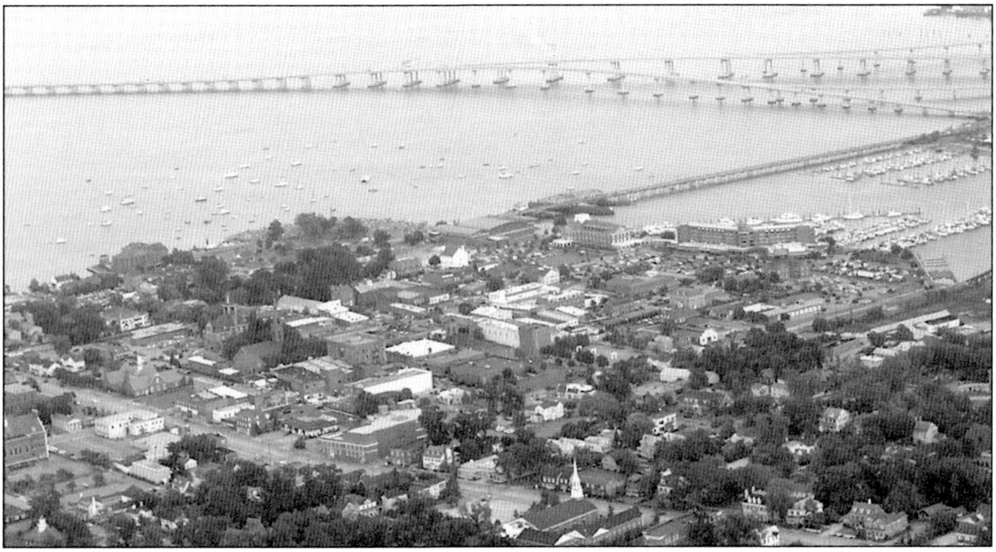

A recent aerial view of New Bern shows many of the town's historic structures, as well as recent commercial additions. New Bern, a small fishing town at the turn of the 20th century, has today become a tourism destination, as well as a retirement community for many Northern transplants who come here to enjoy the mild climate. This aerial view shows changes that has taken place on the Neuse and Trent River waterfronts—docks and fishhouses have been replaced by buildings such as the Sheraton Grand and the newly opened waterfront convention center constructed by Craven County. In the background is the modern-day Neuse River bridge, opened in late 1999. (Courtesy of Bob Murphy and Swiss Bear.)

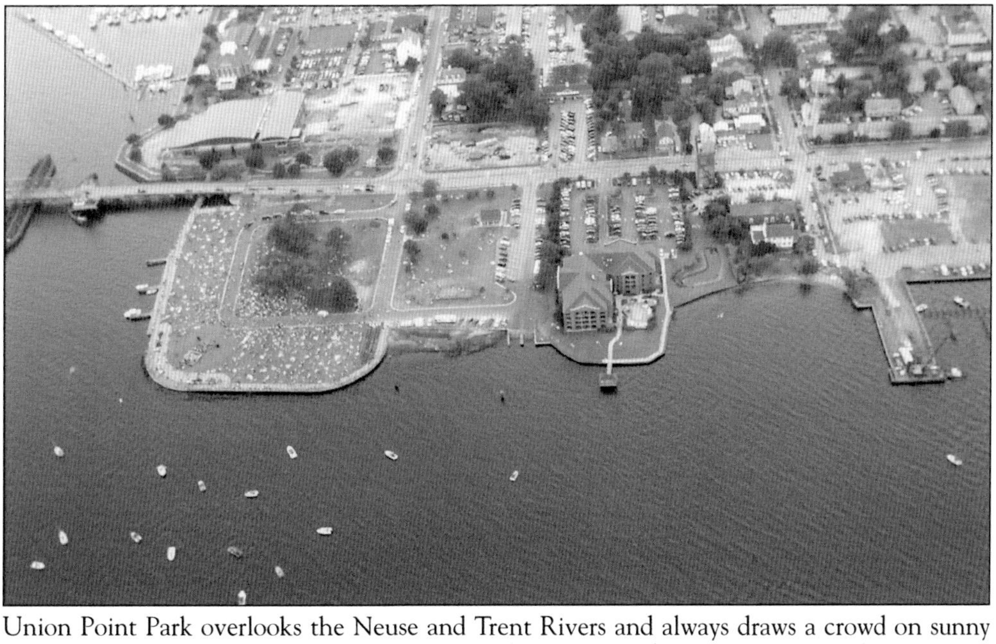

Union Point Park overlooks the Neuse and Trent Rivers and always draws a crowd on sunny summer days. Concerts, festivals, and many other events take place in the park, attracting residents and visitors alike to the downtown area. The park itself earlier in the century served as the town dump. Swiss Bear had a hand in the park's expansion and redevelopment in the latter part of the 20th century. (Courtesy of Bob Murphy and Swiss Bear.)

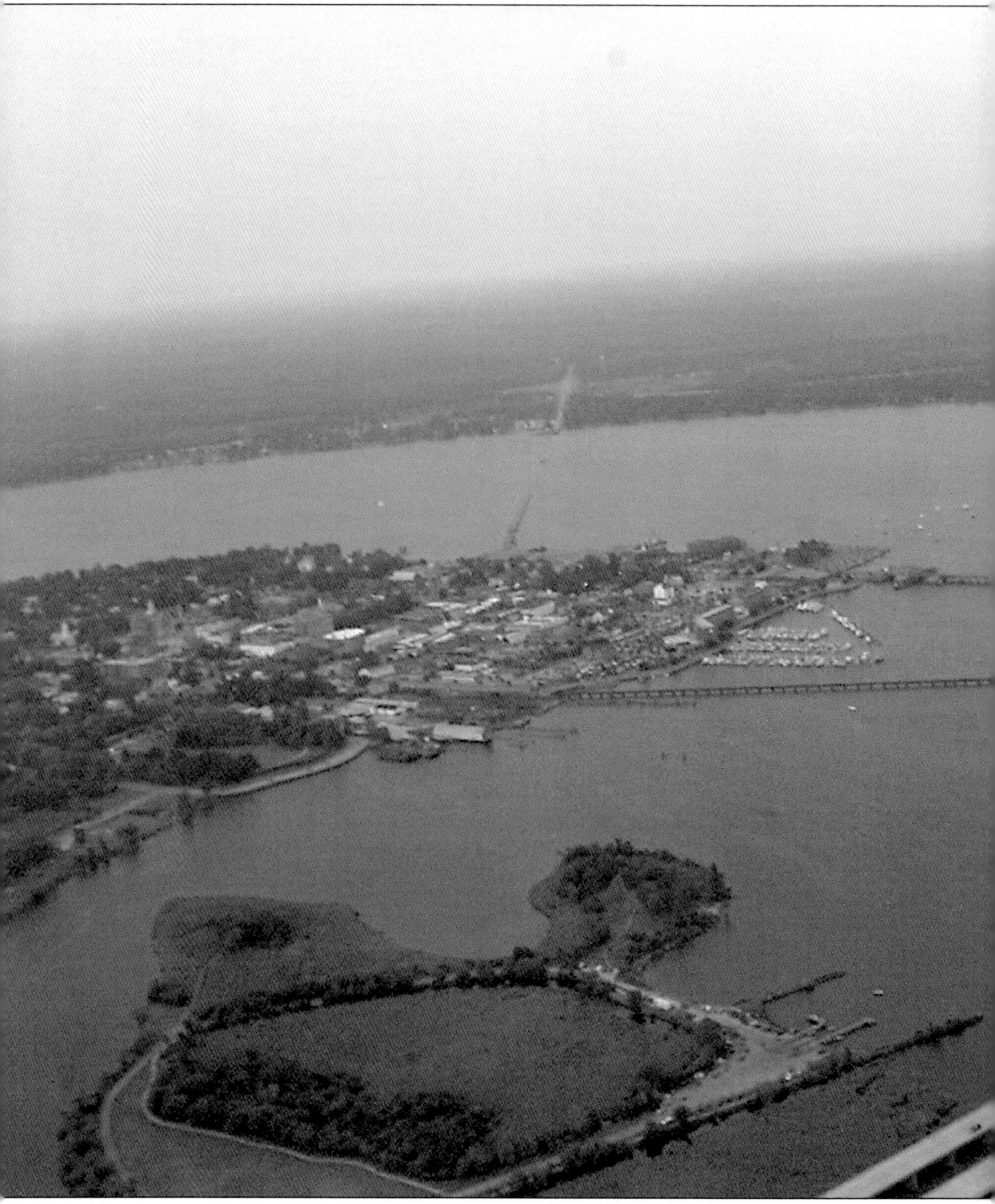

New Bern at the dawn of a new century is a town that celebrates its historic heritage—a town where visitors are always welcome and indeed, treated as long-lost friends. This view takes in

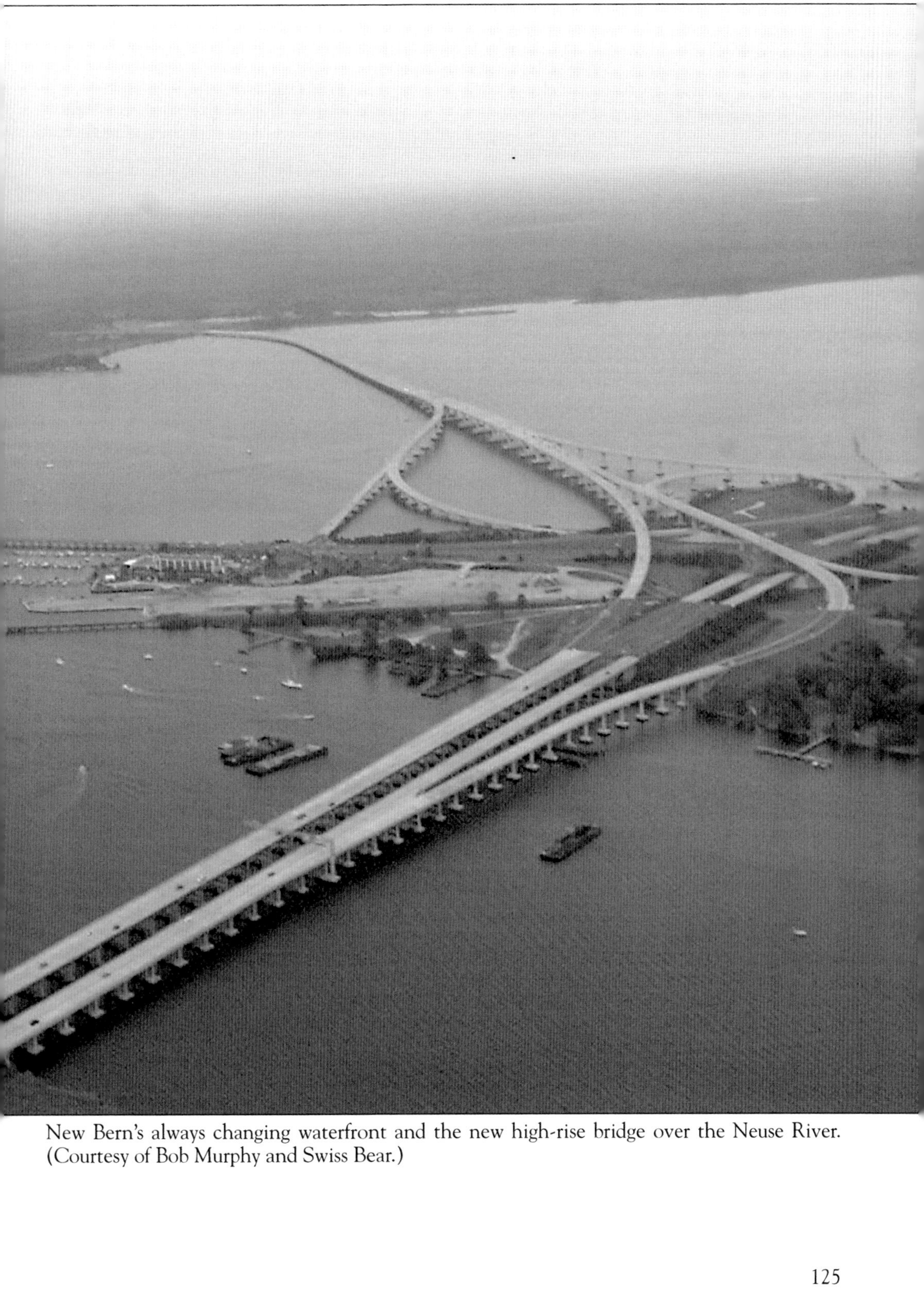

New Bern's always changing waterfront and the new high-rise bridge over the Neuse River. (Courtesy of Bob Murphy and Swiss Bear.)

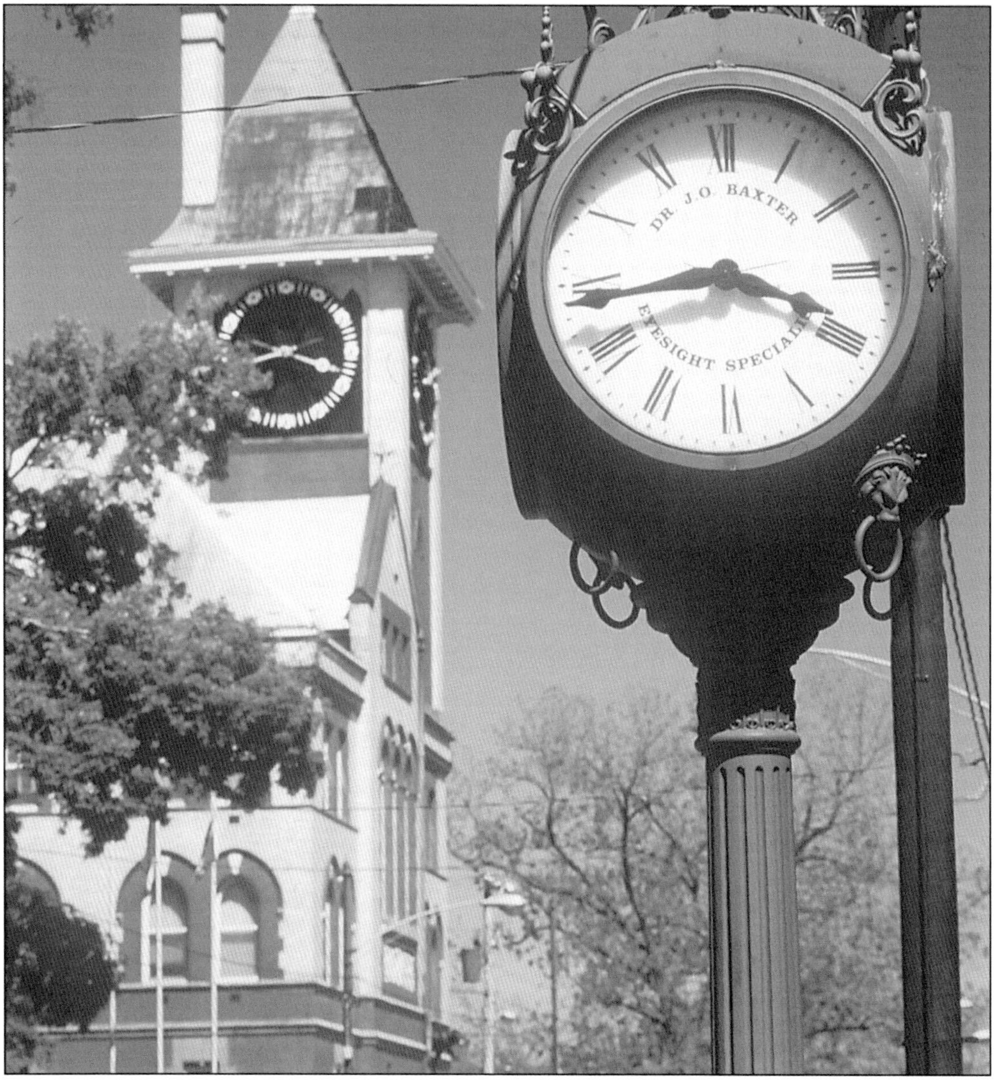

New Bern has two interesting clocks, both located on Pollock Street. The large clock over city hall was actually the second clock for this building. The first clock, a two-faced clock located on the top center of the building, was the subject of many complaints, chief among them that its face was too small to be seen from more than two blocks away and completely not visible from others. In response to the complaints, the first clock was removed and a large four-faced clock, featuring lighted hands and numbers, was completed in 1911. Even today, the clock chimes out the hours and half hours. The second clock, the four-faced Seth Thomas clock located in front of Baxter's Jewelers on Pollock Street, is only one of three still in use in the United States today. The clock, which was rendered inoperable after being struck by a car in 1977, was donated to Swiss Bear by the Baxter family. Swiss Bear, in turn, raised $28,000 to restore the clock to its original glory. (Courtesy of Swiss Bear.)

Acknowledgments

This is my vision of New Bern. While I made an effort to include many important images, my view is only a subjective one. Indeed, one could write volumes about New Bern—it has thousands of stories to tell, each and every one interesting.

This project could not have been completed without the help of some very important and special people. First and foremost, to the people who allowed me to borrow photographs for use in this book: John B. Green III of New Bern, Dean Knight of Tryon Palace Historic Sites & Gardens, Victor Jones of the New Bern-Craven County Public Library, Ben Gaskill of the New Bern Firemen's Museum, Susan Moffat-Thomas of Swiss Bear, JoAnne Gwaltney of the New Bern Historical Society, Tom Faulkenberry of Tom's Coins and Antiques, and Natalie Lee of the New Bern Area Chamber of Commerce. You trusted me with your images and I hope I have done them justice.

To Alanna King, who has demonstrated over the years what it really means to be a loyal and trustworthy friend. Words cannot express my gratitude for the love and support you've always quietly provided.

To my son, Nick—who is more into Nintendo than history, I might add—thanks for being quiet when I needed that, giving a hug and a smile when I needed that, and just being the great kid that you are . . . I love you.

To Debbie "Sunshine" Robinson, who is not only my big sister but also my best friend.

To the Ladies of Lallybroch, including Judie Rouselle, Nancy Varn, and Dawn Faith, who provide me with a great on-line refuge.

And to James, for his devotion and support.

About the Author

Author Vina Hutchinson has lived in North Carolina since 1988, when she moved to Elizabeth City, NC, to work for the local newspaper. Working her way south over the years, Hutchinson has worked in writing and editorial positions for publications such as *The Island Review, Tideland News, Coaster* magazine, and *New Bern* magazine. She is currently co-author of the annual *Insiders' Guide to the Central Coast and New Bern*. A native of Kentucky raised in West Virginia, Hutchinson graduated from Marshall University in 1988 with degrees in journalism and American history. In addition to her full-time and freelance work, she likes to spend time with her son biking, reading, going to beaches and parks, and exploring historic sites.